Narrative Analysis

To Jack and to Lauren
for helping us pay attention
to the whole story.

Narrative Analysis

Studying the Development of Individuals in Society

Editors

Colette Daiute
The Graduate Center, City University of New York

Cynthia Lightfoot
Pennsylvania State University

SAGE Publications
International Educational and Professional Publisher
Thousand Oaks ▪ London ▪ New Delhi

For information:

Sage Publications, Inc.
2455 Teller Road
Thousand Oaks, California 91320
E-mail: order@sagepub.com

Sage Publications Ltd.
6 Bonhill Street
London EC2A 4PU
United Kingdom

Sage Publications India Pvt. Ltd.
B-42, Panchsheel Enclave
Post Box 4109
New Delhi 110 017 India

Printed in the United States of America

Library of Congress Cataloging-in-Publication Data

Narrative analysis : studying the development of individuals in society /
Colette Daiute and Cynthia Lightfoot, editors.
    p. cm.
Includes bibliographical references and index.
ISBN 0-7619-2797-2 — ISBN 0-7619-2798-0 (pbk.)
   1. Discourse analysis, Narrative. I. Daiute, Collette. II. Lightfoot, Cynthia.
P302.7.N364 2004
401′.41—dc22

                    2003015008

Printed on acid-free paper

            06   07   08   09   10   9   8   7   6   5   4   3   2

Acquiring Editor:	Lisa Cuevas Shaw
Editorial Assistant:	Margo Beth Crouppen
Production Editor:	Claudia A. Hoffman
Copy Editor:	Jamie Robinson
Typesetter:	C&M Digitals (P) Ltd.
Indexer:	Kay Dusheck

Contents

Editors' Introduction

Theory and Craft in Narrative Inquiry

Colette Daiute and Cynthia Lightfoot

Yet even those who acknowledge the importance of the broader context wrestle with questions about how to study the complex interactions among changing cultural, historical, and developmental factors. . . . Researchers who are particularly interested in cultural factors in development face the challenge of conceptualizing culture in a way that can be studied empirically. . . . A narrative approach is being recognized as a means of examining the ways in which individuals make sense of their lives within a changing sociohistorical context.

— Phinney (2000, pp. 27–28)

Despite compelling arguments that a narrative approach will advance our understanding of individual development within sociohistorical contexts, the analysis of narratives often seems like a mysterious art to those who are new to narrative inquiry. Narrative analysis assumes a multitude of theoretical forms, unfolds in a variety of specific analytic practices, and is grounded in diverse disciplines. Little wonder that the novice researcher comes away from early encounters feeling too lost in either minutiae or grand theory to transport narrative methods to new projects with confidence.

Nevertheless, social science researchers who have found narrative analyses to be enlightening argue that the theoretical complexity and methodological diversity in narrative modes of inquiry are its major strengths. Narrative analyses tend to be flexible and systematic even as they seek complexity. Where traditional, reductionist approaches see diversity and variation as obscuring underlying processes of interest, and therefore seek to eliminate them, narrative approaches may employ literary tools like metaphors, linguistic devices like pronouns, or cultural conventions like time for insights about diversity within and across participants in their research, and thus create ways to explain phenomena without reducing them. Narrative analysis can be artful and inspired, but narrative researchers rely on more than inspiration to find meaning in their subject matter.

In addition to providing tools with which to examine the complexity inherent to developing systems, narrative approaches offer different ways of conceptualizing cultural/institutional and individual psychological perspectives for developmental research. Narrative psychology and narrative discourse are defined as sites of development as well as sites for examining development, which implicates particular research designs for gathering narratives and as approaches to analyzing them. Researchers who have adopted narrative methods have found them particularly useful for addressing the unmet challenge of integrating culture, person, and change—a challenge that has become especially acute in the last quarter century. Facilitated by advances in medicine, technology, communication, and transportation, the texture of modern life is increasingly defined by weaving together separate generations, life stages, cultures, and social and political ideologies. At the same time, understanding these life systems, in all their complexity and diversity, is essential to such daily affairs as educating our children, caring for our elderly, designing equitable intervention and assessment programs, and formulating policies bent on nurturing the development and well-being of individuals across diverse contexts.

Our overarching aim for this volume is to help researchers and students of research across the social sciences identify and evaluate critically the wealth of rationales, practices, caveats, and values of approaches to narrative inquiry. We are therefore addressing audiences in graduate level courses, undergraduate research seminars, professional research programs, and evaluation projects where readers have some familiarity with the theories, methods, and goals of social science research and are interested to learn about the unique features and potential contributions of narrative inquiry.

In an effort to make explicit the theory-based methods of narrative analysis in the study of human development, we have included contributions from scholars who have extensive experience in various forms of narrative inquiry, and who together describe a range of major, innovative, and inter-disciplinary approaches designed to advance the study of human development rather than define it in narrow terms. But while they all report on the successful use of narrative methods, they also offer critical reflections on what they have done and how their approaches relate to those of others. Thus, the authors explain the problems and limits of narrative analysis, as well as the rationales and methods they have found most compelling, with an eye toward improving future inquiry.

We are therefore pleased to present this collection of theory-based case studies of narrative analysis seeking clarity around the issues of educational inequity, gender and racial discrimination, conformity and agency in response to oppressive institutions, context-sensitive concepts of mental health, citizenship, and ideas about development across the life span. All the chapters address the development of identity and knowledge in some way, and across the chapters different ways of conceptualizing social identity and knowledge. Toward these broader research goals, each chapter offers specific methods of narrative inquiry—such as focusing on imagination; the aesthetic project of adolescent development; cultural frameworks for learning; cultural scripts; the nature and role of audience in narrative writing; the multiple stances of narrators as speakers, subjects, and cultural interpreters; and the issue of research data and their relationship to life.

Although each chapter presents narrating as an important cultural activity in a specific cultural context, different definitions of narrative, narrative analysis, and development come readily to the fore in the analytic approaches employed. We have used these differences to organize the chapters into three main sections that we describe as "readings" in order to account for the epis-temological diversity inherent to each. Part I, "Literary Readings," is com-posed of chapters that emphasize the literary characteristics of narratives and development. Part II, "Social-Relational Readings," contains essays that focus on narrating as a dynamic, interactive process. Part III, "Readings Through the Forces of History," completes the volume and includes chapters that are particularly concerned with individuals' relationships to historically emergent and culturally ubiquitous master narratives.

As a further aid to drawing out the major themes and issues that define contemporary narrative inquiry, we begin each section with a description of its contents. In addition to commenting on the unique contributions of each chapter, these descriptions highlight the major theoretical points and the aspects of development addressed, as well as the range of applications for their extension. Embedded in each section, and drawn out in the prefatory remarks, are the authors responses to such questions as "What is narrative analysis?" "Why do narrative inquiry?" "What is developmental about narrative processes?" "What specific processes are involved in narrative research, at what peril, and with what results?" We address these questions below as an orienting guide to the readings that follow.

What Is Narrative Analysis?

"Narrative analysis" is a place holder for different ways of conceptualizing the storied nature of human development. Narrative may be a metaphor for a life course, a developmental theory, a reference to a totalizing cultural force, and/or the method for interpreting oral or written narrative discourse. Three ways of conceptualizing narrative research are the focus of our discussion, and we use these to organize the contents of this volume.

Narrative analysis is a mode of inquiry based in narrative as a root metaphor, a genre, and discourse. As a metaphor, narrative analysis involves explaining psychological phenomena as meanings that are ordered from some theoretical perspective, like that of a storyteller, and consist of information and comments about the significance of that information. Consistent with this, narrative analysis relies on themes, mostly drawn from literary theory, to explain vicissitudes in the drama of interpreted lives, including time, truth, beauty, character, and conflict. Narratives are also genres, that is, culturally developed ways of organizing experience and knowledge. Feminist and critical psychological researchers have used the concept of narrative as a coherent story line organized implicitly by some dominant force to characterize the values, practices, and controls inherent in groups determining who the heroes are, what life should be like, and what should be heralded or hidden. Narratives are also specific discourse forms, occurring as embodiments of cultural values and personal subjectivities. While these three notions of narrative are not discrete, and researchers do not all use them in the same way, the notions do characterize what we take to be major approaches to narrative analysis.

Drawing on theory from a range of disciplines, the contributors to this volume all view narrating as an active process. Their approaches to narrative inquiry differ, however, as do their definitions of narrative texts. Nevertheless, all consider context in their versions of narrative analysis, and they each offer a different definition to address the specific questions guiding their research and reflection. Narrative is thus always more than words or windows into something else. Narrative discourses are cultural meanings and interpretations that guide perception, thought, interaction, and action.

Narrative discourse organizes life—social relations, interpretations of the past, and plans for the future. The way people tell stories influences how they perceive, remember, and prepare for future events. This meaning of discourse applies to all forms of human communication and symbolization—verbal and nonverbal alike. The view that mental life is comprised of symbols created through the consensus and conflict of social interaction means that sign language, signage, dress, music, and all manner of meaning systems are cultural tools. In this book, we focus on a verbal system, but many of the ideas about the nature of narrative discourse as a social system and the consequences of these ideas for analyzing development can be applied to other symbol systems, including nonverbal communication like dance or photography, although these are not the province of the present work.

The authors whose work appears here are careful to distinguish the materiality of perception, interpretation, and action from the materiality of money, food, and biology, but they explain the basic role of discourse as social relations that create, organize, or limit other material resources. From this perspective, the knives and bullets of war, the hunger of poverty, the privileges of physical health, and the joys of love are not narratives. However, the social relational systems that lead to war, poverty, and well-being occur in discourses and cannot be separated from them. Narrative discourse, like other discourses, is thus of the world not about it. The authors of this volume, one after another, offer their versions of (1) how people make sense of life when telling "what happened," "what happens," or "what will happen," and (2) how the imagining, exaggerating, hiding, performing, joking, and other symbolic activities of narrating support or limit life and its development.

Why Do Narrative Inquiry?

Narrative analysis is a variety of orientations to interpreting varieties of discourse, including narrative texts. Because these varieties are complex and grounded in diverse practices, we describe several approaches as narrative inquiry. Researchers can inquire into subjects of interest by examining narratives, by applying literary tools for understanding, and by integrating diverse types of data with theory-based narratives. The appeal of collecting, eliciting, and creating narratives for research has four major sources.

First, as the chapters in this volume explain or illustrate, *narrative analysis is appealing because its interpretive tools are designed to examine phenomena, issues, and people's lives holistically.* In contrast to survey

xii   Narrative Analysis

methods, for example, which ask participants to give coded or short responses to brief predetermined questions, narrative analysis seeks complex patterns and descriptions of identity, knowledge, and social relations from specific cultural points of view. For this reason, narrative analysts work with natural language; the richness of educational, clinical, and other practices; and the usefulness of narrative research summaries as theories in their own right.

Second, researchers writing for this volume have found that *narrative discourse and metaphor are excellent contexts for examining social histories that influence identity and development*. As a social process, narrating is, in short, a discourse process embodying the people, places, events, motivations, and moralities of life and, as such, narrative in its various forms is ideal for developmental inquiry. For example, Freeman (Chapter 1.4), citing examples from his own life and from his research on experiences of adolescents and artists, takes the broadest view explaining that narrative "data are everywhere." Gergen (Chapter 3.5) reasons that our stories can be more or less flexible and responsive to the particulars of the context in which they are told. Sarbin (Chapter 1.1) understands narratives as expressive behavior, embodied through an imaginative process in social interaction. Other authors employ the language of "genre," "scripts," "counterscripts," "cultural models," and "cultural narratives" to identify the processes by which the details of a life settle into narrative form.

A third source of appeal is that *narrative analysis generates unique insights into the range of multiple, intersecting forces that order and illuminate relations between self and society*. Literary theory makes use of concepts such as plots and subplots (multiple intersecting story lines) and of devices like metaphor (literal and figurative meanings), and narrative theory extends the analysis of complexity in terms of the multiple ways of referencing in narrating. Such referencing is described as (1) "referential" meanings that point to objects, people, events, and other phenomena in the physical world (and linguistic referents to those objects) and (2) "evaluative" meanings that indicate why the story is being told (Labov & Waletzky, 1997). Consistent with this complexity, Lightfoot (Chapter 1.2) refers to "double narrativity" to describe actions outside the narrative, like adolescents' risk-taking and their telling and retelling those experiences to others; Stanley and Billig (Chapter 2.4) and Bamberg (Chapter 2.3) refer to "multiple-positioning"; and Nelson (Chapter 2.1) refers to Bruner's notions of "landscapes of action" and "landscapes of consciousness."

The authors apply understandings of such multiplicity as units of analysis. For example, Stanley and Billig (Chapter 2.4) identify "ideological dilemmas," referring to contradictions evolving from goals and anxieties; Nelson (Chapter 2.1) identifies "cultural selves"; and Daiute (Chapter 2.2) refers to "sociobiographical activities" to connote the interaction of cultural and personal motivations as they play out across narrative genres in children's writing about social conflicts in autobiographical and fictional form. Other authors identify concepts to capture intersubjectivity among people as creating meaning together in conversations, as in Bamberg's (Chapter 2.3) analysis of positionality by adolescent boys making sense of masculinity or across time, as in Lightfoot's (Chapter 1.2) analysis of the time-conflict interaction, and as in Stewart and Malley's (Chapter 3.3) integrative concept of generations.

Finally, narrative analysis *permits the incursion of value and evaluation into the research process.* Two major narrative theorists of the late 20th century found that narrative discourse interweaves two phases of meaning when describing past events (Labov & Waletzky, 1997). In one phase, referential language in narratives points to the physical world—as Nelson (Chapter 2.1) points out, citing Bruner, to "landscapes of action," while in the other phase, evaluative language in narratives contains messages from the narrator to the listener or reader that say why the story is being told. The evaluative phase of narrating is a wealth of meaning for narrative researchers.

What Is Developmental About Narrative Processes?

Our theoretical claim, shared by all who contribute to this volume, is that human development is a social process involving individuals, institutions, and cultures and, therefore, requiring multiple levels of analysis. Beyond this common theme, the authors of the chapters in this volume offer different methods with different theory-based units of analysis to address questions about the development of identity, knowledge, citizenship, and equality.

In addition, the authors give different explanations of how narrating plays a role in development. Some see narrating as developmental because it involves an imaginative process. Others emphasize the developmental implications of narrative as a cultural tool or a means of elaborating knowledge. Still others explain that narrating is developmentally relevant because it creates the conditions for the emergence of complexity, such as multiplicity of perspectives, orientations, and even self concepts.

The Imaginary Quality of Narrating Is Developmental

Narrating is developmental because it is a virtual process that simulates and organizes life and any prevailing view about the life course. Narrative structures provide time- and space-ordered frames that simulate life, and these structures can be altered to reflect complexities of memory, such as flashbacks and foreshadowings. Development is a narrative process because it not only charts the journey through life but also embodies life categories of people, events, motivations, and moral judgments. For example, Sarbin (Chapter 1.1) explains that involvement is the "means through which narrative-inspired imaginings can influence belief and action" (p. 6) and, in particular, that "identity change can occur in response to subtle cues arising from embodied actions performed during attenuated role-taking sequences" (p. 6). The creation of virtual and potential characters, events, motivations, and moralities is a process that creates ideal people and points out the errors along the journeys of those who are less than ideal. Developmental scholars have found that personal extension in the narrating process creates possibilities (Bruner, 1990) that engage new ways of thinking (Sarbin, Chapter 1.1) and transform the psychological and physical states promoted by those who make the rules, such as legal and educational institutions, parents, and health workers. The importance of personal extension in narrative is captured in processes called "as if" (Sarbin, Chapter 1.1), "precounts" (Nelson, Chapter 2.1), and "fantastic" (Lightfoot, Chapter 1.2).

Particularly interesting is the idea across several of these chapters that the fictive and imaginative qualities of narrating are sites of developmental breakthroughs, such as when young people challenge social mores and expectations in their symbolic activities (1) by individual agency in their writing, as explored in the chapters by Daiute, Lee and her colleagues, and Lightfoot and (2) by narrating experiences that mainstream culture tries to suppress or silence, as illustrated in the chapters by Carney, Chandler and his colleagues, and Solis.

As a Cultural Tool, Narrating Is Developmental

Scholars have long equated life with the story of life. Epic poetry imposed order in ancient times. The Bible added moral order. The conflict plot prevalent in some cultures integrates temporal and moral representations, while the spiritual quality of folktales in many cultures, and character-rich moral tales in others, are frameworks for how people perceive and evaluate their lives.

Narrative is a cultural tool in several senses. Narratives are cultural forms often referred to as scripts (or dominant discourses, or master narratives) with embedded values and moralities. Tensions in the practices of cultural and personal narratives provoke the creation of and reflection about individual lives and about the society. It is in these milieu that symbol systems evolve. The culturally relevant symbol systems discussed in this book include genres, event scripts, selves, transcendent scripts, and exclusionary scripts like "illegal" person. These symbol systems are the building blocks of the higher order thinking that organizes identity and knowledge.

The development of the cultural self occurs, according to authors of this volume, interactively, as Vygotsky (1978) describes, in collaboration with those already familiar with the way to do and know things in the culture. Nelson (Chapter 2.1) describes collaborative co-construction with parents, self, and others. She explains how the cultural forms of narrating precede the functional uses, as children's development grows in complexity from repeating the routines and cultural mores of everyday life in their families to forming a native cultural self to eventually becoming individuals whose experiences expand beyond the home culture.

Lee, Rosenfeld, Mendenhall, Rivers, and Tynes (Chapter 1.3) describe development as a social construction process; in particular, they explore the development of literacy via the cultural scaffolding of African American Vernacular English storytelling skills that express Black culture in literary ways with dramatic and figurative language.

This development of multicultural selves is also the focus of the essay by Daiute (Chapter 2.2), who explains how the values teachers convey in their curricula influence the contents of children's narratives about personal experiences of conflict. Explicit and implicit audiences, Daiute explains, are powerful forces shaping the narratives of children who identify as African American, Latino, or European American, yet the fictional narratives by these children express very different orientations to conflict from one another and from those promoted in the curriculum.

Lightfoot (Chapter 1.2) explains that adolescent identity development is a process that mirrors the development of the human self-concept across history, an interaction of "a temporal force and a fictional element that together conspire to create an increasingly hypothetical and imaginative self, subject to revision and critique" (p. 23).

Developmental processes related to issues of power are the focus in several chapters. For example, Stanley and Billig (Chapter 2.4) propose the theory-based unit of analysis "ideological dilemmas" to account for co-constructed narratives that express tensions between the purported values of cooperation in a university setting and the power relations that operate between faculty and students as these tensions emerge in a research interview.

Several authors describe the developmental transition as an interaction of dominant narratives and counternarratives. Solis (Chapter 3.1) describes the counternarrative about rights in the activities and documents of Tepayac, the community-based organization of Mexicans in New York City. Tepayac's counternarrative describes Mexicans as participants in the cheap labor force serving the U.S. economy, and as paying inhabitants of substandard housing, who draw little on social services other than sending their children to public schools as undocumented—that is, unrecognized citizens—rather than illegal.

Carney (Chapter 3.2) identifies the interaction between what she refers to as transcendant narratives and counterstories as one of status, as interviewers of Holocaust survivors in her study pressed for stories of resilient survival, while the survivors themselves suggested in various ways that they had not recovered from the traumas of the Holocaust. The lack of integration between transcendent and counterstories across the participants (and in the culture) is a status which, Carney argues, inhibits the integration of trauma when such integration should be considered developmental and healthy.

Analyzing their interviews with nine women who were college students shortly before World War II, as well as the women's "round Robin" letters, Stewart and Malley (Chapter 3.3) suggest a developmental process that is consistent with this interaction between grand cultural narratives and the more subjective experiences of the details that transform those totalizing descriptions.

Development Is Multiple and Cyclical, Like the Multiple Voicing in Narrative

Related to the sense that narratives provide multiple, often conflicting, cultural models is the notion that the developmental relevance of narrative is to be found in the way that it enables the emergence of complexity. Bamberg (Chapter 2.3) explains that the narrator is involved in creating and maintaining several subject positions across texts as a "subject constantly seeking to legitimate itself, situated in language practices and interactively accomplished, where 'world- and person-making take place simultaneously'" (p. 137). Likewise, Freeman (Chapter 1.4) describes a process he calls "rewriting the self"—a process of narrating a new and perhaps "more adequate" view of who one is as one refashions narratives about one's life.

In her analysis of adolescents' fictional texts, Lightfoot (Chapter 1.2) draws upon Bakhtin's (1986) distinction between two different forms of discourse—one authoritative, one innerly persuasive—to describe how fiction writing constitutes a process through which individuals liberate themselves from the constraints of authority and tradition and reconstruct who they understand themselves to be. Stewart and Malley (Chapter 3.3) likewise explore how young women who lived on the margins of the World War II era fashioned a sense of themselves in relation to but, importantly, distinct from the dominant cultural narrative.

Narrative Skills Require Development

Of course, narrating is also a process that requires the development of various specific culturally defined discourse skills. The authors of this volume link the development of narrative linguistic skills to the development of self-concept and culture-concept. For this reason, we use the term "discourse" to refer to the integration of the cultural, psychosocial, and linguistic strategies involved in narrating. Nelson (Chapter 2.1), for example, focuses primarily on the development of linguistic aspects of narrating by reviewing the case study of Emily, whose crib talk has now inspired several generations of narrative theorists.

Sarbin (Chapter 1.1) offers a developmental sequence of imagining that links language, cognition, and emotion across three phases, involving the ability to imitate the language of an older speaker in the culture, then to imitate an absent model, followed by muted but vividly involved role-taking. These imitations are, according to narrative theorists, wordplay that is meaningful in its creation of culturally meaningful persons and events.

What Specific Processes Are Involved in Narrative Research, at What Peril, and With What Results?

In addition to providing traditional accounts of research projects under-taken in a narrative mode, that is, explaining how the narrative process itself plays a role in constructing psychological phenomena, the authors share their reflections on the *process* of their research—how they negotiate the methodological path between subject and researcher. The authors discuss problems that arise from critical applications of narrative analysis, as well as strategies for dealing with those problems. Critical narrative inquiry involves data analysis processes that build questioning about the analysis into the research design. Such a critical approach, for example, posits multiple units of analysis, ethical questions about the assumption of narrative coherence, and the application of diverse theoretical perspectives to explain narrative discourse analyses. From such a critical perspective, narrative analysis, because it is inherently reflective, implicates an ethical dimension that is typically absent from or unexamined in standard social science research. In contrast to more traditional methodologies, narrative analysis is a mode of inquiry that attempts to integrate theory and ethics through-out the data analysis process. The results of narrative analyses are thus a set of perspectives to answer research questions and represent the central topics of an inquiry.

Overall, this volume argues for the importance of theory to guide the reading of research narratives and the narrative reading of all manner of data. The volume also illustrates ways of using narrative analysis to consider how complex cultural, interpersonal, and aesthetic factors shape individual lives.

References

Bakhtin, J. J. (1986). *Speech genres and other late essays*. Austin: University of Texas Press.

Bruner, J. S. (1990). *Acts of meaning*. Cambridge MA: Harvard University Press.

Labov, W., & Waletzky, J. (1997). Narrative analysis: Oral versions of personal experience. *Journal of Narrative and Life History, 7*(1–4), 3, 38.

Phinney, J. S. (2000). Identity formation across cultures: The interaction of personal, societal, and historical change. *Human Development, 43*, 27–31.

Vygotsky, L.S. (1978). *Mind in society*. Cambridge, MA: Harvard University Press.

PART I

Literary Readings

Padre Emanuele, a character in Umberto Eco's novel *The Island of the Day Before* (1995, Harcourt Brace) makes reference to "that Florentine Astronomer who used the Telescope, or Spyglass, that hyperbole of the eyes, to explain the Universe, & how with the Telescope he saw what the eyes had only imagined" (p. 88). The padre goes on to admit a great respect for the use of mechanical instruments to understand the "Res Extensa," a reference to Descartes's ontological world of objects. But to understand the "Res Cogitans," our way of knowing the world, he argues, we can use only another telescope, which is neither a tube nor a lens but a *weft of words*, "because it is only the gift of Artful Eloquence that allows us to understand this Universe" (p. 88).

To take seriously the idea that knowledge of the world is constituted and transformed through the processes of language, discourse, and narrative is to take up the challenge of understanding the struggle between experience and the telling of it, and between the telling and the story told. Each contribution to Part I sets out from the premise that the narrative study of lives can be moved forward through an appreciation of the relationship between life and literature. Considering this relationship, the authors of the chapters in this part of the book answer the questions "In what sense are literary readings distinct from other narrative approaches?" and "What is to be gained by invoking the literary, as opposed to other narrative forms?" Ordinarily, the *literary* holds out the formal qualities of letters and stories as relevant to if not superseding the significance of their colloquial instantiations.

To some degree, the literary readings collected here are a borrowing, a transportation of methodologies from the humanities, particularly literary history and criticism, to the social sciences. The unit of analysis is often big gulps of text—entire stories—rather than the more discrete units of discourse that are explored later in this book. Likewise, the authors in Part I apply literary concepts such as author, narrator, reader, genre, plot, poetics, metaphor, and aesthetics, as tools for interpreting and analyzing their data. But there is also an emphasis here on the impact of literature itself, that is, how socioculturally relevant literary genre and rhetorical traditions—even specific works of literature—shape individual lives and development. As Lee, Rosenfeld, Mendenhall, Rivers, and Tynes (Chapter 1.3) relate, "the storytellers—the poets, novelists, and playwrights—often wrestle with taboos, with the deeply unresolved questions of the human experience. They act as seers and priests who help us to connect vicariously with experiences that are too difficult for us to take on directly; through imagination, we can enter subjunctive worlds and try on identities that we would not ordinarily be bold enough to assume" (p. 39).

According to the collection of contributions here, attention to the literary aspects of life and experience introduces as significant three interrelated themes held together with a cotter assumption that literary texts and everyday lives, like maps and their territories, are inherently incongruous. The first theme concerns the *resonance* of the text, that is, the extent to which it has meaning beyond the local and personal context of its construction. An example is provided in Sarbin's (Chapter 1.1) discussion of how the publication of Goethe's *The Sorrows of Young Werther*—a story of unrequited love ending in suicide—inspired the suicides of young people on such a scale that the book was banned in several European countries. Likewise, Lightfoot (Chapter 1.2) suggests that the conceptions of self depicted in historically emergent literary genres, such as adventure stories and coming-of-age stories, provide tools with which contemporary adolescents construct representations of the self in written fictional stories. In an examination of the "cultural modeling" of narrative traditions, Lee and her colleagues (Chapter 1.3) explore the ways in which the rhetorical traditions of African Americans—the language, idioms, and sermonic tone—are used as models in the literacy development of African American children.

The resonance of stories—their ability to outlast their tellings—is a notion that Freeman (Chapter 1.4) takes up in his discussion of Ricoeur's theory of time and narrative. According to Ricoeur, meaningful acts have unintended, future consequences of sociocultural significance that outdistance their immediate relevance. While stories are present tellings of past events, their resonance is revealed only in the future. Time is thus a salient concern for those bent on narrative analysis. Related to resonance, and the second general theme addressed in the chapters collected here, is the problematic relationship between texts and both their authors and their readers. Because narrating is an objectification of experience that extends beyond time and authorial intent, the meanings of a text are overdetermined, subject to alternative readings and alternative tellings, each more than the author supposes. Sarbin (Chapter 1.1) develops the concept of imagining as a means for understanding the relationship between author or reader and text. By his lights, imaginings are narrative emplotments—storied sequences of actions—that constitute a form of expressive and embodied role-taking. They are shaped within social contexts and in response to questions such as "What is my role?" and "What story am I telling?" The task of the narrative researcher is to discern the authorial intent of the subject, however shifting it may be.

Freeman (Chapter 1.4), in contrast, has a somewhat different focus. Noting that "narrative analysis of the sort being pursued here moves beyond the confines of the individual as a matter of course and necessity" (p. 78), he suggests that the researcher's ultimate task is not so much the telling of the subject's story as the construction of a story of his or her own making. That is, the researcher aims at a creative rendering of the subject's life according to evidence that may be gleaned from a variety of sources, some strictly narrative, others not. He notes that in his recent work his data do not include discrete texts at all "—or at least no texts possessing an existence independent of, well, *me*" (p. 74). The text, including its coherence and rhetorical appeal (and therefore its scholarly significance), is therefore created by the researcher—its content not necessarily commensurate with the subject's presentational goals or plans but potentially expressive of a "narrative unconscious."

The chapters by Lightfoot (Chapter 1.2) and by Lee and her colleagues (Chapter 1.3) address the cultural and historical constraints on how texts are authored and narrated. Thus, Lightfoot argues that developmental changes in how individuals write fictional stories cohere, in structure and sequence, with the emergence of traditional Western European literary genre. Across the adolescent years, individuals increasingly construct characters who worry about or come to terms with such epistemological issues as self-transformation and subjectivity, as well as the corollary problem of the relationship between the worlds of fact and fiction. Similarly, Lee and her colleagues begin with the understanding that in the multiethnic and multicultural heritage of contemporary America, the Western European literary tradition is but one of many. Using characteristics that have been identified with the African American rhetorical tradition, their analysis of

African American school children shows how specific cultural traditions are inscribed in academic performances. They argue, moreover, that an informed use of culturally appropriate materials in the classroom can facilitate children's academic success.

The third theme that emerges in Part I, and one that is addressed in each chapter, concerns the fictional-imaginal element implicit in the assumption that stories are not "life itself." Thus, Sarbin's (Chapter 1.1) storied imaginings are "as if" constructions. He underscores the imaginative process through which extant works of literature are embodied by readers in ways that move them literally—to tears, to action. In a similar vein, Lightfoot (Chapter 1.2) views adolescent identity development as an inherently aesthetic process through which individuals construct hypothetical selves oriented toward unrealized futures. Lee and her colleagues (Chapter 1.3) argue that African American stories and artifacts engage an imaginative process in which individual children both envision multiple, alternative worlds and develop academic and cultural literacy skills. Freeman (Chapter 1.4) invokes the imagination as a process of articulating meanings that emerge only in the course of retrospective narration.

All of the chapters are fundamentally concerned with the pathway that binds the territory of our lives to the ways in which it is mapped in story and narrative. Whether we read the signs of a life in a story, in a researcher's analysis, or in the rope-scarred hands of a fisherman, the challenge of assessing the epistemological consequences of narratives whose meanings are overdetermined and inherently conjectural remains an inspiration.

1.1

The Role of Imagination in Narrative Construction

Theodore R. Sarbin

T his chapter attempts to clarify the role of imagination in narrative
construction and interpretation. No framework for analyzing narratives can be complete without including the psychological processes usually
subsumed under the generic term "imagination." I have organized the
chapter as follows: First, I show through selected examples that narratives
can have a substantial impact on the identity development, beliefs, and
actions of the reader. (My focus is on narratives read, but the analysis is
equally applicable to stories heard, to dramas performed on the stage or in
movies, and to stories told in other art forms.) Second, I deconstruct the
concept of imagination as a necessary step toward understanding its role in
narrative analysis. This historico-linguistic effort supports the claim that

Author's Note: In the preparation of this chapter, I have borrowed liberally from
some of my earlier work on imagining (Sarbin, 1972, 1998; Sarbin & Juhasz, 1970),
on narrative (Mancuso & Sarbin, 1998; Sarbin, 1982, 1986a, 1997), and on
emotional life and embodiment (Sarbin 1986b, 1989, 1995, 2000; Sarbin & Allen,
1968). The many productive lunchtime discussions I had with Professor Gerald
P. Ginsburg were invaluable to me in formulating the structure and content of the
chapter. I am also grateful to Dr. Ralph M. Carney for his critical reading of an
earlier draft.

imagining (not to be confused with imagery) is not an internal *happening* (such as experiencing "pictures in the mind") but a "doing," a set of actions that can be described as attenuated or muted role-taking. Third, I make the claim that organismic involvement, one of the dimensions of overt role enactment, can be applied, pari passu, to attenuated role-taking. As employed in this essay, the meaning of "organismic involvement" is synonymous with the contemporary meaning of "embodiment." Finally, I posit that organismic involvement is the means through which narrative-inspired imaginings can influence belief and action. The thrust of my argument is that identity change can occur in response to subtle cues arising from embodied actions performed during attenuated role-taking sequences. In this connection, embodiments and their sequelae in emotional roles contribute to the person's assigning credibility to narratively created identities, setting the stage for action.

Stories Have the Potential for Identity Development and Action

In the following pages, I use the term "narrative" as equivalent to "story." A printed or spoken account does not necessarily qualify as a narrative. Shopping lists, road directions, and treasurer's reports, for example, do not qualify as narratives because they fail to meet the essential criteria for telling a story: duration—a beginning, a middle, and an ending—and, importantly, the presence of a moral issue. Current storytelling in print or in the movies, no less than in the ancient fables of Aesop, contains subtexts that deal with one or more moral concepts. Individual differences in the moral codes of readers or listeners to stories determine their appreciation of and responses to such moral issues.

That narratives can have profound influence on identity development and consequent conduct is readily documented. In the domain of literature, Levin (1970) catalogues numerous instances where novelists attributed the identity development of their protagonists to the influence of book reading. The paradigm case is Miguel de Cervantes's *Don Quixote* (1605). The lonely Don, whose pastime is reading tales of chivalry, fashioned an identity for himself based on the exploits of knights-errant of an extinct historical era. He constructs imaginings that replicate deeds of chivalric heroes. In this respect, the Don is like other readers of adventure stories. Skill in imagining enables the reader to enter the pages of the book—sometimes as spectator, sometimes as actor. However, Don Quixote does more than entertain a storied fantasy. To validate his narratively constructed identity, he takes the additional step of performing the social role of knight-errant. His knight-errantry collides with characters who are participants in a 17th-century culture far removed from the feudal institutions of the 12th century, thus invoking humor, pathos, and other dramatic tensions. Labeled the "Quixotic Principle" (Levin, 1970; Sarbin, 1982), *Don Quixote* serves as a model for looking into the frequently observed phenomenon that narratives can mold identities to conform to a protagonist's character and personal style.

The power of narrative to lead readers to action is also illustrated in Johann Wolfgang von Goethe's celebrated novel, *The Sorrows of Young Werther*, published in 1774. In part autobiographical, *Young Werther* is a sentimental story of unrequited love ending in suicide. The publication and circulation of the book increased suicide rates in Europe in the final quarter of the 18th century. Young men adopted as a guiding fiction Werther's struggle with rejection and his ultimate suicide. The book appeared during an era when death and dying, especially dying by one's own hand, was seen as romantic. The literature of the times conferred nobility and heroism on the act of dying, particularly if one could compose one's own death drama. Werther's suicide solution was copied by scores of young romantics suffering the pangs of unrequited love. Suicide rates increased dramatically, so much so that some European countries banned the book. Werther was frequently mentioned in suicide notes. "There was a Werther epidemic: a Werther fever, a Werther fashion . . . Werther caricatures, and Werther suicides" (Friedenthal, 1963, p. 123). One writer noted that "all over Europe large numbers of young people committed suicide with a copy of the book clutched in their hands or buried in their pockets" (Kaufmann, 1975, p. 161). Werther, a fictional character in a novel, had been transfigured to become a model for living and dying. Sociological research lends credibility to the Werther effect and, by implication, to the Quixotic Principle. Studies conducted between 1968 and 1985 reported quantifiable effects on suicide rates that could be attributed to television and newspaper accounts of suicide. The effects were most marked for adolescents (Phillips & Carsterson, 1988).

In 1852, Harriet Beecher Stowe wrote the celebrated novel *Uncle Tom's Cabin*. Employing the literary devices of fiction, the author depicts the evils of the institution of slavery through describing the victimization of Eva, Eliza, Tom, and others. Her descriptions of the cruel practices characteristic of slavery show the dehumanization of innocent and likable human beings. The novel was by far the best-selling book of the 19th century. It was translated into almost every modern language and adapted for the theater. For more than 80 years, *Uncle Tom's Cabin* was a popular vehicle for traveling stage companies (Hughes, 1952). The novel was even more popular in Victorian England, where 1,200,000 copies of the book were sold in its first year of publication. Stowe's poignant portrayal of the dehumanization inherent in the institution of slavery weighed on the conscience of the British readership. A significant outcome of these readers' involvement in the subtext of *Uncle Tom's Cabin*—the moral issue of slavery—was the political decision of the British government not to provide military aid to the Confederacy, despite the economic importance to England of the cotton textile trade with the South (Brock, Strange, & Green, 2002).

The Grapes of Wrath, John Steinbeck's poignant depiction of a family suffering the effects of the Great Depression of the 1930s, was a best-seller. The novel served as the basis for a celebrated motion picture that was seen by millions of people. The narrative reflected the failure of the economic system to provide the means for leading a life of dignity. The following autobiographical account illustrates the power of the narrative to influence the identity development of one person.

> I was completing my graduate studies when I read the *Grapes of Wrath*. I read it in one sitting, until I came to the passage where the old lady died during the migration of the family from Oklahoma to California. I actually sobbed and wiped away tears. I could not bear the sadness and also what I perceived as injustice. It was as if I were a fellow passenger in the old jalopy, sharing the suffering and pain of the family that had been uprooted from their way of life by impersonal economic forces. I became so emotional that I had to close the book before reaching the final chapters. A week or two later, I returned to the book, but not until I had made a decision to become a social activist and try to change the world. My first step was to sign up as a volunteer to a labor union that was on strike at a local industry.

These illustrative examples of the Quixotic Principle generate the question: What are the psychological events that intervene between the story and its often profound behavioral effects on the reader or listener? "The imagination" is frequently cited as the process that intervenes between a person's interacting with the story and his or her adoption of beliefs and actions as a result of that interaction. Typical answers to the question reframe the observation as the reader "projecting" himself or herself into the story or being "transported" by the novel into the world of the story. The observation invites metaphors such as "absorption" and "entrancement," the former representing concentrated attention, the latter representing the effects of reading on beliefs and actions (Nell, 1988). These are useful descriptive metaphors, but they do not contribute much to our understanding of the psychological processes that lead to being transported or entranced. These descriptive metaphors are not primitive terms;

therefore, we are compelled to ask, What are the psychological parameters of imagining? (Note my preference for the gerund "imagining" rather than the substantive "imagination." The gerund "imagining" connotes an active process, something the imaginer *does*. In contrast, the substantive "imagination" suggests a thing-like entity, or a property of the mental apparatus.)

The thrust of the remainder of this chapter is to identify the behavioral processes that redirect attention from the printed page or an oral account to imaginal involvement in the moral dilemmas of historical or fictional characters, to fantasied adventures in uncharted territories, to engrossed participation in times past or times future.

An Etymology of Imagining

To increase understanding of the role of imagination in narrative construction, it is first necessary to sketch out a semiotic analysis. Historico-linguistic study reveals that the roots of the word "imagining" denote copying behaviors, not the popular "pictures in the mind" construction. The history of psychology as a discipline makes clear that Cartesian dualism provided the framework for theorizing about human behavior. From the beginning of psychology as a field of scientific study, the principal task has been to understand the workings of the mind. Imagination, as one of the properties of the mental apparatus that generates images, has been understood as something that happens in the mind. However, to make the Cartesian claim that imaginings are happenings taking place on the shadowy stage of the mind is to affirm a demonstrably futile model of human conduct. A review of theories and research designed to clarify the concept of imagination makes one fact abundantly clear: The model of pictures-in-the-mind has produced virtually nothing in the way of pragmatically useful or heuristically exciting propositions (Sarbin & Juhasz, 1970). The pictures-in-the-mind metaphor collapses when somesthetic experiences are imagined. "Pictures-in-the-mind" becomes an empty metaphor when we consider the rhetorical question: What faculty of the mind would have to be activated in order to imagine the taste of coconut crème pie, the fragrance of a florist shop, or the pain of childbirth?

It is instructive to take a backward glance at the influence of Cartesian mentalism on the later development of imagining as "pictures in the mind." Earlier, the etymological root of imagining, *imago,* had been derived from *imitari,* a form that gave rise to our current word "imitate." The root form did not carry the implication of pictures in the mind but, rather, denoted three-dimensional copying through fashioning a molded likeness, a sculptured statue, or an engraved artifact. *Imago, imitari,* and cognate forms were employed to communicate about such three-dimensional copying. On the basis of a partial similarity between events ordinarily denoted by *imitari* and the copying activities of artisans, *imago,* the root form of *imitari,* was used to denote such copying activities. Image, imago, and similar forms were descriptors only for three-dimensional artifacts such as objects of religious worship and statues of famous persons. When applied in a metaphorical way to those occurrences currently called "imaginings," the tenor was an active constructive process. That is to say, the pre-Renaissance imaginer was a fashioner, an image maker, a fabricator, a doer; no implication was intended that the imaginer was a passive registrant of a mysterious process happening in an equally mysterious mind. Such an implication, however, did evolve when the Cartesian "mind" became the concept of choice to render the theological construction of "soul" philosophically and scientifically credible. The Cartesian perspective assigned imagining, as well as other private and silent actions, to the mysterious domain of mind for which "pictures in the mind" became the preferred metaphor.

The fact is undeniable that a shift in metaphor occurred—a shift from viewing imagining as active three-dimensional imitation to viewing imagining as passive mechanical mirroring in the mind. In linguistic history, post-Renaissance scholars formulated the next step: the transfiguration of imagining as active three-dimensional copying to an interiorized form of *seeing.* Our language is full of instances of this assimilation: "seeing in the mind's eye," "visualizing," "seeing mental pictures," "having a visual image," and so on. These everyday expressions are witness to the fact that we have been captivated by the unlabeled metaphor—we now talk (1) as if there are pictures (alternatively, impressions or representations) and (2) as if there are minds that, like art galleries, provide display space for such mental pictures. Sampson (1996) remarks that the assimilation of imago and similar forms to "pictures in the mind" reflects the preference of Descartes and other Western philosophers for "ocularcentric" metaphors. In reviewing the history of the privileging of vision as an ontological foundation, Sampson further notes that "Descartes built his entire framework upon 'the inner or mind's eye'" (p. 603).

Before proceeding further, I point to an important distinction. Because of lack of precision in the use of vocabulary, the words "imagery" and "imaginings" are often used interchangeably. In current usage, these terms have different referents. The study of imagery is in general the study of experiences of an optical and ocular nature, for example, negative after-images, or the reconstructions of perceptions of absent objects and events, and so on. Most experimental studies of imagery analyze the verbal responses of experimental subjects to instructions such as "visualize a ripe peach." In contrast to imagery, imaginings are storied sequences of actions in which self and others are involved. Imaginings are emplotted narratives carrying implications of causality and duration. They are fashioned from concurrent perceptions of proximal and distal stimulus events, from rememberings, cultural stories, folktales, legends, cultural myths, articulated theories, proverbs, sermons, and experiences with multifarious art forms. In short, imaginings are storied constructions. In another place, I have suggested resurrecting "poetics" as a more apt term in this context than "constructions." "Poetics" more neatly reflects the making of stories, avoiding the architectural connotations of "constructions" (Sarbin, 1997).

Imagining as "As If" Behavior

The contemporary form of Cartesian mentalism is not the only thought model available to students of silent and invisible processes. An alternative view construes human beings as active, exploring, manipulating, inventing, doing creatures. In this view, human beings construct their worlds, within limits, instead of being merely the envelopes of a passive mind and subject to the uncertainties of a capricious world. Human beings' constructions of reality depend upon a skill to function at various levels of hypotheticalness. This skill makes it possible to distinguish between self-reports that reflect ordinary perception ("I heard the voice"), imagining ("It is as if I 'heard' the voice") and metaphor ("I heard the voice of conscience"). That is to say, a hierarchy of hypothesis-making skills liberates human beings from the constraints of the immediate environment. With this "as if" skill, the actor can interact with narratively constructed events that are spatially distant and temporally remote, he or she can relocate self to different times and places.

In this analysis, storied imaginings are fashioned from "as if" constructions. I am using "construction" in the same sense as it is used in Bartlett's formulation about remembering (1932), a formulation that has been revived in current theories of memory, in which individuals actively combine bits and pieces of experience to form rememberings. Through constructing their worlds, human beings are able to place themselves not only with reference to objects and events that are present in the world of occurrences but also with reference to absent objects and events. The behavioral act of constructing absent objects and events is the referent for "as if" or hypothetical construction. Such an act can occur only when the person has achieved some skill in using fictions, such skill following from the acquisition of sign and symbol competences. As outlined in the following paragraphs, the "as if" skill makes possible the formation of narrative plot structures.

A three-stage sequence of child development helps account for the achievement of the "as if" skill, the skill to construct hypothetical worlds. The child acquires knowledge in a number of ways, one of which is imitation. In the developmental sequence, the first stage is the outright copying of the performances of another person. This is the paradigm of imitation. That is to say, to imitate is to copy the actions of a model who can be seen and heard. In the second stage, a complexity is introduced. The child imitates the actions of another, but that other is absent. The child imitates the talk, gestures, and actions of the absent model. This is the paradigm of role-taking. It is a high order achievement to pretend to be Aunt Jane when Aunt Jane is out of sight. A child may set a dinner table with invisible props; he or she may pour "pretend" soup into ephemeral bowls and arrange the seating of unseen guests in unoccupied chairs. Such role enactments follow an unwritten script with recognizable sequences, beginnings, middles, and endings.

The third stage in the development of the skill in imagining is concurrent with another achievement of early childhood: the muting of speech. To talk silently to oneself rather than aloud at first requires only skill in controlling the volume of air that passes over the vocal cords. With practice, the child learns to inhibit most of the overt muscular characteristics of speech. The acquisition of the skill in muting speech and the attenuation of the motoric performances are in the service of reducing the amplitude of the overt actions that comprise the "let's pretend" roles. This third stage—muted and attenuated role-taking—is the ultimate referent for the word "imagining." Note that I have returned to the pre-Renaissance use of the root form of imaginings— the active, constructive, three-dimensional copying of absent models. Rather than artifacts, such as religious icons, the products of such constructional activity are dramaturgical, that is, enacted stories.

Not every story produces the same kind of impact produced by *Young Werther* or *Uncle Tom's Cabin*. This occurs only when the narrative involves the reader in the plot—in the interactions among the characters whose actions make a difference—and where the reader is "moved" by the moral issues portrayed in the story. The moral message of a story will have a different effect depending on the moral status of the reader. When it was first published, *Uncle Tom's Cabin* not only mobilized readers whose own moral development was consistent with that of the author, it was also vehemently rejected by readers who accepted the institution of slavery. Clearly, some stories generate attitudes and conduct that are described as emotional. In this connection, a literary study of 2,000 stories representing many historical periods could be sorted into 36 discrete plot structures, each plot structure representing an "emotion" (Polti, 1916).

Because mentalism is still a powerful influence on our linguistic constructions, when a person, in commenting on a literary work or dramatic production, says "I was moved," the predicate is interpreted as a metaphor implying emotional involvement. It is interesting to note that the etymology of "emotion" contains the root *moti*, a participle form of *emovere*, meaning "to move." In my later discussion of embodiment, departing from the residual influence of mentalism, the sentence "I was moved" can be restored to our lexicon as a more literal descriptor.

To understand how persons can describe their self-perceptions as being "moved" requires a preliminary discussion of observations that carry the label "emotion." In contrast to the conventional view of studying emotions as psychophysiogical happenings (Averill, 1974), I have elsewhere suggested that we direct our attention to *emotional life* (Sarbin, 1989, 1995). This expanded formulation follows from taking into account historical and social contexts, moral imperatives, and rhetorical strategies, as well as the effects of embodied action. From this perspective, episodes of emotional life can be described with the language of narrative construction (Harré, 1986; Sarbin, 1986b), a conception far removed from the tradition of regarding emotions as cranial or visceral objects. The older tradition reflects the ancient myth that emotions are disorganized behaviors, a resultant of our animal heritage and are contrary to logic and reason. The narrative perspective, contrariwise, treats episodes of emotional life as logical, not disorganized. In his exposition directed to undressing the myth of the passions, Solomon (1976) addresses the issue of emotions being logical: "We intend to revenge ourselves in anger, to redeem ourselves in shame, to restore our dignity in embarrassment, to help another person in pity" (p. 190).

deSousa (1980) complements the notion that instances of emotional life are logical. Emotional repertoires are acquired in the context of "paradigm scenarios." These scenarios are prototypes of plot structures, many of which are acquired early in life. A child's reflexive responses to certain stimuli are recruited into an emotional display. "In simple cases the instinctive [read reflexive] response to certain stimuli [such as smiling or crying] becomes an *expression* of emotion (joy, sadness, rage) but it does so only in the context of the scenario" (p. 285).

Because of the dominance of discourses that focus on biological and evolutionary conceptions of emotions as happenings, the discourses that construe emotions as agentic action, such as those of Solomon and deSousa, have been relegated to the periphery of conventional psychology. Applying the concept of agency, contemporary theories view the listener to a storyteller, reader, or theatergoer, as engaged in living out a story, not unlike the person in a real-life emotional drama. Such engagement is more than a cognitive exercise, it is action oriented and thus embodied. A reader who identifies with the moral stance of a fictional protagonist engaged, for example, in a heated quarrel with another character, feels tension in the thrust of the jaw, clenching of fists, contraction of muscles that control locomotion, posture, and so on.

It is a matter of common observation that people overtly enact roles with varying amounts of force and vigor. High involvement in role behavior is illustrated in such conditions as ecstasy, religious conversion, and sexual union (Sarbin & Allen, 1968). An example of moderate involvement would be the case of a novelist struggling to construct a character or a scene—especially if he or she were facing a deadline. The degree of involvement could be noted in the motoric accompaniment of the creative process such as nervous pacing, the speed of writing on the notepad or vigorous striking of the keyboard, disattention to extraneous stimuli, and so on. An example of minimal involvement would be the bored college sophomore acting as subject in a nonsense-syllable experiment.

This action concept, degree of organismic involvement, is as applicable to attenuated "as if" behavior as it is to overt role enactments. Just as we may fruitfully employ "degree of involvement" as a dimension of overt role enactment, so may we employ the same dimension to describe the bodily involvement in muted or attenuated role-taking (i.e., in storied imaginings). A high level of involvement in imagining is illustrated by the reader of *Uncle Tom's Cabin* who tearfully sobs on reading the tragic death of Uncle Tom or who experiences moral indignation at the cruelties of Simon Legree. The role-taking concept "degree of organismic involvement" increases understanding of how silent, attenuated, "as if" behavior can induce the reader or theatergoer to be saddened over the death of a fictional character, or to rejoice when the fictional lovers are reunited after multiple misadventures.

The Embodied Self

In the previous pages, I have centered on the Quixotic Principle, on emotional life, and on attenuated role-taking as a source of identity formation and consequent action that may have profound effects. It remains to demonstrate support for the claim that "degree of embodiment" is a fruitful concept to relate absorption in a story to real-world effects as demonstrated, for example, by the effects on the readers of *Young Werther* and *Uncle Tom's Cabin*.

Like flesh-and-blood actors in emotional life dramas who make use of a large repertoire of verbal and nonverbal actions, the involved reader also makes use of a repertory of embodied actions—crying, laughing, shrugs, postures, gestures, facial expressions, attenuated approach and avoidance movements, and so on. The reader's embodiment of narrative should not be confused with the visceral accompaniments of preparing for action. The embodiments are *expressions* and can serve communicative and rhetorical functions. Visceral changes are adjuncts to experiences that reflect some instances of emotional life that include arousal. Our standard textbooks focus on the arousal activities of the autonomic nervous system as central to understanding emotions. Such a claim reflects a synecdoche, identifying a part of an experience for the whole. The concept of arousal is only a part of the total context of action. Autonomic arousal provides inputs that are antecedent to or concurrent with the strategic recruitment into the ongoing discourse of *expressive* bodily actions, such as crying, laughing, facial gestures, minimal kinesthetic movements, and so on. To be sure, the total context of an emotional experience may include autonomic adjuncts—such as increased respiration, heart rate, and so on—that may have informational value. But these are not the central features that give rise to embodied actions. Embodiment refers to the bodily expressions arising from the reader's placing himself or herself in a particular role. If the reader becomes involved in a story of sadness, embodiments are experienced such as "lump in the throat," tears, postural adjustments, facial displays, and asynchronies of speech as a result of efforts to inhibit crying. If the reader becomes involved in a story in which the protagonist is the object of insult by a villainous character, the reader will make a judgment that the latter character is deserving of retaliatory aggressive actions. These inhibited actions generate proprioceptive sensory inputs in the muscles that would be involved in aggressive action, such inputs becoming part of the reader's cognitive matrix.

I am employing a set of constructions that bears a resemblance to the motor theory of consciousness, a staple of psychological theorizing in the early part of the 20th century (Washburn, 1916). To give body to the motor theory, in the 1920s and 1930s, Jacobson reported a series of experiments that supported the claim that imagining reflected minimal but invisible movements of skeletal muscles (see, e.g., Jacobson, 1930). Typical of his experiments was the recording of action currents when a right-handed subject was told to imagine a task such as throwing a ball. Action currents were generated in the muscles of the right arm but not the left.

On the periphery of standard psychology is an experimental literature that relates expressed feelings to self-perceptions of embodiments created in the act of imagining (Gibbs & Berg, 2002a, 2002b; Laird, in press). In the following paragraphs, I try to show how embodiments arise in social interaction in which participants govern their actions by taking into account feedback from their expressive behavior, but always in the context of concurrent answers to the questions "What is my role?" and "What story am I entering?"

Laird (in press) has reviewed scores of studies, many carried out in his own laboratory, that support the claim, initially laid down by William James (1890), that the often-ambiguous self-evaluation "feelings" follows—rather than precedes—expressive behavior. If laboratory conditions are set up so that experimental subjects smile, or are manipulated to control the facial muscles so that a smile is produced, the subjects' self-reports generally indicate pleasure. Similarly, if the facial muscles are controlled so as to produce a frown, the subjects assess their feeling state as sad or unhappy. Besides facial displays, other expressive behaviors have been studied, such as postures, gaze, tone of voice, breathing patterns, overt actions, and even autonomic arousal. All these experiments lead to the conclusion that when people perform expressive actions that are associated with instances of emotional life, their judgments about self are communicated in the language of feelings. The referents for the impoverished language of feelings are ultimately bodily actions and of necessity are communicated with the aid of metaphors or exclamations. Poets and novelists have acquired the skill in using metaphors and other figures of speech to communicate about feelings and the narrative context. Those who are at a loss for words make use of exclamations. After just completing a marathon, a woman was interviewed by a reporter who asked, "How did it feel when you crossed the finish line?" Her reply was simply, "Wow!"

The gist of Laird's review supports the notion that the "feeling" quality that persons assign to their actions, under some conditions, follows from their perceptions of embodiments from overt or attenuated role enactments. I use the qualifying phrase, "under some conditions," to communicate that the narrative context will determine whether the kinesthetic feedback from a smile will be interpreted as a sign of pleasure or as a sign of one's obligation to appear polite. Hochschild (1983) has observed that women in certain occupations, such as airline cabin attendants, have been required to smile even under degrading conditions, such as sexual harassment. The dialogue partner might misinterpret the smile as a sign of pleasure, at the same time that the woman is experiencing the feeling of disgust or anger. La France and Hecht (1999) have demonstrated unequivocally that power differentials and gender relations affect the form of women's smiles. Careful observation reveals subtle variations in the contraction of subjects' facial muscles when smiling to a peer or to a superior, when smiling as an option or as an obligation. Such variations provide different embodiments, kinesthetic cues that can serve as inputs—given the narrative context—for making an attribution of genuine pleasure or of annoyance, fear, or anger.

Gibbs and Berg (2002a, 2002b) reviewed the experimental literature in cognitive psychology, neuroscience, and psycholinguistics to warrant the claim that mental imagery (their vocabulary for imaginings) is based on embodied action. Drawing from a different database, their conclusions parallel those of Laird. They found that many neuropsychological studies have shown that the physiological processes responsible for embodied action are activated even when no movement can be observed. These studies are reminiscent of those of Jacobson, mentioned before, save that the technologies for assessing activation are more refined. Positron emission topography (PET) studies, for example, have shown that specific areas of the cortex show activity when subjects imagine making different body movements. Gibbs and Berg's (2002a) conclusion is relevant to the proposition that narratively inspired imaginings are affected by perceptions of bodily actions. "The various behavioral and neuroimagery findings highlight that motoric elements are recruited whenever the perceived or imagined object is conceptualized in action-oriented terms" (p. 8).

The foregoing discussion can be applied to understanding why some stories produce profound effects. To recapitulate: My claim is that imaginings are induced by stories read or stories told, that imaginings are instances of attenuated role-taking, that attenuated role-taking requires motoric actions that produce kinesthetic cues and other embodiments, and that embodiments become a part of the total context from which persons decide how to live their lives.

The concept of embodiment is helpful in understanding why some individuals act as if their imaginings are "real," why some imaginings are believed to be of the same character as literal happenings in the distal world. Empathizing with the quasi-reality of the suffering of the protagonist in *The Sorrows of Young Werther* and the tribulations of Eliza in *Uncle Tom's Cabin* is more than an intellectual exercise. The moral posture of the readers together with the artistry of the authors induce embodied imaginings that are integral to the reader's or listener's participation. When the reader becomes highly involved in the text, more organismic systems are engaged and, in the total context of action, proprioceptive sensory inputs become salient (Stepper & Strack, 1993). These sensory inputs are generated primarily in the musculature involved in the attenuated role-taking.

To identify the conditions for persons to act as if they believe (assign credibility to) some poetic imaginings and not others, it is helpful to look into the meaning of the word "believing." An etymological tracing of our modern word "believe" provides some clues to help establish what differentiates believing from imagining, even though they cannot be differentiated in terms of content. This tracing proceeds from an IndoEuropean form, "leubh," translated as "strongly desires" or "love," through Latin forms that gave us "libido" and various other forms meaning "to love" (Needham, 1973).The etymological connection between "belief" and the various words for "love" is central to my thesis: that believings are highly valued imaginings. Thus, within the cognitive term "belief" resides variants of "love," a concept associated with emotional life. In this context, I am interpreting the word "love" not in its romantic sense but in its more general sense of "being highly valued."

The argument can be made that a well-constructed story is automatically given credibility unless an effort is made to disbelieve. William James (1890) put it succinctly: "Any object which remains uncontradicted is ipso facto believed and posited as absolute reality" (vol. 2, p. 289). "We never disbelieve anything except for the reason that we believe something else which contradicts the first thing." (vol. 2, p. 284). The Jamesian proposal is supported by a series of studies that demonstrated that both children and adults automatically assign credibility to fictional accounts unless they make an effort to disbelieve (Gerrig, 1993; Gerrig & Pillow, 1998).

The foregoing analysis leads to the conclusion that the act of reading or listening to a story, in the context in which the reader's moral constructions are engaged, produces embodied self-perceptions. The greater the degree of embodied involvement in narrative-inspired imaginings, the more likely that the reader or listener will "feel with" or identify with the protagonist"s efforts to resolve the moral issues central to a particular plot.

References

Averill, J. R. (1974). An analysis of psychophysiological symbolism and its influence on theories of emotion. *Journal for the Theory of Social Behavior, 4*, 147–190.

Bartlett, F. (1932). *Remembering: A study in experimental and social psychology.* Cambridge, UK: Cambridge University Press.

Brock, T. C., Strange, J. J., & Green, M. C. (2002). Power beyond reckoning. In M. C. Green, J. J. Strange, & T. C. Brock (Eds.), *Narrative impact: Social and cognitive foundations* (pp. 1–16). Mahwah, NJ: Lawrence Erlbaum.

deSousa, R. (1980). Self-deceptive emotions. In A. O. Rorty (Ed.), *Explaining emotions* (pp. 283-298). Berkeley: University of California Press.

Friedenthal, R. (1963). *Goethe: His life and times.* London: Wiedenfeld & Nicholson.

Gerrig, R. J. (1993). *Experiencing narrative worlds.* New Haven, CT: Yale University Press.

Gerrig, R. J., & Pillow, B. H. (1998). A developmental perspective on the construction of disbelief. In J. de Rivera & T. R. Sarbin (Eds.), *Believed-in imaginings: The narrative construction of reality* (pp. 101–120). Washington, DC: American Psychological Association.

Gibbs, R. W., Jr., & Berg, E. A. (2002a). Mental imagery and embodied activity. *Journal of Mental Imagery, 26,* 1–30.

Gibbs, R. W., Jr., & Berg, E. A. (2002b). Finding the body in mental imagery. *Journal of Mental Imagery, 26,* 82–108.

Hochschild, A. R. (1983). *The managed heart.* Berkeley: University of California Press.

Harré, R. (Ed.). (1986). *The social construction of emotions.* Oxford: Basil Blackwell.

Hughes, L. (1952). Introduction. In H. B. Stowe, *Uncle Tom's cabin.* New York: Dodd, Mead. (Original work published 1852)

Levin, H. (1970). The Quixotic Principle. In M. W. Bloomfield (Ed.), *Harvard English Studies: I. The interpretation of narrative: theory and practice.* Cambridge, MA: Harvard University Press./

Jacobson, E. (1930). Electrical measurements of neuromuscular states during mental activities: IV. Evidence of contraction of specific muscles during imagination. *American Journal of Physiology, 95,* 703–712.

James, W. (1890). *Principles of psychology* (Vol. 2). New York: Henry Holt.

Kaufmann, W. (1975). *Without guilt and justice: From decidophobia to autonomy.* New York: Delta.

LaFrance, M., & Hecht, M. A. (1999). Option or obligation to smile: The effect of power and gender on facial expression. In P. Philippot, R. S. Feldman, & E. J. Coats (Eds.), *The social context of nonverbal behavior* (pp. 45–70). Cambridge, UK: Cambridge University Press.

Laird, J. (in press). *Feelings: The perception of self.* New York: Oxford University Press.

Mancuso, J. C., & Sarbin, T. R. (1998). The narrative construction of emotional life. In M. F. Mascolo & S. Griffin (Eds.), *What develops in emotional development?* (pp. 297–316). New York: Plenum.

Needham, R. (1972). *Belief, language, experience.* Chicago: University of Chicago Press.

Nell, V. (1988). *Lost in a book.* New Haven, CT: Yale University Press.

Phillips, D., & Carsterson, L. L. (1988). The effect of suicide stories on various demographic groups. *Suicide and Life-Threatening Behavior, 2,* 100–114.

Polti, G. (1916). *The thirty-six dramatic situations.* (L. Ray, Trans.). Boston: Writer, Inc.

Sampson, E. E. (1996) Establishing embodiment in psychology. *Theory and Psychology, 6,* 601–624.

Sarbin, T. R. (1972). Imagining as muted role-taking: A historico-linnguistic analysis. In P. Sheehan, *The function and nature of imagery* (pp. 333–354). New York: Academic Press.

Sarbin, T. R. (1982). The Quixotic Principle: A belletristic approach to the psychology of imagining. In V. L. Allen & K. E. Scheibe (Eds.), *The social context of conduct: Psychological writings of Theodore Sarbin* (pp. 169–188). New York: Praeger.

Sarbin, T. R. (1986a). The narrative as the root metaphor for psychology. In T. R. Sarbin (Ed.), *Narrative psychology: The storied nature of human conduct* (pp. 3–21). New York: Praeger.

Sarbin, T. R. (1986b). Emotions and act: Roles and rhetoric. In R. Harré (Ed.), *The social construction of emotions* (pp. 83–97). Oxford, UK: Basil Blackwell.

Sarbin, T. R. (1989). Emotions as narrative emplotments. In M. J. Packer & R. M. Addison (Eds.), *Entering the circle: Hermeneutic investigation in psychology* (pp. 185–201, 312–314). Albany: State University of New York Press.

Sarbin, T. R. (1995). Emotional life, rhetoric, and roles. *Journal of Narrative and Personal History, 5,* 213–220.

Sarbin, T. R. (1997). The poetics of identity. *Theory and Psychology, 6,* 67–82.

Sarbin, T. R. (1998). Believed-in imaginings: A narrative approach. In J. de Rivera & T. R. Sarbin, *Believed-in imaginings: The narrative construction of reality* (pp. 15–30). Washington, DC: American Psychological Association.

Sarbin, T. R. (2000). Embodiment and the narrative structure of emotional life. *Narrative Inquiry, 11,* 217–225.

Sarbin, T. R., & Allen, V. L. (1968). Role theory. In G. Lindzey & E. Aronson (Eds.), *Handbook of social psychology* (Vol. 1, pp. 488–507). Reading, MA: Addison-Wesley.

Sarbin, T. R., & Juhasz, J. B. (1970). Toward a theory of imagination. *Journal of Personality, 38,* 52–76.

Solomon, R. (1976). *The passions.* New York: Doubleday.

Stepper, S., & Strack, F. (1993). Proprioceptive determinants of emotional and non-emotional feelings. *Journal of Personality and Social Psychology, 84,* 211–220.

Washburn, M. (1916). *Movement and mental imagery: Outlines of a motor theory of the complexer mental processes.* Boston: Houghton Mifflin.

1.2

Fantastic Self

A Study of Adolescents' Fictional Narratives, and Aesthetic Activity as Identity Work

Cynthia Lightfoot

I'd like to begin with a retelling of the story of Adam and Eve and what happened before they were banished from Eden and sent off to the east. You recall that in the original narrative, God gave Adam dominion over all; over all the beasts, the birds, the fishes—over every living thing that moveth upon the earth. Adam's first act was to give everything a name. The second chapter of Genesis reads, "[The Lord God brought all the creatures] unto Adam to see what he would call them: and whatsoever Adam called every living creature, that was the name thereof" (Gen. 2:19). Shortly thereafter, God crafted the woman from Adam's flesh. "And they were both naked, the man and his wife, and were not ashamed" (Gen. 2:25).

Everything was fine until that business with the apple. One day, God noticed that Adam and the woman had covered themselves with fig leaves—they knew they were *naked;* they about *it*. And God said (and I paraphrase), "Adam, did you eat from the tree of knowledge even though I warned you against it?" Adam, you may remember, blamed the incident on the woman because it was after all she who had tempted him with the apple. They were both punished. They were to endure, according to his or her kind, the pain of childbirth, the subjugation of one to the other, desire, the need to eat bread and herb from the field and, of course, mortality. In the language that Margery Williams used to describe a not dissimilar transformation of the velveteen rabbit, we could say that Adam and the woman were made to become "really real."

To finish the story, God had words with Adam. After "the talk," Adam named the woman "Eve," and after that they were banished from the Garden. That's the original narrative in a nutshell. Ursula Le Guin (1987) wrote a thought-provoking revision of how the story ends. It goes something like this: One day, Adam and Eve were hanging about the crib. Adam was preoccupied, as usual, with Adam sorts of things, and Eve was tidying up, something that she never really took to. Somewhere in the middle of this ordinary day, Eve was inspired to gather all the creatures—every beast, every fowl, every fish, every living thing that moveth upon the earth—and un-name them. She then gave back to Adam and his father her own name, "Eve," thereby un-naming herself. Her final act in this chapter of Le Guin's Genesis was to throw open the gate to the east and sally forth. And here we are—smack dab in the middle of the woman's great adventure.

The title of Le Guin's short story is "She Un-Names Them." Thickly interpreted, it is a commentary about power and patriarchy and resistance. More generally, it is about the role of language, naming, and narrative in defining who we are and how we change. Our understanding of human development has profited significantly from two decades of work focused on exploring narrative and language as a principal way through which we make sense of ourselves and our experience. In light of the fruitfulness of this scholarship, it is something of an oddity that written texts have received relatively scant attention from developmentalists, particularly given the extent to which literate societies lean on the written word and work so hard to place it in the hands of children.

My special interest in fiction writing as a developmentally relevant form of self-expression and exploration arose in the context of my studies of the relationship between adolescent risk-taking and peer culture (Lightfoot, 1997). In talking with teenagers about the personal and social meanings of their risk-taking, I was struck by the functional continuities between their risk-taking and the play of younger children as it has been described by developmental psychologists, anthropologists, and folklorists. Both risks and play are sources of fun and excitement; both convey "don't have to" or "just for the hell of it" attitudes; both stand in a fragile and ambiguous relationship to the "real world" of non-risk and non-play; and both are forms of commentary—on the individuals engaged, and on their relationships with each other and with the social order.

So I set out to explore adolescent risk-taking as a form of play and, as such, a means of generating and maintaining a sense of self and peer culture. From risks and play it was an easy segue to drama and narrative. Indeed, in a way that departs importantly from the play of younger children, the risk-taking of adolescents introduces a double narrativity; its meaning is inscribed not only in the act of taking a risk but also in the telling and retelling of the experience to others. This particular approach to adolescent risk-taking cuts a path from the social sciences to the humanities, signposted by the insights of literary historians and critics.

In this chapter, I mean to unfold an interdisciplinary approach to exploring our selves, especially as we represent them in writing. I want to provide an account of how the understanding of selves has become, in history and in ontogenetic development, invested with a temporal force and a fictional element that together conspire to create an increasingly hypothetical and imaginative self that is increasingly subject to revision and critique.

First, I will trace out the broad changes of self-representation in Western cultural history, with special reference to written narratives. Informed by insights from the disciplines of literary history and criticism, this historical analysis provides a conceptual frame for examining developmental changes in how the self is portrayed in contemporary adolescents' fictional stories. In both explorations of self-representation, I emphasize how the infusion of time and the emergence of a fiction-imaginal element set what I believe to be an important stage in the ability to conceive of hypothetical selves projected into possible futures.

Selves in History

There have been several recent examinations of how ways of writing the self have changed over time that seem to me relevant to understanding the role of ficionalized selves in adolescence. Much of this work has been undertaken by literary critics and historians who trace a fascinating path that begins somewhere around the 17th century with an objective, atemporal self who moves through life event by event, deed by deed, leaving nothing behind but a reputation, and taking nothing away but a good night's sleep. There is little evidence at this point of a self embedded in time or subject to transformation. In early examples of the genre of life writing, the dramatic element is played out in a simple exaggeration of proportion; the author "creates a heroics of life in an epic-like battle against mankind" (Nalbantian, 1994, p. 8). People didn't pay much attention to subjective selves or their formative experiences; they weren't the stuff of contemplation, or of angst.

The 19th century, however, became a watershed for interest, opinion, and theorizing about the self—especially how it changed through time (Lightfoot & Lyra, 2000). Emerson described the era as the "age of the first person singular." A new sense of a self embedded in time framed development as a succession of interior awakenings and subjectively transforming experiences. This view stood in sharp contrast to the old way of describing a life as a collective Aesthetic Activity of events and accomplishments fed out on a line, item by item, like so much laundry.

That the cultural revision of self was but a symptom of modernism writ large is apparent in the extent to which the new autobiographies inscribed a reflective understanding of the autobiographical form itself as a means of portraying a life (McKeon, 2002). Rousseau, for example, on writing what is generally taken to be the first example of modern autobiography—a singular instance that presaged a future genre—comments on his lack of confidence in being able to get straight the facts and dates of the events in his life. He argues, in fact, that his goal is entirely otherwise. The chief subjects of his story are, rather, his own feelings: "It is the history of my soul that I have promised to recount" (cited in Nalbantian, 1994, p. 14).

The elaboration of psychic facts and formative experiences continued into 20th-century autobiography. But recently a new form seems to be taking shape. Life writing of the past 20 years has seen an incursion of fiction into autobiography. This hybrid of fact and fiction has been dubbed "aesthetic autobiography" by Suzanne Nalbantian (1994), who shows the form to coalesce "life fact and artifact in a movement away from the gauge of extrinsic verification" (p. 25). With direct correspondence to the "really real" thus defrocked as the criterion of merit, principles of art and aesthetics emerged as the new gold standard.

Of course the fictional and imaginary did not insert themselves unannounced into life writing. Their first arena of influence was not the subjective self but the material body (Lightfoot, 2003). The Romantic period courted the imaginary, the visionary, and the utopian not as figments of mind but as forces actively engaged with the material world. So, for example, the fields of theoretical embryology and teratology gave pride of place to the imagination in accounting for fetal anomalies. Eminent physicians, surgeons, and midwives of the period believed that when the pregnant woman's imagination was occupied with objects of beauty, she bore a beautiful child. Likewise, if her imagination was overtaken by objects of fear and loathing, her unborn child would be affected in kind.

The fragile boundary between the real and the imaginary was nowhere more evident that in the storm of public reaction to the report that "sometime in October 1726, Mary Toft, the illiterate wife of a poor journeyman cloth-worker, gave birth, in Godalming, Surrey, to her first rabbit, and that she went on to deliver sixteen more" (Todd, 1995, p. 1). The story of Mary Toft, although subsequently revealed as a hoax, was the talk of London simply because it was believable. Indeed, a substantial literature from the period catalogues a veritable zoo of monstrous offspring: frogs, worms, snakes, harpies, and rodent-like creatures. From the reptilian to the mythological, monsters were paraded across Europe inspiring both public awe and scientific study of the distinctiveness of mind and body and of the "mysterious intercourse" between them.

Right on the heels of the popular obsession with Mary Toft and her ilk was the birth of literary fantasy. Its kissing cousin in philosophy, which emerged around the same time, was the doctrine of philosophic speculation (Calvino, 1977). Founded on what is described as the "coherence theory of truth," the doctrine aims to understand reality as composed according to principles of self or mind. By Calvino's analysis, literary fantasy is similarly motivated. That is, its broad intention is to represent the reality of the interior, subjective world of the imagination. This world draws its credulity not from its direct correspondence to a material world of everyday life but from the degree to which it represents an emotional truth and a fidelity to human experience that outdistance its fantastic content (Calvino, 1977, p. ix). As Attenbery (1980) notes, "We enter the Other World only when there is air to breathe, food to eat, and ground to walk on" (p. 35).

Initially, the fantastic tale represented the subjective world by constructing imaginative spaces and populating them with ghosts, ghouls, and other visionary apparitions that play central roles in early 19th-century fantasy. In the next century, however, another dimension of the interior becomes manifest. In the wee hours of the 1900s, there emerged a fantasy genre in which the narrative tension is no longer contained by encounters with supernatural figures. Instead, the tension itself is interiorized. The spooks are not entities but mental shadows. The conflicts are not of the type that results in loss of life or limb; they are of an abstract, psychological nature that result in loss of self or mind.

Once germinated, the theme of inner conflict ripened to produce some of the most noteworthy literary treatments of a self divided. In a remarkable historical analysis, *Medicine, Mind, and the Double Brain,* Harrington (1987) provides a telling list of major 19th-century writers who, in one fashion or another, addressed the themes of duplicity, multiplicity, and inner moral conflict. The list includes Johann Wolfgang von Goethe, Jean Paul Richter (who coined the word *doppelganger*), George Buchner, E.T.A. Hoffmann, Guy de Maupassant, Franz Kafka, Fyodor Dostoevsky, James Hogg, Edgar Allan Poe, and Oscar Wilde. Robert Louis Stevenson's (1886/1996) *The Strange*

Case of Dr. Jeckyll and Mr. Hyde is a penultimate example of the cultural preoccupation with duality, captured here in the oft cited rumination of Jekyll:

> With every day, and from both sides of my intelligence, the moral and the intel-
> lectual, I thus drew steadily nearer to that truth, by whose partial discovery
> I have been doomed to such a dreadful shipwreck: that man is not truly one,
> but truly two. I say two, because the state of my own knowledge does not pass
> beyond that point. Others will follow, others will outstrip me on the same
> lines; and I hazard the guess that man will be ultimately known for a mere
> polity of multifarious, incongruous, and independent denizens. (p. 82)

The janus-faced soul of Stevenson's tale attaches the prospect of madness and depravity to a loss of self-continuity occasioned by a radically split personality. Indeed, as Foucault (1973) suggested, an era's conceptions of self touch tangibly on its understanding of madness, and physicians and medical practitioners of the period were quick to interpret a variety of mental illnesses to "a fundamental dividedness in the patient's intellectual and moral fiber" (Harrington, 1987, p. 108). The split personality was one of the most widely discussed clinical disorders of the 19th century (see also Hacking, 1995; Showalter, 1997; 1999). In modern societies, the individual's capacity to at least envision, if not outright represent, the self as fractionated and multiple is given yet further scope through the self-anonymity and dissembling enabled by contemporary technologies (Sass, 1997).

The brisk historical review presented here is meant to suggest that shifting conceptions of self and mind—in life writing, literary fantasy, embryology, and teratology—come of a piece and are in an important sense epochal, traversing science and the humanities. In addition to being interesting in their own right, the historical analyses provide a map for exploring the territory of conceptions of self emergent in the development of contemporary children.

Selves in Adolescents' Fiction Writing

My students and I have collected more than 100 stories from elementary school, high school, and college students. All the stories were written as a part of normal, English course requirements. I will focus here on a subset written by ninth grade boys and girls (13–14 years of age) and men and women college students (20–22 years of age).

The stories were analyzed in light of the historically emergent cultural conceptions of self described above. We were thus particularly attentive to

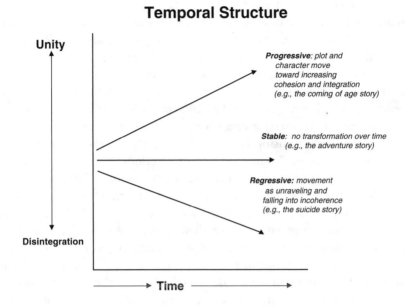

Figure 1.2.1   The Temporal Structure of Stories

how characters are placed in relation to time and circumstance, as well as in relation to their own selves. Our concerns focused on such issues as fate versus agency, event versus transforming experience, mortal conflict versus moral crisis, and evidence of preoccupation with self-fragmentation, duplicity, and authenticity.

Time and Conflict

Because the representation of time in literature has undergone profound historical change and is tightly coupled with notions of self and transformation, it seemed appropriate to examine the stories in terms of their temporal structures. Borrowing from Gergen and Gergen's (1983) typology, the temporal structure of each story was identified as progressive, stable, or regressive (see Figure 1.2.1).

In progressive narratives, the central character undergoes a transformation that is resolved in coherence and integration. The calculation of self across the events of the story results in a non-zero sum—a new understanding, a new way of relating. The best case example is the coming of age story. In one such story that we analyzed, an American girl travels to England in order to "find herself." While there, she witnesses a folk celebration of a holiday and remarks on the passage of music and dance from one generation to the next. The event inspires a process of self-reflection regarding her own location in time and space. Indeed, references to time, coherence, progress—all accoutrements of an identity quest—are infused throughout the narrative. Fully half of the college students produced narratives whose temporal structure was identified as progressive, compared to 20% of the high school students.

In contrast to progressive narratives, stability narratives are characterized by little or no transformation over time. The events of the story are related as "happenings" that have no lasting effect on characters who are variously witness to or victims of the particular episodes that compose the plot. The stability narrative is typical of what Bakhtin (1986) described as "adventure narratives." The events of such tales are detached and isolated from the broader contexts in which they occur. Once they have run their adventurous course, things and selves settle back more or less cozily into their original places. In one of our stories, for example, a narrator tells of how he and his brother drove a stake into the heart of their father, who had become possessed by an attic demon. The story ends, "That was it. Timmy and I now live with Grandma and Grandpa Griswald." The stability narrative was the temporal structure of choice for the high school students in the sample, characteristic of 43% of their stories. Of the college students, 29% produced stability narratives.

The regressive narrative is the third temporal structure examined in the stories. In this case, the change over time was marked by increasing disintegration and incoherence. Characters in these stories are undone; they unravel in the face of what is usually overwhelming adversity. The weight of life events may lead to suicide; unrequited love may lead to emotional limbo. Somewhat more than a third of the high school students produced stories of this nature, compared to 21% of the college students.

In addition to analyzing the temporal structure of each story, an effort was made to characterize the nature of the dramatic element, which was here defined in two ways. The first concerned the location of conflict. A distinction was made between stories of external conflict, in which the dramatic tension exists between the central character and some outside force, as in a battle, and those of internal conflict, in which a character is portrayed at odds with himself or herself, that is, engaged in some type of mental or moral crisis. Nearly 80% of the high school students produced stories of external conflict. One of the most distinctive features of the college students' stories, in contrast, was the interiorization of the conflict. References to mental states and inner turmoil, with the narrator often at odds with himself or herself, characterized 57% of the stories. We find in

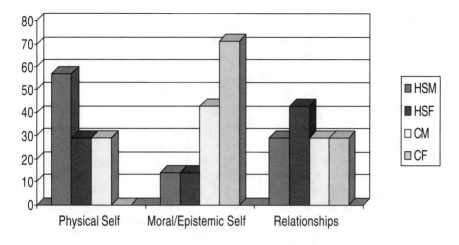

Figure 1.2.2   The Nature of Conflict and Loss in Student Stories, by Student Age and Gender

Note: HSM stands for high school male; HSF stands for high school female; CM stands for college male; and CF stands for college female.

these stories a preoccupation with genuineness, sincerity, and showing an authentically true and moral self.

Beyond the inner or outer location of conflict, the dramatic element was also examined with respect to potential loss, the threat of loss inherent to any notion of conflict. Three categories of potential loss were identified: loss of physical self, loss of a significant other, and loss of a moral or epistemic self. For example, the dramatic tension that carries a story of mortal combat may feature a potential loss to the physical self; and so might a story of suicide. In contrast, the drama of a potboiler romance may feature a potential loss of a significant other. A story focused on a central character torn between conflicting moral choices may reflect a potential loss of a moral self.

As shown in Figure 1.2.2, high school males typically produced narratives in which the physical self is threatened, whereas high school females produced narratives in which social relationships are on the line. College students, particularly females, produced narratives in which the moral or epistemic self is at risk.

Narrative Form

Time and conflict are but aspects of the overall narrative form that shapes the representation of self and experience in the students' stories. Aiming for a more integrative view, an effort was made to characterize the general narrative form of the stories. For example, some of the stories read like historical, factual records of events encountered by happenstance. The dominant motif is the heroic myth in which the central character clashes with an enemy—a terrorist, a ghost, a terminal disease. The hero reigns supreme in some stories, but in others he or she is made a tragic victim. Typically, forces of fate or whimsy drive the narrative, as in the story "Life or Death" below, which was written by a 13-year-old boy.[1]

> As I stand here on the edge of the twelve-story building, I wondered how it had all gone wrong. I grew up a healthy and well-treated child. . . . My dad was in real estate and my mom was a high school teacher. . . . I got a job at IBM as a accountant. . . . I met the girl of my dreams. Diane and I immediately fell in love. . . . My youngest sister was close to becoming very wealthy at her job. My parents had retired and moved to Florida. . . . Life was great!
>
> Then everything came crashing down like an avalanche My . . . . sister . . . had lung cancer. . . . I lost my job at IBM. . . . Hurricane Bob had destroyed my parent's home. . . . Diane was shot in the crossfire gang fight and died instantly. . . . A week later my sister Shell died of the lung cancer before she could get treated.
>
> The breeze blowing across my face feels relaxing. Life is not important. No one cares about me. It'll only hurt for a second. Hardly any traffic . . . now it's time to go. . . .
>
> (Witnesses to the suicide remark): "I can't believe he did it." "Yeah, why do people do that? I mean, is life that bad?" "I guess he had problems, but there's always someone who's willing to care." "I mean how bad could it have been?"

In "Life or Death," the central character is an innocent and powerless bystander to an avalanche of tragedy. There is no agent here. Even those who witnessed the event and "can't believe he did it" posit no resource capable of derailing the outcome other than the presence of some external, ephemeral other "who's willing to care." The problem and its solution reside in a material world that plays host to the central character but makes little accommodation for will, motive, or act.

Another suicide story (there were, interestingly, quite a few of them in both the high school and college samples), "In My Room," chronicles a girl's battle with drug addiction. In many ways it is similar to "Life or Death." There is a polarization of life circumstances and a fatalistic lack of control over them. Both stories also end by calling into question the inevitability of the outcome.

> When people ask me, do I remember Thursday night in the summer of 1994, I force myself to say yes. It's hard for me to say yes, because that night was the worst night of my life.

My friends and I arrived at a party. . . . The next thing I know I was being carried out of the party on a stretcher. . . . My life was a total mess because all I would do was go to parties and come home high and drunk. No one could tell what was going on because I would hide myself in my room until I was better, and then I would go out and do it again. Then one night I was really bad, I was so high that I tried committing suicide. . . .

So now as I sit here in my room (at the home for uncontrollable teenagers) I ask myself why I did it, because I was a great student and I could go places in my life. Now I hate myself for what I did. At night I cry myself to sleep, because when I get out I ask myself, "Will I do it again?" For now I don't know. I guess I'll have to wait and see. (I hope I don't.)

The polarization of "great student" and suicidal drug addict and the fatalism reflected in "I guess I'll have to wait and see" coincide with the general thrust of "Life and Death." The difference between being a victim of circumstance and a victim of one's own behavior is more apparent than real. In both cases, there is a sense of a detached and helpless witness to the tragic events unfolding. Likewise, in both stories the uncomprehending detachment carries over to the social realm: "Why do people do that? How bad could it have been?"; "No one could tell what was going on because I would hide myself in my room."

In a second narrative form, events are construed in terms of their subjective meanings for the central character. Hard work pays off, and the character achieves her dream; a particular event, meeting a certain significant other, deflects a course of action. In contrast to the previous form in which the central character is tossed about on waves of fortune and circumstance, there is a goal structure and an agent at work. For example,

It was Giai's senior year. She was so excited that high school was almost over. She had a great life. She felt her family was the best. She had a good-looking boyfriend. She was also way popular. However the one thing she wanted, she couldn't have.

Giai loved the game of basketball. It was her life. . . . She always made the team, but she sat the bench. . . . Her plan was to play for Syracuse University. . . . Giai knew that if she was to play this year she would have to practice twice as hard. . . .

The team was going to the State Championships. . . . When the game was over, Giai had 40 points, 10 steals, 20 assists, and 9 blocks. Her team won. . . . Everyone was happy and proud.

About 2 weeks later, Giai received a letter from Syracuse asking her to play basketball for them. They indicated they would offer a scholarship to assist with college tuition. Hard work and perseverance had paid off—Giai's dream finally came true.

Nearly all of the stories produced by the high school students were of the two types described above. High school males typically produced some variant of the heroic myth, whereas high school females more often produced stories that played out themes of subjective relevance. Although somewhat less than half of the college students also wrote stories addressing themes of personal, subjective relevance (in which no gender differences were apparent, however), most composed narratives that were variants of a third form.

If the first two narrative forms can be said to comment on issues of agency, control, and the subjugation of self to events or desires objectively defined—be they events of circumstance or personal goals and desires—the third narrative form takes issue with the subjugation of self to the way the world is interpretively framed. Here, the events of the story are taken to comment on or challenge fundamental and transpersonal notions of reality, truth, beauty, and morality. Doubt figures prominently in references to duplicity and the distance between objects and symbols, selves and their guises, real worlds and virtual worlds. An example is provided in a story set in an electronic chat room. It is titled "Reader, Are You There?" and begins, appropriately enough, with Reader entering the "room" in the middle of a conversation:

Reader has just entered the chatroom

RealMcCoy: Entirely invisible?

TeleBob: How's it going, Reader?

SaidSadly: Not entirely. Animals see me. . . .

RealMcCoy: Invisible animals, or all animals? . . .

SaidSadly: You're mocking me. . . .

RealMcCoy: No, but if you're typing, I'm sure someone can see you.

TeleBob: I think you're nuts, buddy.

SaidSadly: I type therefore I am? . . .

RealMcCoy: When did you become invisible?

SaidSadly: Shortly after I retired. . . .

RealMcCoy: So, where do you live? . . .

SaidSadly: In a little apartment that you've never seen,

                On a road you've never driven,

                In a town you've never heard of. . . .

SaidSadly: In this chatroom, I am a name without a face. In the real world, I'm barely even that much. Real people belong in the real world. This is the perfect place for invisible people like me. In here, you're just as invisible as I am.

RealMcCoy: What is your real name, by the way? . . .

SaidSadly: Sid Sadler.

                [It becomes apparent that Sid intends to kill himself; RealMcCoy tries to reason with him.]

SaidSadly: You're a good man for trying (to dissuade him from taking his life), but I've wasted my life to an irreparable point. I'm so pathetic that I don't even exist. When I log off, you will only know a man named Sid Sadler that a character named SaidSadly told you about. Our entire conversation, what you know of me may have been made-up. You don't even know for sure that my real name is Sid Sadler.

RealMcCoy: This is a pretty sick joke it if is one!

SaidSadly: Goodbye, RealMcCoy.

                SaidSadly has just left the chatroom

RealMcCoy: Sid, please!

TeleBob: Reader, are you there?

                Reader has just left the chatroom

The relationship between the real and virtual is a pedal point of tension in several stories. The excerpts below come from a story titled "Living on Paper." In it, the narrator juxtaposes his life in the "real world," unformed and lacking in meaning, with the more deeply felt world of comic book superheroes:

Paper—a wonder of the ages. . . . Very few people today appreciate the real value of paper as a transcendental medium—but I do. . . . Of course, I wouldn't go on like this about just any paper. Today, I'm only thinking of a very particular vintage: the endearingly cheap grade of newspaper used to make comic book pages. Sure, it's coarse and grainy . . . but I've always felt that the true worth of paper, as with anything else, is not in its material quality. It's in its applications. After all, two sticks of wood are just kindling by themselves— but fasten them together perpendicularly, and you've got yourself a symbolic object that can ward off vampires, execute messiahs, and launch crusades of love and hate that last for centuries and kill millions.

The narrator spends an imaginatively absorbing and emotionally animated afternoon at a "Comic back-issue mega-sale," where vintage comic books are sold by weight. He continues,

> . . . but my joy ends quickly as I hit the sidewalk. The sky above is gray and formless and unending, without even the threat of rain to give it character. Down the street, everything is oppressively ordinary—no foiled bank heists or alien invasions, not so much as a cape or cowl anywhere in sight. Sadly, I take a look back at the colorful warmth of the Hoard (comic book store). In there, where myths of transcendence are on sale by the ounce, I feel like there's some substance to my life; out here, there's nothing but trees and cars, storefronts and trash cans, fences and parking meters, plastic and concrete, streets to cross, classes to worry about, appointments to keep, decisions to make, relationships not to have, and the nebulous throngs of my supposed peers, strolling along in their little herds of two or three, all laughing at some huge private joke (me, probably) and feeding on an invisible ambrosia of life the likes of which I've never tasted. There's no moral, no climax, no unifying theme; just "real life," in all its chaotic banality, happening all around me.

In another story, "Clown Day Afternoon," a young man is recruited to play a clown at a child's birthday party. The narrative makes much of the ineffective transformation—the suit fits badly; the young man sports the rubber nose but neglects to apply the makeup; he introduces himself by his real, un-clownlike name, James; because he doesn't know how to make balloon animals, he offers the increasingly disaffected crowd of 10-year-olds a string of skinny balloons that he absurdly declares to be paramecia, eels, and linear monkeys. As the situation goes from bad to worse, he notices a child in a wheelchair who, legless, hairless, and sickly, surveys the catastrophe with mild interest and a forgiving attitude. Several weeks later, the narrator reads the child's obituary in a local paper. His name was Timothy Robinson. The narrator is overtaken by guilt, despite acknowledging to himself that "he was not to blame—he wasn't the one who made Timmy die. It was the cancer. It had agency beyond behavior, beyond language." Nevertheless, he undertakes to write a story about the party from the dying boy's point of view, and then he submits it to an "irregularly published comedy magazine." The story ends with the clown and the boy becoming fast friends. "Then Timmy died. It was the cancer."

The story is rejected:

> We regret to inform you that cancer isn't funny, clowns are. The only success-fully humorous moments in your manuscript are achieved through seemingly unintentional non sequiturs. The diction is often overblown in decidedly unfunny incidences of exaggeration utterly devoid of verisimilitude. The end-ing is neither an effective twist (void of surprise) nor coherent with the piece (syntactically or otherwise). Keep trying!

The narrator reflects on the rejection note and his poor effort to commit the boy's life and experience to paper. The reader is left with these ruminations:

> But it [the story] was not reality. This was his problem—he wanted to expand Timothy's life into language, but that wasn't possible—the word and the flesh were irreconcilable. . . . Language does not equal life; in some sense the two were at odds. All he had was the story that Timmy produced from him—not even Timmy really; he never got to know the kid (not even his name while he was alive), but the idea of Timmy, the concept of the character Timmy. Not Timothy Robinson, whoever that may have been, ineffable to him now, but Timmy. In this sense, James found the rejection satisfying and oddly appropri-ate. Besides, the absurd was always difficult to accept as a fundamental underpinning of daily life.

In true modernist fashion, many of the college students' stories reflect a preoccupation with the process of writing itself and its relation to the events and characters that it inscribes. These stories reach beyond singular events and their subjective meanings to explore transpersonal, aesthetic questions regarding the imaginative realm of possibility defined by the disjunction of the world and the interpretive point of view through which it is narrated.

Aesthetic Activity as Identity Work

Bakhtin (1986) argues that during adolescence the individual engages in what is, psychically and developmentally speaking, a nearly life or death struggle against what is imposed from without—from the authority and traditions of family, culture, and history. In his words, there is a struggle between an "authoritative discourse" and an "innerly persuasive discourse" that leads ultimately to the birth of an ideological consciousness. Authoritative discourse is encountered with its authority already attached. It is compelling only because of its authority. It is closed to growth, change, and scrutiny. History, including cultural stories and genres, conforms to this notion. Our personal as well as our collective histories are in an important sense not of our making or our choosing; these histories, these stories, are imposed, yet we are bedded down with them for the long haul. Innerly persuasive discourse, on the other hand, is compelling because it is persuasive. "Half-ours and half-someone else's," to quote Bakhtin (1986), it is a personal orchestration, elaboration, and reconstruction of the discourses of others and of our own inner speech. Unlike history and the discourse of authority, innerly persuasive discourse has an aesthetic and fictional quality. In contrast, our histories and experiences, our fictions, indeed all aesthetic projects—art, play, literary works—are our comment on history and experience, and sometimes our revenge.

Bakhtin (1981) suggests, as have others—Winnicott (1971), for example—that we experience ourselves within a liminal space between what is and what could be. I hope that the work presented here has you thinking about two things. First, there are developmental and cultural limits to the proprietary claims of subjects/authors on the construction of their stories and lives. Developmentally, there is an emergent ability to imagine ourselves as different from who we are, and to construct and reconstruct ourselves as different from how we have been imagined and how we have been named. This, I think, defines the context of the great adventure—this defines the struggle to be really real somewhere east of Eden.

Note

1. All of the stories excerpted below have been abbreviated; deleted content is indicated by ellipses.

References

Attenbery, B. (1980). *The fantasy tradition in American literature.* Bloomington: Indiana University Press.

Bakhtin, M. (1981). *The dialogic imagination.* Austin: University of Texas Press.

Bakhtin, M. (1986). *Speech genres and other late essays.* Austin: University of Texas Press.

Calvino, I. (1977). Introduction. In I. Calvino (Ed.), *Fantastic tales: Visionary and everyday*. New York: Pantheon.

Foucault, M. (1973). *Madness and civilization: A history of insanity in the age of reason*. New York: Random House.

Gergen, K., & Gergen, M. (1983). Narratives of the self. In T. Sarbin & K. Shiebe (Eds.), *Studies in social identity*. New York: Praeger.

Hacking, I. (1995). *Rewriting the soul: Multiple personality and the sciences of memory*. Princeton, NJ: Princeton University Press.

Harrington, A. (1987). *Medicine, mind, and the double brain*. Princeton, NJ: Princeton University Press.

The Holy Bible: King James Version. Oxford, UK: Oxford University Press.

Lightfoot, C. (1997). *The culture of adolescent risk-taking*. New York: Guilford.

Lightfoot, C. (2003). Breathing lessons: Self as genre and aesthetic. In T. Brown & L. Smith (Eds.), *Reductionism and the development of knowledge*. Mahwah, NJ: Lawrence Erlbaum.

LeGuin, U. (1987). She unnames them. In *Buffalo gals and other animal presences*. New York: New American Library.

Lightfoot, C., & Lyra, M. (2000). Culture, self and time: Prospects for a new millennium. *Culture and Psychology, 2*, 99–104.

McKeon, M. (2002). *The origins of the English novel*. Baltimore, MD: Johns Hopkins University Press.

Nalbantian, S. (1994). *Aesthetic autobiography*. New York: St. Martin's.

Sass, L. (1997). The consciousness maching: Self and subjectivity in schizophrenia and modern culture. In U. Neisser & D. Jopling (Eds.), *The conceptual self in context: culture, experience, and self-understanding*. New York: Cambridge University Press.

Showalter, E. (1997). *Hystories: Hysterical epidemics and modern media*. New York: Columbia University Press.

Showalter, E. (1999). Dr. Jekyll's closet. In E. Smith & R. Haas (Eds.), *The haunted mind: The supernatural in Victorian literature*. Lanham, MD: Scarecrow.

Stevenson, R. L. (1996). *The strange case of Dr. Jekyll and Mr. Hyde*. Charlottesville, VA: University of Virvinia Library Electronic Text Center; Boulder, CO: NetLibrary. (Original work published 1886)

Todd, D. (1995). *Imagining monsters: Miscreations of the self in eighteenth-century England*. Chicago: University of Chicago Press.

Winnicott, D. (1971). *Playing and reality*. New York: Tavistock.

1.3

Cultural Modeling as a Frame for Narrative Analysis

Carol D. Lee, Erica Rosenfeld, Ruby Mendenhall, Ama Rivers, and Brendesha Tynes

N arrative is a universal genre of both oral language and written texts (Turner, 1996). Some have argued that through narrative, humans impose meanings on experience (Bruner, 1990). Such meanings are individual and also capture cultural models of human agency—as well as cultural schemas for relationships, culturally appropriate goals, and subsequent actions to fulfill those goals (D'Andrade, 1987). Most national and/or ethnic cultures carry forward from generation to generation archetypal themes and plots that are interrogated and reworked with each new generation (Berman & Slobin, 1994). With the above assumptions, we can view patterns of narratives as opportunities to view what a group of people deem important in the conduct of human affairs. The storytellers—the poets, novelists, and playwrights—often wrestle with taboos, with the deeply unresolved questions of the human experience. They act as seers and priests who help us to connect vicariously with experiences that are too difficult for us to take on directly; through imagination, we can enter subjunctive worlds and try on identities that we would not ordinarily be bold enough to assume. Narrative, then, is a powerful tool that, although universal, unfolds and acts in culturally specific ways. Amy Tan's (1989) wrestling with the winding way of chi from the past through the hybrid spaces of the present carries subtle messages that someone who is not Chinese or Chinese American may have difficulty understanding. More important, the authorial audience of *The Joy Luck Club* is composed not merely of those who are Chinese or Chinese American in terms of ethnic heritage but also of those who understand basic tenets of Taoist and Confucianist thought, as well as the tensions between old culture and new. That is to say, the authorial audience (Rabinowitz, 1987) is defined by their beliefs and practices (Gutierrez & Rogoff, 2003).

In a country like the United States, understanding the culturally specific nature of any activity, including narrative, is complicated by the diverse nature of ethnic culture (Lee, Spencer, & Harpalani, 2003). Depending on many factors, people are both American and of some other ethnic origin. Pan-ethnic groups often represent political categories more than categories of actual ethnic practice. Ethnic groups are often a hybrid of old world practices and new world adaptations. Because of the legacy of what African American historians have termed the "African American Holocaust of Enslavement," people of African descent face special challenges—their having for centuries been identified by others on the basis of race alone clouds the ability of some to recognize those qualities of belief and practices that are ethnic and of African descent (Lee, Spencer, & Harpalani, 2003). Among the most visible indices of ethnic beliefs and practices among people of African descent living in the United States (and in other parts of the Diaspora) is how the vast majority of them use language. There is a significant body of research documenting both the systematic features of what is called African American English (AAE) or African American Vernacular English (AAVE) (Baugh, 1983; Morgan, 1993; Smitherman, 1977) and the African origins of its syntax, phonology, and lexicon (Mufwene, 1993; Rickford & Rickford, 1976). It is indeed ironic how what some call this Africanized English has been both vilified and lionized simultaneously. It is vilified as nonstandard English, as an indicator of a lack of intelligence or competence, and as a barrier to upward mobility (see Labov, 1972; Smitherman, 2000a). It has been lionized in great literature (e.g., by Toni Morrison, AliceWalker, Amiri Baraka, Haki Madhubuti, Sonia Sanchez, August Wilson, Paul Laurence Dunbar, Sterling Brown, and Zora Neale Hurston, to name a few) (Jones, 1991), commodified in advertisements, reified in music across the generations, and dramatized around the world through hip-hop culture (Smitherman, 1973). Aspects of AAE have been the language of liberation for African Americans through the civil rights movement, for Polish workers, for Chinese dissidents, and for the war against apartheid in South Africa. By these examples, I mean not merely the theme of language but the very structure of genres and the syntax aimed to inspire ordinary people to take bold actions.

In this chapter, we consider the semiotic potential of African American narrative traditions for literacy development among African American children. Children are in the process of learning the narrative traditions of their families and communities. They have incomplete and evolving knowledge of such narrative traditions. Different communities apprentice children into what Heath (1983) calls "ways with words," or ways of using language, specifically through capturing experience in narrative. In Heath's (1983) classic study, African American children in a southern working-class community learned that in order to get adults to listen to their recounts of experience, the children needed to articulate the meaning of public experiences rather than to simply recount events that both the children and the adults have witnessed. This narrative socialization focused on examination of the internal states of actors as stepping-stones to goal-directed behaviors (i.e., the plot). In addition, children were socialized both through their opportunities to tell stories and through listening to the stories told by adults and older peers that the form of the message (i.e., the creativity in ways of using language) was as important as the content of the message (Smitherman, 1977). This emphasis on creative ways of using language has been codified by Smitherman (2000b) in what she calls the "African American Rhetorical Tradition." This tradition is often captured in narrative forms, although it can be found in expository forms as well (Ball, 1992, 1995). According to Smitherman (2000a), the African American Rhetorical Tradition includes:

1. rhythmic, dramatic, evocative language

2. reference to color-race-ethnicity (that is, when topic does not call for it)

3. use of proverbs, aphorisms, Biblical verses

4. sermonic tone reminiscent of traditional Black Church rhetoric, especially in vocabulary, imagery, metaphor

5. direct address-conversational tone

6. cultural references

7. ethnolinguistic idioms

8. verbal inventiveness, unique nomenclature

9. cultural values-community consciousness

10. field dependency; involvement with and immersion in events and situations; personalizing phenomena; lack of distance from topics and subjects. (pp. 86–87)

Culturally Responsive Narrative Analysis and Instructional Design

We have argued that narrative is a way of imposing meaning on experience and that the forms of narrative—including the cultural models, schemas, and scripts that they capture—are culturally specific. We have also noted that African American English and by extension the children for whom this is a first language have been vilified and underserved in public education. We have reasoned that because of narrative's role in life-course development and its centrality to literate practices, we can learn much by examining and ultimately influencing the narrative practices of African American children who are speakers of AAE. This orientation is situated in what we call the "Cultural Modeling Framework" (Lee, 1993, 1995a, 1995b, 2000, 2001).

The aim of Cultural Modeling is to facilitate students' learning generative concepts in academic subject matters by helping them to make connections between the target knowledge and forms of knowledge they have constructed from their home and community experiences. The design of instruction according to Cultural Modeling principles involves a careful analysis both of the target academic task and of the everyday practices of students. The goal is to make connections that may be based on similar strategies, analogies, or naïve concepts. Previously, Cultural Modeling conceptualized similarities in the strategies used by speakers of African American Vernacular English to produce and interpret figurative language—such as symbolism, irony, and satire—and the strategies expert readers use to interpret such tropes in literature. We have made similar connections between the strategies used to interpret irony, satire, symbolism, and the use of unreliable narrators in rap lyrics and other products of popular culture (many emanating from African American culture) and the strategies used to interpret canonical works of literature. In both instances, the Cultural Modeling Framework required unique analyses of literary as well as everyday practices. In our investigations of everyday narrative practices as a scaffold for writing narratives, we needed both theory and analytical methods to evaluate and characterize narratives, and the theory and analytical methods had to be sensitive to the cultural specificity of uses of African American English in both oral and written narratives.

Several bodies of research proved useful in these efforts. One body of research situated how African American children's narratives were positioned in school contexts. Among the classic research in this area are the sharing time studies by Michaels (1981) and Cazden (Cazden, Michaels, & Tabors, 1985). They found that the oral narratives produced by African

American primary school children were not being understood by teachers. "Sharing time" is an activity where children bring objects from home and tell the class stories about these objects. The White middle-class children in the study told stories that had linear plot configurations. The teachers understood this structure, as it mapped onto the school essay tradition to which they were trying to apprentice students. The teachers were then able to give the children immediate feedback as to ways to make their descriptions more explicit and their plots more detailed. Michaels calls the structure of these stories "topic centered." The African American children, on the other hand, told what Michaels calls "topic associative" stories. The scenes of the plot changed in non-linear fashion, and the teachers could not perceive any order to the stories. As a result, they were not able to provide the African American children with feedback for improving their stories. In a follow-up study, Cazden (1988) found that topic centered and episodic narratives were evaluated differently by Black and White adults. Whites thought that episodic narratives were ill formed and indicated low achievement; whereas, Blacks found value in both forms. This research raises important questions about how the oral narratives of African American children should be analyzed, both in theory and in practice. Gee (1989) challenged the findings of the sharing time research. He reanalyzed the narrative of one of the children, Leona, and posits a different interpretation of the structure and quality of her story and, by extension, of the topic associative narrative style. Gee's narrative analysis drew on literary theory to divide the story into stanzas and to examine the rhetorical function of each stanza in relation to every other stanza. Gee argues that the topic associative narrative developed by the children is an emergent form of a more literary narrative structure, one that children would not be expected to address until much later in their school careers. Fundamentally, Gee claims that the emergent structure of the topic associative narrative is more complex than the linear topic centered narrative structure that the primary school valued. Gee's analysis makes evident the difference that theory can play in the evaluation of narrative structures, particularly in the school context.

Since the sharing time studies of Michaels and Cazden, other researchers have documented the range of narrative structures employed by African American children (Hyon & Sulzby, 1994). These include, especially as children get older, a more widespread use of what are termed "classic structures," which are more akin to Michaels's topic centered narratives than the sharing time studies implied. In addition, Champion (1998, 2003) has found that the contexts under which narratives are elicited can make a difference in the structure and length of the oral stories told by African American students. In particular, Champion emphasizes that the use of an interlocutor who responds to the storyteller ("Un huh," "Is that right?") appears to engage African American children. Among the range of narrative features that Champion found in several studies of African American children's storytelling styles is a performative aspect. Performative aspects of African American children's narratives include a high use of dramatic intonation, gesture, and rhythmic prosody. These features are consistent with those found in other research on speech genres within the African American English speech community, including signifying and loud talking (Mitchell-Kernan, 1981; Smitherman, 1977). Signifying is a form of ritual insult that includes use of figurative language and hyperbole (Lee, 1993). Smitherman observes that African American rhetoric spans a spectrum from the secular to the sacred. These performative features can be found in secular genres, such as signifying, as well as in sacred genres, such as the structure of sermons delivered in African American churches (Moss, 1994).

The Cultural Modeling in Narrative Project

To test our hypothesis that the range of features of narratives in the African American Rhetorical Tradition were part of the narrative repertoire of African American children who are speakers of African American English, and that scaffolding these features in instruction could lead to the development of complex written narratives, we designed the Cultural Modeling in Narrative Project (Lee, Mendenhall, Rivers, & Tynes, 1999). A key lever in this work was to be able to translate the research on African American English and African American children's narratives both into analytic methods for evaluating children's narratives and into the design of prompts and other supports that would help to develop the quality of narratives we imagined possible.

The design principles of the Cultural Modeling Framework required that we develop supports that would lead children to reflect on their prior knowledge and its relevance to writing narratives. In Cultural Modeling, this process usually occurs through the careful selection of what we call "cultural data sets" (Lee, 1999). Children should already be very familiar with the cultural data sets and the analysis of the cultural data sets should involve the same strategies and/or concepts that are demanded to carry out the target academic task. In the selection of cultural data sets for this work in written narratives, we were influenced by two bodies of research. The first is that of Hillocks (1986, 1995). Hillocks argues that writers need declarative, procedural, and conditional knowledge of forms. The term "forms" here refers to the structure of genres, for our purposes, narrative.

This includes the knowledge of (1) internal states of characters and how their goal-directed behaviors are an outgrowth of those internal states and (2) how to describe dialogue, setting, and actions. "Declarative" knowledge involves knowing that narratives have people, a sequence of actions, a setting, dialogue, and so on. "Procedural" knowledge involves knowing how to translate these elements of narratives into written language. This process of translation into written language is no easy feat for the best of writers. "Conditional" knowledge involves knowing when to use particular sources of knowledge and how to evaluate their effectiveness in relation to the writer's purpose. In *Observing and Writing*, Hillocks (1975) describes a series of activities that engage students in writing descriptions (of objects, such as shells, of scenes from pictures to elicit dialogue, etc.). Hillocks calls these "gateway activities."

The lessons of Hillocks's research in composition are reinforced by Sadoski and Paivio's (2001) dual coding theory of reading and writing. Sadoski and Paivio make the claim that reading and writing involve similar cognitive processes. This linking of reading and writing is important because of our interest in ultimately influencing both the reading and writing competencies of students. As part of the Cultural Modeling in Narrative Project, students both read and produced written narratives. In addition, Sadoski and Paivio (2001) make a case for the importance of imagery to both the encoding and retrieval of knowledge in long-term memory. They state that

> imagery can serve as a structural vehicle that inspires, organizes, and carries a written work regardless of its genre. . . . Certain images can stand for an abstract idea and as a retrieval cue for associated images and language. . . . The imagery system provides a way to store concrete memories of the world and to transform and manipulate those memories free from the sequential constraints that characterize language. (pp. 157–158)

On the basis of these two bodies of research, we selected as cultural data sets pictures that captured cultural scripts from African American life. In particular, we used pictures from the famed African American artist Annie Lee. Annie Lee has created an array of works of art depicting scenes from the Black Church, of the historical act of jumping the broom, of African American grandmothers working in the kitchen. We postulated that these scenes captured cultural scripts with which many African American children would be deeply familiar; that these images would elicit concrete memories of scenes, smells, and dialogues, as well as an understanding of the internal states of characters; and that these images would therefore act as generative cultural data sets to serve as prompts for writing.

In the instructional design, children heard African American storytellers, watched video clips of African Americans in film engaged in culturally familiar ways of telling stories (one example was a clip from August Wilson's *The Piano*), and finally were presented with Annie Lee pictures. In each case, students were supported in the process of translating the visual image into written products. These supports included instruction in how to punctuate dialogue, how to create paragraphs, and how to find new words to express descriptions and feelings. Students first developed oral narratives and then translated their oral narratives into written narratives.

In evaluating the children's written and oral narratives, we drew on Smitherman's (2000c) work on the African American Rhetorical Tradition that we described in an earlier section of this chapter. Smitherman examined 867 writing samples from elementary aged African American children based on National Assessment of Educational Progress (NAEP) writing assessments for 1984 and 1988 to 1989. Smitherman found that the African American children in her sample produced better quality narratives than expository writing. Further, she found a positive correlation between the presence of features of the African American Rhetorical Tradition and the quality of the writing as judged by NAEP evaluators. Interestingly, she also found a decline in use of AAVE syntax features over time. Using Smitherman's methods for narrative analysis and the work of Peterson and McCabe (1983) on narrative structures, we evaluated the corpus of written and oral narratives produced by the children in our sample.

Research Site

This research was conducted in two elementary sites in a large urban school district. Each school served an all African American student population. The research reported in this chapter focuses on a combined third and fourth grade class of students at McDonald Elementary School. McDonald School has 97% low income students and a mobility rate of 34%. Many of the combined third and fourth graders in this class have failed first or second grade more than once. Most of the 25 children in the class were 10 and 11 years old, and yet they had not fully mastered basic decoding. Their spelling was definitely more like that of emergent writers in the first and second grade. They were not designated as special education, but they were a unique class of students in the school in that in the primary grades they had experienced repeated academic failure. By contrast, McDonald School was known as one of the best schools in the system, having beaten the odds in terms of their students' achievement in reading comprehension. However, the gains of the school as a whole had not yet profited this particular group of students.

We report on this class because they represent a special illustration of cultural scaffolding for children who are in greatest need of academic support. We see the work with this class as a classic case of Vygotsky's (1978) concept of a zone of proximal development (ZPD). The idea of the ZPD is to understand the difference between what these children can do by themselves and what they can do with support.

Data Analysis and Findings

Instruction involving the cultural data sets as prompts for writing was carried out by both the teacher and the members of our research team. The students' engagement with the Annie Lee cultural data sets is captured in field notes:

> We then asked the students to talk about what was happening on the cards (in the Annie Lee picture called Six Uptown). I wrote their responses on the chalkboard, using capital letters and underlined words for emphasis. Black English was also used with the Standard English version written directly above it so the students could distinguish the two. Some of the students' responses included the following:
> Precious shouted, "OH LORD!"
> Precious threw her head back and said, "talk to the hand."
> Denise cried, "I'm gonna [going to] win this *time*."
> Claudia shook her head and said, "You betta [better] stop cheating!!"
> (R. Mendenhall, field notes, December 9, 1999)

Not only are the children engaged in the activity of looking at the pictures, but they are also able to use their funds of knowledge (Moll & Greenberg, 1990) and personal experiences to make meaningful inferences from the pictures that become the base for their generation of details in the narratives. This gives them access to a much larger toolkit for writing than is generally available with more traditional writing prompts.

In the current study, we collapsed several of Smitherman's features, resulting in the following coding categories for what we call "African American Discourse Features":

- Use of dramatic language
- Use of or description of body language and gesture
- Sermonic tone
- Cultural references
- Use of direct speech
- Use of ethnolinguistic idioms
- Field dependency

Students were encouraged to work together. Of the 25 students, 16 submitted 13 stories based on the Annie Lee pictures, 4 were written in pairs and 9 were written individually. Based on what Boykin (1994) calls an "Afro-cultural ethos," he has demonstrated that for African American students, it is working collaboratively in groups, without extrinsic rewards, that leads to the largest gains in learning. Boykin (1994) posits that for African American children, group work appears to activate "intrinsic motivational processes" (p. 134). In a similar vein, we found that the children gravitated to work in cooperative groups, even without prompting. Two researchers independently coded their stories for presence of the African American Discourse Features. Initially, interrater reliability was 85%. On areas of disagreement, raters discussed their differences and came to consensus.

All the students employed African American Discourse Features (AADF) in their narratives. Researchers coded a minimum of 2 instances of AADF in these stories, with an average of 5.7 instances per story. Stories ranged in length from 7 sentences to 15. We believe that the scenes in these pictures were so familiar to the students that they were able to use their available cultural resources in constructing narratives based on the pictures.

Presence of African American Discourse Features

Use of Dramatic Language and Field Dependent Style

The use of dramatic language and the presence of a field dependent style was prominent in students' narratives. There were 6 out of 13 stories that contained dramatic or provocative language, while 8 of the 13 showed evidence of field dependency. "Field dependency" is defined as the tendency to put one's self inside a situation and to view elements relationally. Dyson (1997) discusses the degree of permeability of the "official world of school" as the key factor in determining children's success in merging home and school worlds. A curriculum that creates such a space increases the likelihood that writers will develop confidence with narrative structure. We see the same phenomenon occurring with the Annie Lee narratives. Due to the familiarity of the scene, students were invited to bring the world of their families, friends, and neighborhoods into their narratives in ways that went beyond an explicit written prompt asking them to write about a familial topic. In the examples of field dependency below, each student has inserted himself or herself as the character.[1]

"Gabriel is just getting off work."

"Kenneth is playing a banjo."

"Nathaniel is playing checkers. . . . "

"Andre is drinking pop and bouncing the ball."

Randall is dancing his butt all over. Takanna is standing on the corner. . . . "

To illustrate the level of inferencing by students, we will include the pictures on which the children's descriptions are based. The following picture of an old man sitting in his chair prompted descriptive detail. There were 6 different stories that gave a sensual description of the day and season implied in this picture:

"It was a hot, sunny day. . . . " (G.N.)

"It is a long sunny day. . . . " (R.B., I.L.)

"It was one long, hot, sunny day." (A.C.)

"It was a hot sunny day. . . . " (L.D., J.P.)

"It all started on a hot summer day. . . . " (A.N.)

"This is a hot sunny day in the summer. . . . " (D.C.)

While each description includes a reference to the fact that the sun was shining, there are interesting syntactic differences in how the students appropriated this detail. A.C.'s reference to "one long, hot sunny day," has an emphatic air very replete with an expected AAVE prosody that emphasizes "long" as a modifier. In addition, the attributes of long and hot are not explicit in the picture but must be inferred by the children. It is also interesting to note that all of these phrases are the first sentence of each story and are nearly identical. While we do not see the typical "Once upon a time . . ." as an introduction to any of their stories, the students' alternative beginning certainly serves the same rhetorical purpose, as a marker not only of the setting but of the start of the story. It is possible that the familiarity of the scenes in the Annie Lee pictures, coupled with the structure of the narrative writing lessons, has forged a link between culturally relevant material and the structure of narrative writing. This pattern certainly demands further exploration.

Some students extended their use of dramatic language beyond the introductory phrase. The next story provides a dramatic description of the day and employs parallel structure as an emphatic device to dramatically capture the actions of the character.

"This is a hot, sunny day in the summer. Harry was sitting on the chair, just sitting on the chair changing channels and eating popcorn, crackers, and chips. . . . " (D.C.)

Figure 1.3.1   Annie Lee's *Daily Snooze*. Used by permission.

In the picture used as the prompt for this narrative, there is no television, and there are no popcorn, crackers, and chips—there is simply an old Black man falling asleep in a chair with a newspaper falling from his hands. The addition of details from the child's imagination, presumably based on lived experience, is another example of the semiotic potential of these visual prompts. Our suspicion is that these vivid scenes from scripts of African American life have a very different potential for stimulating the imagination of these children—and therefore their ability to generate the kinds of descriptive detail that characterize good written narratives—than, for example, postcards of Impressionist paintings of French men and women walking in the park, the women wearing long, bustled gowns.

The Use of a Sermonic
Tone and Cultural Referents

Of the 16 students, 4 incorporated the sermonic tones of the African-American church and cultural referents. These were additional features

Figure 1.3.2   Annie Lee's *Eb-body Say Amen*. Used by permission.

identified by Smitherman (2000c) as elements of the African American Rhetorical Tradition, and they were used by the older elementary students whose NAEP writing samples she examined. African American writers such as James Baldwin in *Go Tell It On the Mountain* and Richard Wright in *Black Boy* also effectively invoke the sermonic tone of the Black Church. It is interesting to note that when the students, as emergent writers, attempted to create sermonic tones, they often did so by creating dialogue. Remember, they were responding to pictures that have no words. This picture by Annie Lee is the prompt that invited students to capture in written narrative the talk, the sounds, the feelings of a Pentacostal Black Church experience.

"I want the Lord to help me love. . . . then she said, 'I want the Holy Ghost.'

Then she said, 'I want you to help me Lord.'" *(A.S.)*

"She is saying 'Oh Lord help me.'" (R.B.)

Again, our argument is a cultural one. These students gain access to schema and cultural scripts they know well as a scaffold for the production of dialogue, descriptive detail, and actions that capture the internal states of character types they know well. These prompts support the development of the kinds of procedural skills for narrative production that Hillocks (1995) describes.

Another way in which students activated cultural scripts was through the use of cultural referents in their narratives. One of the pictures captured an activity called "jumping the broom." During the era of the enslavement, lynchings, and burnings of Blacks in this country, the African American Holocaust of Enslavement, Blacks were not even legally allowed to marry. So to mark the ceremony of entering into the sacred institution of marriage, couples would jump over a broom. That ceremony has been maintained within contemporary African American culture. It is not uncommon for couples today to follow up a church marriage ceremony by jumping over a broom. In G.N.'s narrative based on this picture, she recognizes and names the ceremony. She creates dialogue and gives names to the man and woman being married, drawing on her cultural scripts to construct action in the plot.

"The wedding looked so pretty. There was dancing [and]

Mr. Johnson said to his wife, 'I love you.' 'I love you, too,' Ms. Sara Lee said.

Figure 1.3.3   Annie Lee's *Jumping the Broom*. Used by permission.

"Mr. Johnson threw up his Bible and said, 'Thank you Jesus! For giving me a wonderful ceremony' and Ms. Sara said, 'Amen to that.'" (G.N.)

. . . They both were happy. They jumped over the broom." (G.N.)

The following picture depicts a woman working in the fields. She is wearing a headdress and long skirt. L.D. and J.P., working together,

Figure 1.3.4   Annie Lee's *100% Cotton*. Used by permission.

extrapolated from the one woman to the "Black people" and chose for the woman's work to drive the plot. Their use of the phrase "the white man" has common usage in the African American community and communicates a point of view about power relationships between Blacks and Whites.

> "The Black people went to work for the white man . . . picking cotton. . . . "
> (L.D., J.P.)

The last example of a cultural referent involves a variety of foods commonly called "soul food." The following scene depicts a diner. The cultural scripts evoked by the picture lead the students to identify specific foods that they would expect to be served there. As with the other pictures, there are not sufficient details in the picture for the students to name particular foods. Rather, they use imagination to name and describe the food they would expect to find served at the corner restaurant. In addition to A.N.'s referents, other students also talk about ham hocks, smothered chicken, short ribs, candied sweet potatoes, and catfish—all items on a typical soul food menu.

> "Claudia was eating some fish with hot sauce." (A.N.)

A.N. goes on to create characters with names, describe what they were wearing, state the time of day (5:00 p.m.), and give the address of the diner.

Figure 1.3.5   Annie Lee's *Compliments to the Cook*. Used by permission.

Direct Address and a Conversational Tone

The use of direct forms of address and conversational tone are other features of the African American Rhetorical Tradition. As many students incorporate dialogue into their stories, the characters speak through direct forms of address about love, feeling tired, the weather, and prayers to God.

"Mr. Johnson said to his wife, 'I love you.' 'I love you, too,' Ms. Sara Lee said." (G.N.)

"She is saying, 'Oh Lord help me.'" (R.B.)

"Lard said, 'It's very hot.'

Boy Willy said, 'Yes, it is very hot.' . . . Zahkiyah said, 'I'm going with my mom.' Takanna said, 'I am going with my mom'" (N.A.)

" . . . Harry was sitting on the chair changing channels, eating popcorn, crackers, and chips, saying, 'I am so tired. I have a full stomach. . . .'" (D.C.)

"I am tired." (D.L., J.P.)

Integrating African American Discourse Norms

We have provided illustrations of isolated uses of African American discourse features across the corpus of the children's narratives in response to the Annie Lee pictures. The following story by G.N. was a response to the jumping the broom picture described earlier. It is a well-formed narrative that integrates many of the African American discourse features we have described in rhetorically appropriate ways.

It was a hot, sunny day. Ms. Sara Lee and Mr. John Johnson were getting married. It was back in 1895, March 31. Ms. Sara looked so pretty [and] Mr. John looked handsome. The wedding looked so pretty. There was dancing. Mr. Johnson said to his wife, "I love you." "I love you, too," Ms. Sara Lee said. They both were happy. They jumped over the broom. Mr. Johnson threw up his Bible and said, "Thank you Jesus! For giving me a wonderful ceremony." Ms. Sara said, "Amen to that." They had a beautiful background and the most beautiful wedding. She had on a beautiful wedding dress. It was so pretty. Mr. Johnson had a suit on that shined up the place. Ms. Sara Lee's dress was sort of a marble color, and her dress shined up the place also. They looked so happy together. (G.N.)

In addition to establishing the setting (hot, sunny day; March, 1895; a wedding), naming the characters (Ms. Sara Lee and Mr. John Johnson), describing their dress (sort of a marble color), and creating the coda (they looked so happy together), G.N. also creates dialogue for the characters in a sermonic tone (Mr. Johnson threw up his Bible and said, "Thank you Jesus! For giving me a wonderful ceremony." Ms. Sara said, "Amen to that."). This exchange reflects a clear cultural script of call and response. Also, her use of hyperbolic descriptions of Mr. Johnson's suit and Ms. Sara Lee's dress, that they "shined up the place," is an ethno-linguistic idiom with great drama. Finally, her reference to Ms. Sara Lee as Ms. Sara is another ethno-linguistic idiom. It has been traditional in the African American community to refer to an older woman in the community as Ms. and her given name. G.N.'s story meets the criteria for a well-formed story that is also replete with uses of African American discourse features.

Discussion

In this chapter, we have tried to make a case for the ways that the use of cultural data sets as prompts for narrative writing can extend the potential of the quality of written narratives produced by a group of severely under-achieving African American third and fourth graders. These students, who had repeated first, second, or third grade more than once, had been isolated from their peers in a special class. While we have documented their use of features of good narrative writing, their skill in spelling, the use of punctu-ation, and the formation of sentences and paragraphs remained severely impaired. In many respects, these surface features of poor spelling and punctuation hid from the teacher's and the school's view the strengths these children had available to bring to their writing. To the extent that severely remedial students, such as these at McDonald School, experience writing instruction that focuses primarily on surface features, without balancing attention on the skills and strategies necessary to create well-formed narra-tives—such as descriptions of setting and the creation of characters (espe-cially of their internal states), of dialogue, and of action—they could well remain severely remedial writers of the sort described by Shaughnessy (1977). Flowers and Hayes (1981) argue that developing writers need a mental model of the product and operations of composition. Bereiter and Scardamalia (1987) argue that procedural cues could facilitate the compos-ing and editing skills of novice writers. Hillocks (1995) argues that novice writers need supports for developing the procedural skills that will allow them to competently produce the elements of the genres of narratives, argu-ments, and extended definition. In the Cultural Modeling in Narrative Project, we attempted to enter this on-going conversation by posing an argument for the ways that cultural prompts and facilitation cues can help children make links to existing schemata and cultural scripts. The Annie Lee pictures, the video clips from narrative dialogues in movies such as August Wilson's *The Piano*, and oral storytelling by African American storytellers all served as artifacts or tools that extended the resources available to the children to use in composing their narratives. In many respects, these particular artifacts function like the tertiary or imaginative artifacts described by Cole (1996), which by their very nature invite imagination and an envisioning of other possible worlds. By invoking such cultural scripts, students are able to use imagination to construct inferences that form the base for the explicit use of language and detail. In our study of the field testing of this curricular approach in another school, with students without the extensive remedial needs of the students reported in this chapter, we found positive correlations between the quality of students' writing and their use of African American discourse features, as did Smitherman with NAEP writing samples.

With the Cultural Modeling Framework, we attempted to design learning environments that explicitly connect deep disciplinary knowledge and problem solving with the competencies students develop as they participate in routine cultural practices outside of school. With the Cultural Modeling in Narrative design, we tried to link what the cognitive literature on the act of composing says about the process with those competencies that young speakers of African American Vernacular English develop as they hear and tell oral stories outside of school. In addition, with the Cultural Modeling Framework we attempted to design participation structures (Phillips, 1983) that offer students opportunities to use multiple mediational means for attacking problems. Boykin's (1994) work on the intrinsic value that working in groups affords the African American students he documented across multiple controlled studies led us to design explicit opportunities for collaborative work in composing narratives. For this particular group of severely remedial students, the opportunities to compose narratives in pairs proved engaging for them. We found that the use of African American discourse features increased as students worked in pairs.

In addition to the design principles described, we also needed analytic methods to capture features of the narratives. Our methods of narrative analysis were informed by sociolinguistic literature on African American English and prior work on African American children's narratives. Based on Sadoski and Paivio's (2001) theory of dual coding in reading and writing, we selected prototypical scenes of African American life as captured in the Annie Lee pictures. Our methods of narrative analysis and prompts were symbiotically related. The prompts were intended to elicit the features that our methods of narrative analysis were intended to capture. Smitherman's (2000c) research documenting correlations between the presence of African American discourse features and the quality of African American student writing on NAEP samples led us to believe that facilitating these cultural features in student writing would result in better narratives. We found that images also spark the imagination of the best of our writers. As Murray (1978) explains,

> When Gabriel Marquez was asked what the starting point of his novels was, he answered, "A completely visual image . . . the starting point of *Leaf Storm* is an old man taking his grandson to a funeral. . . . Joyce Carol Oates adds, "I visualize the characters completely; I have heard their dialogue, I know how they speak, what they want, who they are, nearly everything about them." (quoted in Sadoski & Paivio, 2001, p. 152)

Alice Walker says that Celie in *The Color Purple* speaks in the voice of her great-grandmother. The children from the McDonald School observed the scenes of their lives, heard the voices, smelled the odors, knew the characters. Despite the limitations of their decoding skills, they told stories of African American life, using the creative rhetorical strategies of the African American tradition, and in the process created narratives that shed light on the meaning of their membership in the African American community.

Note

1. For purposes of clarity, we have transcribed the students' stories with correct spelling and punctuation. The words, however, are the children's, and their actual initials follow their work.

References

Ball, A. F. (1992). Cultural preferences and the expository writing of African-American adolescents. *Written Communication, 9*(4), 501–532.

Ball, A. F. (1995). Text design patterns in the writing of urban African-American students: Teaching to the strengths of students in multicultural settings. *Urban Education, 30,* 253–289.

Baugh, J. (1983). *Black street speech: Its history, structure and survival.* Austin: University of Texas Press.

Bereiter, C., & Scardamalia, M. (1987). *The psychology of written communication.* Hillsdale, NJ: Lawrence Erlbaum.

Berman, R. A., & Slobin, D. (1994). *Relating events in narrative: A crosslinguistic developmental study.* Hillsdale, NJ: Lawrence Erlbaum.

Boykin, A. W. (1994). Harvesting culture and talent: African American children and educational reform. In R. Rossi (Ed.), *Educational reform and at risk students.* New York: Teachers College Press.

Bruner, J. (1990). *Acts of meaning.* Cambridge, MA: Harvard University Press.

Cazden, C. (1988). *Classroom discourse: The language of teaching and learning.* Portsmouth, NH: Heinemann.

Cazden, C., Michaels, S., & Tabors, P. (1985). Spontaneous repairs in sharing time narratives: The intersection of metalinguistic awareness, speech event and narrative style. In S. Freedman (Ed.), *The acquisition of written language: Revision and response.* Norwood, NJ: Ablex.

Champion, T. (1998). "Tell me somethin' good": A description of narrative structures among African-American children. *Linguistics and Education, 9*(3), 251–286.

Champion, T. (2003). *Understanding storytelling among African American children: A journey from Africa to America.* Mahwah, NJ: Lawrence Erlbaum.

Cole, M. (1996). *Cultural psychology, A once and future discipline.* Cambridge, MA: Belknap Press of Harvard University Press.

D'Andrade, R. (1987). A folk model of the mind. In D. Holland & N. Quinn (Eds.), *Cultural models in language and thought* (pp. 112–147). New York: Cambridge University Press.

Dyson, A. H. (1997). *Writing superheroes: Contemporary childhood, popular culture, and classroom literacy.* New York: Teachers College Press.

Flowers, L., & Hayes, J. (1981). A cognitive process theory of writing. *College Composition and Communication, 32,* 365–387.

Gee, J. P. (1989). The narrativization of experience in the oral style. *Journal of Education, 171*(1), 75–96.

Gutierrez, K., & Rogoff, B. (2003). Cultural ways of learning: Individual traits or repertoires of practice. In C. Lee (Ed.), Re-conceptualizing race and ethnicity in educational research [Special issue]. *Educational Researcher, 32*(5), 19–25.

Heath, S. B. (1983). *Ways with words: Language, life and work in communities and classrooms.* New York: Cambridge University Press.

Hillocks, G. (1975). *Observing and writing.* Urbana, IL: National Council of Teachers of English.

Hillocks, G. (1986). *Research on written composition: New directions for teaching.* Urbana, IL: National Conference on Research in English/ERIC Clearinghouse on Reading and Communication Skills.

Hillocks, G. (1995). *Teaching writing as reflective practice.* New York: Teachers College Press.

Hyon, S., & Sulzby, E. (1994). African American kindergarteners' spoken narratives: Topic associating and topic centered styles. *Linguistics and Education, 6*(2), 121–152.

Jones, G. (1991). *Liberating voices: Oral tradition in African American literature.* New York: Penguin.

Labov, W. (1972). *Language in the inner city: Studies in the Black English vernacular.* Philadelphia: University of Pennsylvania Press.

Lee, C. D. (1993). *Signifying as a scaffold for literary interpretation: The pedagogical implications of an African American discourse genre* (Research report series). Urbana, IL: National Council of Teachers of English.

Lee, C. D. (1995a). A culturally based cognitive apprenticeship: Teaching African American high school students' skills in literary interpretation. *Reading Research Quarterly, 30*(4), 608–631.

Lee, C. D. (1995b). Signifying as a scaffold for literary interpretation. *Journal of Black Psychology, 21*(4), 357–381.

Lee, C. D. (1999, April). *Supporting the development of interpretive communities through metacognitive instructional conversations in culturally diverse classrooms.* Paper presented at the annual conference of the American Educational Research Association. Denver, CO.

Lee, C. D. (2000). Signifying in the zone of proximal development. In C. D. Lee & P. Smagorinsky (Eds.), *Vygotskian perspectives on literacy research: Constructing meaning through collabative inquiry* (pp. 191–225). New York: Cambridge University Press.

Lee, C. D. (2001). Is October Brown Chinese: A cultural modeling activity system for underachieving students. *American Educational Research Journal, 38*(1), 97–142.

Lee, C. D., Mendenhall, R., Rivers, A., & Tynes, B. (1999). *Cultural modeling: A framework for scaffolding oral narrative repertoires for academic narrative writing.* Paper presented at the Multicultural Narrative Analysis Conference at the University of South Florida, Tampa.

Lee, C. D., Spencer, M. B., & Harpalani, V. (2003). Every shut eye ain't sleep: Studying how people live culturally, In C. Lee (Ed.), Re-conceptualizing race and ethnicity in educational research [Special issue]. *Educational Researcher, 32*(5), 6–13.

Michaels, S. (1981). "Sharing time": Children's narrative styles and differential access to literacy. *Language in Society, 10,* 423–442.

Mitchell-Kernan, C. (1981). Signifying, loud-talking and marking. In A. Dundes (Ed.), *Mother wit from the laughing barrel* (pp. 310–328). Englewood, Cliffs, NJ: Prentice Hall.

Moll, L., & Greenberg, J. B. (1990). Creating zones of possibilities: Combining social contexts for instruction. In L. Moll (Ed.), *Vygotsky and education: Instructional implications and applications of sociohistorical psychology* (pp. 319–348). New York: Cambridge University Press.

Morgan, M. (1993). The Africaness of counterlanguage among Afro-Americans. In S. Mufwene (Ed.), *Africanisms in Afro-American language varieties.* Athens: University of Georgia Press.

Moss, B. (1994). Creating a community: Literacy events in African-American churches. In B. Moss (Ed.), *Literacy across communities* (pp. 147–178). Cresskill, NJ: Hampton.

Mufwene, S. (Ed.). (1993). *Africanisms in Afro-American language varieties.* Athens: University of Georgia Press.

Murray, D. M. (1978). Write before writing. *College Composition and Communication, 29,* 375–381.

Peterson, C., & McCabe, A. (1983). *Developmental psycholinguistics: Three ways of looking at a child's narrative.* New York: Plenum.

Phillips, S. U. (1983). *The invisible culture: Communication in classroom and community on the Warm Springs Indian Reservation.* New York: Longman.

Rabinowitz, P. (1987). *Before reading: Narrative conventions and the politics of interpretation.* Ithaca, NY: Cornell University Press.

Rickford, J., & Rickford, A. (1976). Cut-eye and suck teeth: African words and gestures in new world guise. *Journal of American Folklore, 89*(353), 194–309.

Sadoski, M., & Paivio, A. (2001). *Imagery and text: A dual coding theory of reading and writing.* Mahwah, NJ: Lawrence Erlbaum.

Shaughnessy, M. P. (1977). *Errors and expectations: A guide for the teacher of basic writing.* New York: Oxford University Press.

Smitherman, G. (1973). The power of the rap: The Black idiom and the new Black poetry. *Twentieth Century Literature,* 259–274.

Smitherman, G. (1977). *Talkin and testifyin: The language of Black America.* Boston: Houghton Mifflin.

Smitherman, G. (2000a). Ebonics, King, and Oakland: Some folks don't believe fat meat is greasy. In G. Smitherman (Ed.), *Talk that talk: Language, culture and education in African America* (pp. 150–162). New York: Routledge.

Smitherman, G. (Ed.). (2000b). *Talk that talk: Language, culture and education in African America.* New York: Routledge.

Smitherman, G. (2000c). African American student writers in the NAEP, 1969–1988/89 and "The Blacker the berry, the sweeter the juice." In G. Smitherman (Ed.), *Talk that talk: Language, culture and education in African America* (pp. 163–194). New York: Routledge.

Tan, A. (1989). *The Joy Luck Club.* New York: Random House.

Turner, M. (1996). *The literary mind.* New York: Oxford University Press.

Vygotsky, L. (1978). Mind in society: The development of higher psychological processes (M. Cole, V. John-Steiner, S. Scribner, & E. Souberman, Eds.). Cambridge, MA: Harvard University Press.

1.4

Data are Everywhere

Narrative Criticism in the Literature of Experience

Mark Freeman

Life and Literature

In much of my recent work (e.g., Freeman, 1997, 1998a, 1998b), I have spoken of the "narrative fabric" of the self and have argued further that human life is itself narratively structured. As against those who imagine life to be essentially formless, and narrative to be an imposition from without, my own perspective is that it may profitably be understood as a kind of *literature*. What this suggests, in turn, is that there exists the need to approach (a portion of) the "data" of human lives in a manner that differs significantly from that of traditional social science.

Without wishing to overstate the distinction at hand—there are significant continuities as well—the approach suggested herein tends more toward the *qualitative* than the quantitative; it is more *idiographic,* focusing on the individual person, than nomothetic, focusing on generalities across individuals; it looks more toward interpretive *understanding* than explanation; and, not least, it relies more on *poetic* than scientific modes of writing and is thus oriented not only toward the cognitive and discursive functions of language but also toward the emotional and evocative. On the face of it, this shift of emphasis would seem to take narrative inquiry away from psychology's customary aim of portraying objectively a given phenomenon; it seems more ambiguous, indefinite, "subjective." But it may very well be that only through more interpretive modes of inquiry and more poetic modes of writing can there emerge that sort of fidelity to the phenomena that is the first requirement of the narrative analysis of human lives. Put more quaintly, this shift of emphasis seeks to practice greater fidelity to the *reality* of human experience and thereby to tell a more *truthful* story about it.

One significant source of inspiration for the perspective offered here is the seminal work of the philosopher Paul Ricoeur. Ricoeur (1981a) maintains that human action might usefully be framed on the model of the literary text. Among the many reasons for doing so, several deserve emphasis. The first has to do with what might be termed the "semantics" of human action. "Meaningful action," Ricoeur (1981a) states, "is an object for science only under the condition of a kind of objectification which is equivalent to the fixation of a discourse by writing" (p. 203). Second, Ricoeur (1981a) speaks of the "autonomization" of action: "In the same way that a text is detached from its author, an action is detached from its agent and develops consequences of its own" (p. 206). As Ricoeur goes on to explain, "our deeds escape us and have effects which we did not intend," the result being that they are "read" anew by others with whom we are engaged as well as by ourselves. Taking this idea one step further, Ricoeur (1981a) considers the ideas of relevance and importance, noting that "a meaningful action is an action the *importance* of which goes 'beyond' its *relevance* to its initial situation" (p. 207). Fourth, and finally for the time being, Ricoeur speaks of human action as an "open work, the meaning of which is 'in suspense'" (p. 208).

It is this last characteristic of the text that leads Ricoeur to thereafter focus explicitly on the issue of *narrative,* especially in relation to the issue of *time* (e.g., Ricoeur, 1981b, 1984, 1985, 1988; with reference to developmental psychology, see also Freeman, 1984, 1985, 1991). Human action consists of events that are, essentially, "episodes in the making"—that is, events that will *become* episodes, retroactively, by virtue of their interrelationship with other events, both antecedent and subsequent, as well as with those "endings" that will ultimately serve to transfigure them into the stuff of narrative. In a distinct sense, one often does not know "what is happening" until the moment is past, until it can be located within some broader constellation of events, read for its significance in some larger whole.

There is something of a paradox entailed in the process at hand, one that is related to the notion of the "hermeneutical circle" (e.g., Gadamer, 1975; Ricoeur, 1981a). On the one hand, it may be said that the beginnings and middles of stories determine their endings. At the same time, however, it can also be said that endings determine beginnings and middles; for only when a story has ended—whether the ending in question is temporary, as in life, or permanent, as in death—is it possible to discern the meaning and significance of what has come before. There must, again, be a synoptic act of *reading*, whereby events are seen together in their interrelatedness as episodes in an evolving narrative. Ricoeur (1981b) thus speaks of two distinct dimensions of narrative: the "episodic," which refers to the events of which a story is comprised, and the "configurational," which refers to this process of seeing- or grasping-together, "eliciting a pattern from a succession" (p. 174). He also speaks of a "temporal dialectic" that may be said to characterize the unique temporality of narrative. By virtue of the episodic dimension, there is, in every story, a tendency toward the linear representation of time—this happened, then that happened, and so on. The model is one of succession, adhering to clock time. By virtue of the configurational dimension, however—Ricoeur speaks of the process of "emplotment" (see also Brooks, 1985; White, 1978)—there is a different temporal movement altogether, one that looks essentially backward rather than forward. Indeed, Ricoeur (1981b) suggests,

> It is as though recollection inverted the so-called natural order of time. By reading the end in the beginning and the beginning in the end, we learn also to read time itself backward, as the recapitulating of the initial conditions of a course of action in its terminal consequences. In this way, a plot establishes human action not only within time . . . but within memory. (p. 176)

Alongside the defining characteristics of texts enumerated earlier, Ricoeur (1981b) therefore gives us another set of criteria by which we might characterize human experience as a kind of literature: "Reading" human action partakes of the same temporal dialectic that is involved in reading literature. What Ricoeur calls "narrative time" may thus be regarded as a constitutive feature of human experience.

Thus far, I have called attention largely to "formal" reasons why human experience may profitably be understood as a kind of literature: In some fundamental ways, human experience resembles literary texts. It should not be forgotten in this context, however, that literary texts are *themselves* modeled on human experience. Crites (1970) puts the matter well: "Life is not, after all, a work of art. An artistic drama has a coherence and a fullness of articulation that are never reached by our rudimentary drama. But the drama of experience is the crude original of all high drama" (p. 303).

This brings to me to a final set of reasons for considering human experience as a kind of literature, and it is one with which we are all familiar: Our very lives are bathed in stories, in comedies and tragedies, with happy endings and shocking, or unanticipated, or disappointing ones. I do not wish to overdramatize human experience. It can be uneventful and quite tedious. It can also be truly chaotic, possessing no discernible meaning at all, even in retrospect. But much of the time it is quite different than this. Stories abound and proliferate. Data are everywhere.

Social Science and Beyond

In order to show how I have arrived at this particular vision of narrative inquiry, it may be useful to present some sense of the path my own work has gone through during the course of the past 20 or so years. It began, in fairly traditional fashion, with a mixture of questionnaire and interview data exploring aspects of life history along with data that sought to provide something of an experiential snapshot of particular periods of the lives in question. In one study, for instance (Freeman, Csikszentmihalyi, & Larson, 1986), adolescents' experience in various domains of their lives (with family, with friends, and alone) was charted at two points in time, 2 years apart, via the Experience Sampling Method (ESM), which asked them to rate and comment upon the quality of immediate experience in these domains. Through this method, my colleagues and I obtained a kind of map of these adolescents' experiential worlds at the two points in time and were therefore in a position to discern what sorts of changes, if any, had occurred. At around the time of the second sampling, extensive interviews with the same individuals were also carried out, asking them to reflect on how they perceived their experience in each of the aforementioned domains to have changed during this span of time. The results proved to be interesting. While there had been virtually no significant changes in their experience as gauged by the ESM self-reports, the interviews suggested that they had gone through considerable positive change. Moreover, the adolescents were able to substantiate this change, to explain the ways in which they believed it to have occurred and how it had served to transform the fabric of their lives.

For present purposes, the details of the data gathered are less significant than the methodological framework employed. By virtue of having acquired both forms of data, one oriented toward immediate experience and the other toward recollection, we were able to get some sense of what was being *done* in and through the adolescents' process of narrating the stories of their lives. The virtues of this particular methodological approach notwithstanding, I eventually came to feel that aspects of it were overly contrived. I do not wish to offer an indictment of the approach; within its sphere, it was of great value. But having had a taste of what interview data could bring—namely, a recognizable sense of people's actual lives—I found myself drawn toward more open-ended modes of narrative inquiry and analysis.

This led to my becoming involved in a study of artists carried out at the University of Chicago in conjunction with the School of the Art Institute of Chicago (under the direction of Mihaly Csikszentmihalyi, J.W. Getzels, and Stephen P. Kahn). In one wave of the project, carefully designed questionnaires geared toward gathering life history information had been sent to the artists in question. Not surprisingly, the data proved to be interesting and informative. But in my own mind, these data simply didn't *live*. Not only wasn't there enough space on any given page for people truly to speak, but the very structuredness with which the relevant questions were presented had led to a too-artificial form of interrogation and, in turn, a kind of objectification of those on the receiving end. They were not partners in dialogue about their lives and their art; they were the objects of questions, tied to *our* interests. To a greater or lesser extent, of course, this is always the case. One speaks to whomever because of a question or an interest one has; the other, therefore, becomes a means to one's own ends. But some narrative methods do this in a cruder, more ethically questionable way. That, at least, was how I came to feel about it. I wasn't alone either. Some of the artists to whom we had sent the questionnaires had clearly been put off by having been asked to serve as the instruments of social scientists' empiricist designs about their art and creativity.

Here, too, I do not wish to offer a blanket indictment of the methodological approach employed in this first wave of the study. Questionnaires have their place, and there is no inherent need to exclude artists and the like from the burden of filling them out every now and then. It should also be emphasized that, as questionnaires go, this one was composed with a good deal of care, both for the instrument and for the artists themselves. In fact, I am fully prepared to say that my own alienation from this sort of method had more to do with *me* than anything else. I simply could not "get near" the basic approach employed. That was my last encounter with it.

The next wave of the study was much more appealing. We would go to artists' studios or homes and speak with them, at length, about their lives and work. We were armed with discrete questions, of course, for, among other reasons, a number of dissertations had to be completed. But we were to proceed in as dialogic a way as possible, trying as best we could to ensure that there emerged a natural flow of conversation in which the artists themselves had ample opportunity to speak their minds. The resultant data were extraordinarily rich and informative. There was also an immense quantity of data. By the project's end, there were transcripts from some 54 artists, with some of the transcripts being upwards of 30 single-spaced pages. What were we to *do* with all of this information? How might we begin the difficult process of narrative analysis?

The plan was to build an elaborate coding scheme designed to encompass as much of the data as possible. We would also look at word frequencies and other such ostensible indices of (possible) meaning and significance. And, sensibly enough, we would try to determine ways of cataloguing the data in order that they might be related to earlier data sets. Basically, therefore, the aim was to take this voluminous quantity of data and boil it down as best we could to the clearest, most manipulable categories in order, subsequently, to undertake the most rigorous and systematic analysis possible. This is in fact how most of those working on the project proceeded. There would also be narrative analysis of a sort, for instance, in the form of a brief case history. But it would likely be presented as a supplement, designed to flesh out or to substantiate the main, quantitatively derived findings.

In principle, I have no qualms whatsoever about quantitatively derived findings. I also want to emphasize that many of those working on the project in largely quantitative fashion did some excellent and important work. But there were several problems that came to plague me at the time. The first was that the elaborate coding scheme on which we were working seemed overly reductive, serving to flatten some of the richest and most significant information into generic categories. Second, this way of proceeding also tended to break the narrative order: An episode that might have been an integral part of a given person's story had been extracted from the story and transformed into an instance of this or that codable phenomenon. Another set of problems had to do with the kinds of analyses being done. For lack of a more graceful way of putting the matter, it sometimes felt as if we had taken information that was meaningful, significant, and revealing, broken it down in such a way that many of its most interesting features were no longer recognizable, and then tried to reassemble it to determine whether in fact anything notable emerged. There was also the sense that the quantitatively derived information was the *real* stuff and that the rest was somehow decorative, ornamental. Why should this be?

Much to the chagrin of some of those with whom I had been working, I resolved to do a purely qualitative dissertation that would place people's stories at the forefront. In addition to all of the methodological reasons that have been identified, there was another, more substantive reason for doing so, and it is one that brings us closer to one of the aims of the present volume, that of studying the development of individuals in society. As I went on to suggest in the book that eventually emerged from this work, *Finding the Muse: A Sociopsychological Inquiry Into the Conditions of Artistic Creativity* (Freeman, 1993a), what life narratives reveal frequently extends well beyond the psychological plane. In addition to serving as vehicles for understanding the unique trajectories of individuals' lives, they also serve as means of access to social reality, signifying the worlds through which people have moved.

One related methodological issue that I brought up in *Finding the Muse* deserves mention before we move on. In a very basic and obvious sense, life narratives deal with *subjective* meanings; they are individuals' *perceptions* of their past, their interpretive renditions of the past from the standpoint of the present. But this subjective dimension of narrative inquiry is by no means the only dimension. "As with any text," I had suggested, "the interest is not only in what the *author* himself or herself may have meant by a particular utterance but what the *text* itself means: We want to understand what is being said and what this something is about" (Freeman, 1993a, p. 34). Following the aforementioned reflections of Ricoeur (1981a) on the text as an appropriate model of human action, the project of narrative understanding and analysis expands greatly. "For in moving beyond subjective meanings, localized in the person of the author, we immediately have before us a much larger range of possible interpretations, emerging in line with the essential openness of discourse itself" (Freeman, 1993a, p. 34). The narrative analysis undertaken, therefore, would not rest with subjective meanings alone; the aim would be "to extend their reach, through interpretation, to the social realities constitutive of them" (p. 35).

There is a corollary to this set of ideas that can present a difficult interpretive and indeed ethical challenge for those pursuing narrative analysis. It is one, in fact, about which there may be considerable disagreement. In some of the work I have carried out, I explore possible meanings that the people in question may find unrecognizable or, for that matter, completely disavow. In some of the stories provided by the artists, for instance, it became clear to me that they had bought into a myth about the struggling genius, at odds with the world, that had actually stunted their creativity. They themselves may not have been fully aware of this myth and, had I presented this interpretation to them, they might have rejected it. Now, it is of course true in this context that *my* word is hardly the last. But neither, I would argue, is theirs. And sometimes it can be extremely valuable to look beyond intended meanings and pursue the possibility of different ones altogether. In recent years, some narrative researchers have taken to presenting their own renditions of people's lives to the people themselves. This is a way of trying to ensure that what the researchers have said is faithful to what they have been told, but it is also a way of "giving back" to those being studied. The motives are surely noble ones. I would nevertheless question the necessity and even, in some instances, the desirability of returning one's interpretations in this way.

The story continues. Once I had decided to pursue a purely qualitative approach, the narrative-analytic challenge loomed before me. What exactly should be done with these 50-plus interviews? As an initial step, I decided that I would transform the interview transcripts into narrative form, using the artists' own words as much as possible in the service of fashioning stories adequate to what they had said. Had the artists read these preliminary narratives, they would likely have found them recognizable and acceptable. In this first phase, in other words, the primary aim was to translate into story form what the artists themselves had said, following their own narrative leads. Subsequently, the task—not unlike the task of categorizing and coding in some sense—was to determine what went with what (for instance, which pieces of one person's story seemed to go with which pieces of another's), which of the narratives would be turned into full-blown case histories (perhaps for their richness or tellingness), and, finally, how to tell the "collective" story within which these individual stories emerged. I need not recount the details of the analyses pursued. But basically, I commenced dealing with the interviews and the resultant narrative texts as one would deal with works of literature, on the lookout for plot structures and themes and literary tropes. The entire process—which, in a distinct sense, had become a kind of literary criticism—proved to be terrifically exciting, for a vast new realm of possibilities for narrative analysis had been opened up.

In speaking of literary criticism here, I refer to that sort of broad interpretive undertaking that seeks to unpack literary texts for their meaning and significance. Following one of the basic distinctions often made in contemporary literary criticism, some of my interpretive analyses were largely "formalist" in nature, "close readings" that remained within the perimeter of the text, seeking to explicate what was being said. In these instances, careful attention was paid to the use of language and to the formal properties of the texts in question. Other analyses were more "historicist" in nature, seeking instead to situate the texts within some broader cultural/historical constellation of issues—for instance, the problem of women artists trying to gain entry into a male-dominated art world or the problem of artists trying to make art in an artistic climate that had become so pluralistic as to actually undermine creativity. Other kinds of analyses were employed as well. None of these analyses, I should avow, were the product of a discrete method of extracting the relevant information, of the sort that might be given to someone else to use. I do not mean to suggest that the analyses just discussed were unmethodical. In carrying out this kind of work, there is always an approach to inquiry involved, a methodological perspective, geared toward trying to understand the phenomenon in question and trying to say something meaningful about it. But the perspective employed is not determined ahead of time. Nor is it determined by any one technique or set of techniques for carrying out the analysis. It is determined instead by the nature of the phenomenon, what's interesting about it, and what's worth saying.

What Are Legitimate Data for Narrative Analysis?

I begin this section with a somewhat contentious assertion: Social scientists—including psychologists interested in narrative—have generally been unduly restrictive in their conception of what constitutes legitimate data. Likewise, there has been too much restrictiveness in terms of method, that is, in terms of how one goes about acquiring one's data. Consequently, ways of meaningfully expanding the scope of narrative inquiry ought to be pursued.

From the analysis of life narratives derived from interviews, it was but a short step to examining memoirs, autobiographies, and other personal documents. In *Rewriting the Self* (Freeman, 1993b), I examined nonfictional literary texts, ranging from St. Augustine's *Confessions* (397/1980) to Helen Keller's *The Story of My Life* (1902/1988). These texts were selected not just on the basis of how interesting or important they were but on the basis of what sorts of methodological and theoretical questions and problems, pertinent to narrative analysis, they presented. In the case of *Confessions,* for instance, much of the focus was on the problem of memory and, specifically, on the difference between life as lived and as told in retrospect, through narrative. In the case of *The Story of My Life,* the focus was on the interrelationship of language and personal identity. Insofar as *Rewriting the Self* remained attentive to psychological issues, it could still plausibly be called "psychology." But by this time it had become difficult to differentiate this work from literary criticism itself. Was there a need to?

More and more, it strikes me as essentially irrelevant whether narrative inquiry, in psychology and beyond, continues to be subsumed under the rubric of *science.* I used to care about this. In fact, in some of my earlier work, I tried to suggest that, appearances notwithstanding, I really was doing a kind of science. I even had a rationale for why I was able to call it that: In line with what was said earlier regarding fidelity to the phenomena, my aim was to be faithful to the human experience. And so, if science is about faithfulness to reality, then surely I was doing it. In fact, I would sometimes argue that it could be that what I was doing was *more* scientific than what they were doing ("they" being whoever my positivist opponents were)—at least there were some signs of *life*.

I also insisted that I was doing *psychology*. A very brief autobiographical excursion may be appropriate here. One time, in my own department after I had given a presentation on some issues related to those being explored here, one of my colleagues had come up to me and said something like, That was interesting. But why do you call what you're doing psychology? Why not literary criticism? Another, more "playful" colleague had also found the presentation interesting. He liked fiction a great deal, he explained, and by all indications that's what I was doing. The same fundamental question had emerged from each of them: What is it that allows you to call yourself a psychologist? At the time, I had an entire arsenal of answers prepared, for why I should still be considered part of the club, why the club had to expand its membership, and so forth. Recollections of this sort can be extremely humbling.

At this point, in any case, I am not entirely sure how important it is for this sort of work to be considered science. Strictly speaking, it's probably not. I am also not sure whether it is important for it to be considered psychology. Although a good deal of contemporary work in narrative is in fact being carried out by psychologists, much of it intersects with fields other than psychology, such as sociology, anthropology, history, philosophy, and literature. I believe this is a potential plus. The question that needs to be asked is not whether a given piece of work is or isn't psychology (though of course this sort of question may well be pertinent to job placement, tenure decisions, etc.) but whether it is adequate to its own aims, and whether the aims themselves have any value.

Now, it is true that analyzing a literary text involves somewhat different interpretive assumptions and requires somewhat different interpretive strategies than analyzing texts produced by interviews and other such methods. In the case of autobiography, for instance, it has likely been written for a reason of some sort (demonstrating how a sinner can become a saint, showing how a deaf and blind child can triumph over adversity), and the writer has likely shaped the resultant story with as much attention to its aesthetic qualities as its informational value. Cruder issues may be involved as well. Some autobiographies, in the present moment especially, may be crafted with an eye toward what will sell (a lot). But all this means is that in undertaking narrative analysis of these kinds of texts, one needs to be aware of and attentive to the relevant rhetorical issues.

The same may be said in regard to the analysis of fictional texts. Of the six texts explored in *Rewriting the Self,* only one—Jean-Paul Sartre's

Nausea (1938/1964)—was a work of fiction. Not too long after completing this work, I turned my attention to another fictional text, Tolstoy's novella *The Death of Ivan Ilych* (1886/1960; see Freeman, 1997). With fiction, the methodological challenges became more pronounced. Among the many reasons for why this is so, there is the simple fact that the story in question is not *true* and that the situations depicted, however much they may rely on the author's knowledge of "real life," also rely on his or her imaginative reworking of it. More problematically still, we often meet up with characters in works of fiction that could not exist in the real world. They may be Martians or cyborgs or just inordinately quirky. What is one to say about *them?* In some cases, perhaps nothing. But in other cases, it may well remain possible to discern what is being said about the world, the *real* world, in and through the imaginary vision being presented. As Ricoeur (1983) has suggested, fictional texts entail the suppression of a first-order reference to the world as the condition of possibility for disclosing a second-order reference. The empirically unreal and untrue thereby become a means of articulating the real and true on a deeper, more fundamental plane. To the extent that one wishes to say something (meaningful) about the psychological sphere via narrative analysis of fictional texts, one needs to proceed very cautiously, being attentive to the specifically literary dimensions of the texts at hand. But it can surely be done. Literary critics, who may know very little about psychological matters, have been doing it for many years. Psychologists and other social scientists can, and should, add to the mix.

There are other sources of data as well. They are rich and indeed limitless (and don't even require extensive funding from granting agencies). Here, I refer to that which we colloquially call "life itself," that is, the world of our everyday encounters with others as well as ourselves. There are several significant reasons for exploring such data. First, there is the opportunity to move beyond the rarefied atmosphere of the interview, along with other discrete social scientific methods. As suggested already, I certainly would not want to say that the interview is without value or that it should be abandoned—far from it. But to a greater or lesser degree, the resultant data are bound to be an artifact of the questions and presumptions we, the researchers, bring to the situation, and the situation itself is bound to be (more or less) contrived. Put in more positive terms, there are aspects of trying to explore people's lives *outside* the research context that allow a different kind of relationship to the data.

A second, more substantive, reason for writing about life itself is that it sometimes serves to bind together more closely the world we live in and the world we study. To reiterate a point made earlier, we are surrounded by stories all the time, and many of them are not only fascinating but telling. That is to say, we can *learn* something from them. Here, one might plausibly ask: What? And my answer to this question, also once more, would be that it depends entirely on the nature of the narrative in question. For the sake of making this answer more concrete, I now turn briefly to several recent pieces that draw from the bountiful literature of life itself.

The Challenge of Exploring the Lives We Lead

In one recent piece of autobiographical reflection, titled "The Presence of What Is Missing: Memory, Poetry, and the Ride Home" (Freeman, 2002a), I tried to say something about the nature of memory, specifically about the way in which certain outcomes or "endings" can condition and monumentalize views of earlier life events. It is the story of a ride home from college I took with my father at the end of my sophomore year in which he and I *spoke* to one another, made some connections, for the first time in years. In a sense, we ratified one another's existence. A month or so later, he was gone. Had my father lived beyond that fateful summer, had there been more rides home together, more points of contact, that particular one might have faded into the oblivion of memory or simply have become a nice episode to recount in the history of a relationship. But because it was virtually the last experience he and I shared, it became something else, something more. One might of course deem this conviction a consolatory fiction, for at the time the event occurred, it had hardly been monumental. But memory, I suggested, is ordinarily not about returning to an earlier time and narrative is not about telling it "as it was." Imagination is involved, *poiesis,* a process of articulating meanings that could not possibly emerge except in retrospect, through narration.

It is important to emphasize that I had little interest in revealing something about *me* in this autobiographical exercise (although I am sure I did so on some level). The aim was instead to "use" me, to use my experience, as a vehicle to explore something else: memory, the poetic process of fashioning a connection between past and present, the building of psychical monuments. This brings me to a more general point about method. In much of my recent work, not only is there no discrete method being relied upon, but the data themselves are unplanned and the process of analysis highly exploratory and speculative. It should also be noted that, in most of these instances, there are no discrete texts involved—or at least no texts possessing an existence independent of, well, *me*. This is true of all autobiographical reflection to the extent that it takes place in the absence of material documents such as diaries or journals: The "text," such as it is, is itself one's own creation, one's own imaging and imagining of the past. On some occasions, I do rely on some rough notes. But on other occasions—in the case of that ride home with my father, for instance—all I had were memories, and distant ones at that. The outlines of these memories had become blurred, the details murky, and they were surely suffused with my wishes, my desire for the story to have a particular meaning, one that was redemptive, that allowed me some measure of solace and rest. In this sort of situation, all one can do is to be candid about what one remembers and what one does not, about the blurriness and the possible wishes, about one's very position as a teller and a writer. The resultant story may not please those who insist on following strictly the rules and expectations of empirical social science. This would be their loss, for there is much to be gained, I believe, from carrying out such work.

In order to show concretely what might be gained, let me now discuss in some detail a piece I did several years ago that dealt with someone else's life, a friend of mine, who had gone through some very tough times. The piece is called "Culture, Narrative, and the Poetic Construction of Selfhood," and its argument is that, even though the "tools" employed in the construction of selfhood are social in nature—by virtue of language, prevailing ways of understanding human conduct, prevailing genres of narration, and so on—the acts through which this process of construction occurs are better conceived in poetic terms, as what I call "imaginative labor" seeking to give form and meaning to experience (Freeman, 1999b). A secondary argument in the piece is that there are ways of understanding this poetic, imaginative process that do not necessarily return us to the Romantic, sovereign self, creating his or her own private world of meaning, but that point instead toward the relational dimension of autobiographical self-fashioning. In fact, what I tried to suggest is that the central source of inspiration for this process of autobiographical construction is not so much the self as the Other—in this case, another person.

The man about whom I wrote, a colleague and friend, had been known by people as a vital, strong, bigger-than-life figure, someone remarkably good at what he did. He was also known for his sharp intellect, his quick wit, and his refusal to suffer fools gladly. There had been a few wrinkles for him at work in recent years, but overall things had gone well. As for his life beyond work, I referred to there having been "one great, big, chaotic, unruly happy family" with him at the center. He had been their "rock," as he eventually put it to me. Things suddenly changed when his wife, herself a model of strength and vitality, was diagnosed with cancer. Even then, he had been able to maintain some semblance of his usual persona, if only as a way of reassuring himself and others that the situation was less than dire. The guise was hardly foolproof: On occasion, his fear and misery would break through. But, for a time, he hung tough, believing that God played a significant role in allowing him to do so.

What sent him over the edge was his own trip to the doctor. An x-ray had revealed a shadow, and although it was likely nothing to worry about, or so he was told, everything suddenly came undone: He too was going to die, and his children would be alone, forever. How could this *be*? How could their good fortune have changed so radically? And, where was God? He had brought these questions, and more, to me, in my office, shortly after the doctor visit. We talked about numerous things, from Kierkegaard's reflections on dread and despair to the all too mysterious ways that God often worked. But his main focus was the children, and the injustice that seemed to be hurtling their way, so suddenly and inexplicably. I had never seen this man so vulnerable. Nor had he seen himself this way. He wondered if perhaps he wasn't the tower of strength he had imagined himself to be. He didn't say this outright, but the meaning of his response to this horrific situation was clear enough: Even I can be broken. I *am* broken. I am not all that I appear to be. The scene of that conversation was an unusual one. Ordinarily, he wasn't given to self-disclosure, certainly not with me. I wasn't a best friend but only a friend, and colleague, the philosophically oriented psychologist down the hall who had kids of his own and often seemed to think about these kinds of issues.

The doctor turned out to have been right about the shadow on the x-ray. It was nothing. Normalcy returned, after a fashion. But there had been a change, too—significant and perhaps permanent; much had been disclosed during that awful time. I knew this by his silence, by the fact that we never revisited that scene, the ideas we had exchanged, the emotions we had felt. Someone is now on to me, he might have thought. Someone has witnessed me at my most vulnerable. Narrative analysis can take a strange turn at times like these. What is not said may be every bit as important as what is.

Because we never "processed" our exchange, I do not know for certain what he made of it. But in all likelihood, he had to fashion for himself a somewhat new story, a new version of who and what he was, one that was more adequate to the multiple fields of his existence. This doesn't mean that he had been engaged in self-deception earlier or that this new version somehow falsified the previous one or that, finally, after all these years, he had stumbled onto the definitive truth of his life. Rather, the conditions of his life had changed in such a way that regions of his own being, heretofore uncharted and unarticulated, had suddenly come into view. Along these lines, he himself had undoubtedly *learned* something through this series of events, about his own life and, perhaps, about life itself. Not only were he and his wife mortal, but they could die at any moment, leaving their children behind to suffer their absence. How shocking and strange. I eventually asked him if it was okay for me to write about his situation, discreetly of course, to which he agreed. He never asked me to read the piece, and I never volunteered to show it to him. And I never will. Since the time I wrote the essay, there has been a death in his family, not of his wife and not of him but of a child. Although there is a great deal that might be said about this story, it is highly doubtful whether I will ever write about it. In my own mind, it is simply out of bounds. This, I suppose, is one of the liabilities of writing about real life. There are, however, some significant assets as well. Let me therefore try to unpack some of the different dimensions of analysis this brief narrative called forth.

The first dimension has to do with interpretation. As I suggested earlier, the man being discussed had been forced to come to terms with new "data," new evidences of self, and he had to find some kind of interpretive context within which these new data would fit. I also had to do so on some level. The data that I had before me were much the same as those he had, and I too had to craft an interpretive context that would begin to make sense of things. I should note here that there was an avowedly speculative nature to this particular interpretive endeavor. The truth is, I don't know for sure whether he engaged in exactly the interpretive process that I have attributed to him. In fact, as I also noted earlier, I relied as much on his silence as his words to frame this very interpretation. But all that this underscores is the frequently speculative and ambiguous nature of the interpretive endeavor itself, particularly when there is no written text to consult.

The second dimension has to do with the idea that self-*interpretation* is at one and the same time an act of self-*construction*, or *poiesis*—self-articulation and self-discovery entail self-creation as well. What they also entail is the idea of *development,* that is, the fashioning of a new, and perhaps more adequate view of who and what one is. Far from implying that this process is somehow leading to some absolute endpoint or *telos,* all that is being implied is that the understanding at which one has arrived is, arguably, *better*—fuller, more comprehensive, more adequate—than the one that had existed previously. What I call *rewriting the self,* therefore, may often be regarded as a developmental process and project, broadly conceived (see Freeman, 1991, 1993b). It is a process of refiguring the past and in turn reconfiguring the self in a way that moves beyond what had existed previously. The backward movement of narrative therefore turns out to be dialectically intertwined with the forward movement of development.

A third dimension has to do more directly with culture. This man's dread and despair—along with his discomfort in revealing this dread and despair to me—was related to his bravado, his status as the "rock" of the family, and the expectation that he ought to hang tough through it all. He was like a dam that had suddenly sprung some serious leaks, leaks that, because of the pressure they had been under, threatened to burst forward and flood him. There were other cultural narratives at work as well, having to do, for instance, with the nature of the happy American family, suddenly undone, and the quintessential Mother-Provider, suddenly felled. All of these narratives may be thought of as cultural resources, cultural tools, with which people make sense of things.

A fourth dimension has to do with the imaginative labor that this man had himself employed, using these cultural tools, in order to refashion his self. In a sense, he had come to realize how pervasively his own attitudes, his own self, had been shaped by certain prevalent social expectations and cultural storylines. With this in mind, part of his challenge was precisely to identify how these had been operative in his stoicism and, ultimately, to challenge and resist them. Narratives don't simply maintain and uphold the status quo; they can also change it, revise it, exactly through the kind of imaginative labor that had been exercised in this case. In some ways, the process was one of *de*construction followed by *re*construction. That, at least, is how I came to understand some of what had gone on.

Finally, I want to call attention to the social dimension of this man's very self. Social relationships loom large in all facets of the story: with his wife and children; with others, both real and imagined, who might learn of his fragility; and, of course, with me, his partner in dialogue. In addition, there is the wider world—the world of the individual in society—within which his story took place. This is the world of doctors and x-rays, norms and values, wives and children, life and death. There is no story apart from this world. Narrative analysis of the sort being pursued here moves beyond the confines of the individual as a matter of course and necessity.

Theory, Writing, and the Project of Narrative Criticism

Narrative analysis of the sort being considered here also moves beyond the confines of "theory" as it is ordinarily conceived. I emphasize the phrase "as ordinarily conceived." Ordinarily, theory is conceived in rationalistic, scientific terms. One develops a theory, about this or that, in order to rationally account for a particular sphere of reality. One then goes on to test the theory, which may in turn lead to further refinement and differentiation of its terms or, if the data prove to be too recalcitrant, abandonment. Narrative analysis of the sort I have been pursuing aims at something somewhat different. In its very concern with the concrete particularities of individual cases, it is as much about the "possible" as the "actual," its aim being more to *suggest* than *convince,* to open a "region" of truth rather than seek to present a definitive one. So it is, I have also suggested (Freeman, 1999a; see also Freeman, 2000), that at least a portion of writing about life narratives might move from *argument,* based on the logic of theoretical postulates, to *appeal,* based on the poetic resonances of the narratives in question, on their aesthetic texture and their evocative power. I offer this perspective not out of some sort of antiscientific, aestheticist fervor but, rather, out of a conviction that narrative analysis, insofar as it seeks to depict the concrete particularities of individual cases, lends itself more readily to *poetics,* to the project of articulating and explicating meaning, than to theoretical knowledge.

Taking this last idea one step farther, I want to claim that being attentive to the poetry of human lives on some level *requires* more poetic modes of writing, ones that are closer to those modes of writing found in literature. The reason is straightforward. Life itself is variously quite beautiful and very messy, and literature generally does well to embody it in its full measure. It also does well in dealing with the emotional side of things, allowing us not only to *think* but also to *feel.* In emphasizing the importance of feeling, I am suggesting that narrative analysis, in addition to supporting the customary scientific aim of increasing knowledge and understanding about the human realm, can support the aim of increasing compassion and sympathy, and a sense of connection to others. It can therefore provide readers with much the same kind of experience that literature and literary criticism can provide when they orient readers toward the reality of people's lives. Hence my suggestion that a portion of narrative psychology be devoted to *narrative criticism,* geared toward addressing the literature found not only in actual texts but also in the very fabric of human experience.

This sort of project isn't for everyone. For some, however, working in this way sometimes allows there to be more of a bridge between work and life, between the academic and the lived realm of narrative. The two become continuous: Trying to make sense of experience and trying to think about narrative become one and the same undivided process. Maddening though this can sometimes be, it helps ensure that narrative analysis remains anchored in the world we most intimately know.

References

Augustine, St. (1980). *Confessions*. New York: Penguin. (Original work published 397)

Brooks, P. (1985). *Reading for the plot: Design and intention in narrative*. New York: Random House.

Crites, S. (1971). The narrative quality of experience. *Journal of the American Academy of Religion, XXXIX*, 291–311.

Freeman, M. (1984). History, narrative, and life-span developmental knowledge. *Human Development, 27*, 1–19.

Freeman, M. (1985). Paul Ricoeur on interpretation: The model of the text and the idea of development. *Human Development, 28*, 295–312.

Freeman, M. (1991). Rewriting the self: Development as moral practice. In M. B. Tappan & M. J. Packer (Eds.), Narrative approaches to moral development [Special issue]. *New Directions for Child Development, 54*, 83–101.

Freeman, M. (1993a). *Finding the muse: A sociopsychological inquiry into the conditions of artistic creativity*. Cambridge, UK: Cambridge University Press.

Freeman, M. (1993b). *Rewriting the self: History, memory, narrative*. London: Routledge.

Freeman, M. (1997). Death, narrative integrity, and the radical challenge of self-understanding: A reading of Tolstoy's *Death of Ivan Ilych*. *Ageing and Society, 17*, 373–398.

Freeman, M. (1998a). Mythical time, historical time, and the narrative fabric of the self. *Narrative Inquiry, 8*, 27–50.

Freeman, M. (1998b). Experience, narrative, and the relationship between them. *Narrative Inquiry, 8*, 455–466.

Freeman, M. (1999a). Life narratives, the poetics of selfhood, and the redefinition of psychological theory. In W. Maiers, B. Bayer, B. Esgalhado, R. Jorna, & E. Schraube (Eds.), *Challenges to theoretical psychology* (pp. 245–250).Ontario: Captus.

Freeman, M. (1999b). Culture, narrative, and the poetic construction of selfhood. *Journal of Constructivist Psychology, 12*, 99–116.

Freeman, M. (2000). Theory beyond theory. *Theory and Psychology, 10*, 1, 71–77.

Freeman, M. (2002a). The presence of what is missing: Memory, poetry, and the ride home. In R. J. Pellegrini & T. R. Sarbin (Eds.), *Between fathers and sons: Critical incident narratives in the development of men's lives* (pp. 165–176). New York: Haworth Clinical Practice.

Freeman, M. (2002b) Charting the narrative unconscious: Cultural memory and the challenge of autobiography. *Narrative Inquiry, 12*, 193–211.

Freeman, M., Csikszentmihalyi, M., & Larson, R. (1986). Adolescence and its recollection: Toward an interpretive model of development. *Merrill-Palmer Quarterly, 32*, 167–185.

Gadamer, H.-G. (1975). *Truth and method*. New York: Crossroad.

Keller, H. (1988). *The story of my life*. New York: New American Library. (Original work published 1902)

Ricoeur, P. (1981a). *Hermeneutics and the human sciences.* Cambridge, UK: Cambridge University Press.

Ricoeur, P. (1981b). Narrative time. In W. J. T. Mitchell (Ed.), *On narrative* (pp. 165–186). Chicago: University of Chicago Press.

Ricoeur, P. (1983). Can fictional narratives be true? *Analecta Husserliana, 14,* 3–19.

Ricoeur, P. (1984). *Time and narrative* (Vol. 1). Chicago: University of Chicago Press.

Ricoeur, P. (1985). *Time and narrative* (Vol. 2). Chicago: University of Chicago Press.

Ricoeur, P. (1988). *Time and narrative* (Vol. 3). Chicago: University of Chicago Press.

Sartre, J.-P. (1964). *Nausea.* Norfolk, CT: New Directions. (Original work published 1938)

Tolstoy, L. (1960). *The death of Ivan Ilych.* New York: New American Library.(Original work published 1886)

White, H. (1978). *Tropics of discourse: Essays in cultural criticism.* Baltimore, MD: Johns Hopkins University Press.

PART II

Social-Relational Readings

The careful reader hears many voices in and around narrative texts. Each contribution in Part II focuses on the social-relational quality of narrating and the value of reading narratives as conversations. A central story line organized by time, characters, and setting always speaks to other story lines—within the text and outside, across time and space. Some of the voices are clear and loud, others whisper, still others only mouth behind the scenes. No voice is isolated, and none are innocent, as all work in some relation to the whole. In short, we read narrative texts in the context of those voices that have in some way influenced narrators, those that would want to silence them, and those who might be influenced by them. Authors of the chapters in this section analyze as narratives a range of diverse kinds of empirical data, including interview dialogues, peer group conversations, written narratives, and researchers' summaries.

The contributors here tend to write about narrating to emphasize dynamic expression from specific points of view interacting with other points of view across the confines of time and space. Drawing primarily on discourse psychology and sociohistorical theory, each chapter identifies central theoretical concepts to bring narrative social relations to life. Nelson (Chapter 2.1) describes a person-in-the-making process in which parents provide verbal facts, forecasts, and excitement as the data their child uses to craft a cultural self. Daiute (Chapter 2.2) focuses on sociobiographical activity as the shifting of personal and cultural points of view in figure-ground relations shared in the context of public school. Bamberg (Chapter 2.3) illustrates the multidynamic of positioning, showing how to read diverse points of view in and around narratives. Stanley and Billig (Chapter 2.4) offer the concept of "ideological dilemmas" to identify the motivations that organize people's performance of social actions when they tell stories.

These authors focus on the interactional details of narrating as a way to excavate the ubiquitous yet not always obvious influences of the culture, society, and individuals that shape narrative texts. Emily's crib talk echoes her parents' histories and hopes for the future (Nelson, Chapter 2.1). Narratives by students in third and fifth grade classrooms belie their audiences as the young authors narrate their "personal" experiences in terms of the values their teachers had promoted (Daiute, Chapter 2.2). Conversation and context are integrated as they operate across the three positions of the characters' conversations, the filmmaker's visual narration, and the author's own research summary of the normative frame serving as a counterpoint to the characters' and filmmaker's narratives (Bamberg, Chapter 2.3). A conversation between doctoral students focuses closely on language to identify the silenced power relations in higher education (Stanley & Billig, Chapter 2.4).

Across these contributions, "social relations" refers to interactions—of individuals in society; of individuals with different roles, rights, and resources in educational institutions, in families, and in peer groups; and among individuals who may experience some tension as members of different age groups, ethnic groups, or status groups. "Social relations" is also a theoretical concept for representing the complexity of narratives, including, for example, the multiple roles of narrators and listeners/readers as points of view and subjects, as well as the focus on subjective perspectives organizing narratives in relation to societal meanings, which some of the authors refer to as "ideology," others "culture," and others "society."

What Are Narratives?

These contributions present different kinds of narratives to illustrate the dynamic interaction of individuals in society. All the chapters offer narrative texts in context to illustrate the conversational nature of thought, identity, and development. The chapters all isolate and analyze some specific narrative sequence—formal or informal, oral or written, with single or multiple narrators—and they demonstrate the more and less explicit links outside those texts to actors, settings, times, and powers. Nelson (Chapter 2.1) explores a toddler's "crib talk" in response to her parents' talk as they tucked her into bed. Daiute (Chapter 2.2) looks across written narratives by elementary school children to show why readers should not take for granted any normative features of genres like autobiography and fiction. Bamberg (Chapter 2.3) illustrates how researcher-created narratives help interpret the meaning of conversations in context that involve narrations from different points of view or positions. Stanley and Billig (Chapter 2.4) represent a conversation between researcher and subject as a narrative.

These different ways of focusing on the social-relational quality of narratives in context suggest the idea of internarratives—intersubjective symbolic spaces of individual and shared discourse as they resonate in a narrative text and as a narrative thread across time.

Social-Relational Language

Researchers seeking tools for analyzing meanings in discourse can find them in the chapters in Part II, which apply linguistic devices as tools to understand the dynamics of human interaction, purpose, and meaning. However, these scholars use not just any words in their inquiries but evocative words that reach beyond any single context for their meaning. In particular, they use referential devices like names, and pronouns like "I" and "we," that reach outside of texts to individuals in time, space, and social relations. Likewise, they use markers of psychological states and causality that have meaning only in reference to cultural agreements or tensions. As Stanley and Billig (Chapter 2.4) point out, in Hanako's shift from referring to her Ph.D. advisor as "supervisor" to calling him "Pete," language is neither transparent nor an accident but the embodiment of social relations, culture, and ideology. These chapters thus offer cautions for researchers who want to identify themes without worrying too much about how those themes are expressed. The chapters in Part II highlight an argument across this volume that the most revealing information may be lost when human discourse is analyzed in ways that separate its content from the form of its expression.

Identity and power relations also become interesting issues here. Bamberg (Chapter 2.3) and Daiute (Chapter 2.2) urge readers to craft an understanding of identity that is not literal, either as "personal stories and self-thematizations that, unfortunately, have become the privileged site for identity analysis" (Bamberg) or merged with any particular genre, like autobiography (Daiute). For example, Daiute explains that given the pressure to conform in institutions like public schools, autobiographical narrating offers only limited insight into subjects' self-reflections—because of the high stakes of public exposure in such explicitly revealing media—while personal information abounds in students' writing outside the public gaze, like fictional accounts. For Stanley and Billig (Chapter 2.4), the interplay between expression and silence, normative expectation and observation, can point to identities but never reveal them fully. Nelson (Chapter 2.1) points out that personal identities are possible only following cultural forms.

Power relations is another theme across these contributions. Seeking to move beyond vague notions of social representation, these authors describe units of analysis that capture institutional motivations organizing individuals' discourse. For these authors, power relations are those social forces that shape, require, model, and guide narrators to present themselves according to certain normative ideals. For Nelson (Chapter 2.1), a child learns to fit the details of her life within cultural scripts provided by her parents in their own special, loving way. Daiute (Chapter 2.2) reads the audience in older children's narratives, and this audience is the mainstream culture promoted via public education as teachers implement the institution through the curriculum. For Bamberg (Chapter 2.3), power resides in cultural images of masculinity, and for Stanley and Billig (Chapter 2.4), it resides in the Ph.D. advisor who, although we never meet him in the interview, is an ever present guide to the reflections of the student, Hanako, the focus of the interview. In the details of narrative analysis, we can see that although cultural and institutional norms can be oppressive at worst or persuasive at best, power does not flow only one way. Emily has an imagination. The third and fifth graders in urban schools find ways to express subjective perspectives and unconventional social values in fiction-writing assignments, which few expect to read as autobiographical. Hanako finds subtle ways of expressing disapproval of her advisor's delays—while maintaining a discourse of respect. The film *Stand by Me* crafts diverse commentaries on masculinity.

All of these chapters are concerned with the grand and particular moments and meanings in life. The chapters thus suggest how narrative inquiry can appreciate the details of lives as they are lived in everyday events and clarify the larger meanings that make those lives worth living.

2.1

Construction of the Cultural Self in Early Narratives

Katherine Nelson

N arratives serve as a storehouse of shared knowledge and beliefs in human societies and as an essential source of cultural learning (Bamberg & Moissinac, 2003; Bruner, 1990; Donald, 1991; Fivush & Haden, 2003). Autobiographical memory narratives also form the basis of self-history, emerging in the early childhood years through collaborative reconstruction of the self in the past with parents and others. Children's own proto-narrative constructions reveal the influence of cultural stories (Nelson, 2003a; Nelson & Fivush, 2000; Nicolopoulou & Weintraub, 1998). Narrative thus plays a formative role in the development of the "cultural person" (Nelson, 2003a, 2003b, 2003c).

In this chapter, I return to an important source of insights into the process whereby the "cultural self" emerges from memory reconstructions—the study of the crib monologues of the child Emily between the ages of 21 and 36 months. Emily's monologues, together with parental dialogues at Emily's bedtime, were analyzed by myself and a group of colleagues and reported in the book *Narratives From the Crib* (hereafter *Narratives*; Nelson, 1989c). These analyses varied, focused on issues of language acquisition, grammar, and narrative; my contributions ranged from memory (to begin) to self and time (at the end), revealing my changing understanding of the person in the monologues. Initially my focus was on how a child might represent her own memory of her experiences in the unfolding world around her, and this interest was well repaid. The richness of the monologues and dialogues revealed a complex interweaving of the child's memory with problematic issues, parental forecasts, imagination, fictional and factual stories, and play. Out of this mix emerged a person-in-the-making in a specific cultural world. At the present remove from the project's inception, a new look at the processes involved in the developmental admixture of culture and self through a reconsideration of the data seems warranted.

In this chapter, I consider several issues of method and content arising from this reconsideration. Two unique aspects of the original study are the data themselves, which provided insight into the private thoughts of a child in transition from infancy to early childhood, and the group reconstruction of the meaning of the data, which considered issues of the cultural sources for the construction of narrative and the construction of self. These issues have taken on new significance in recent years as contrasting positions have been explored on the status of narrative as a cognitive universal or a variable cultural form, as well as on the nature of the culturally differentiated self.

The first issue examined here is the contribution of the group analysis that first revealed the emergence of narratives in the transcripts. Next, I consider focal transcripts from the perspective of the development of narrative in terms of form and content, the former concerning the use of voices and the storytelling register, the latter including aspects of the "landscape of action and the landscape of consciousness." The final analysis highlights sources of narrative constructions—in personal experience and cultural genres through parental accounts, storybooks, personal memory, and imagination—that provide differential contributions to the cultural construction of self. Two points in particular stand out in these analyses: that the forms of narrativising precede its functional uses and that the source of form lies in parental discourse—this is especially evident here in talk about the future, which is called "precounting."

Group Analysis of Monologues and Dialogues

My goal at the outset of the study was to locate evidence of memories from previous experiences and to describe their form and content. I did not anticipate interpreting the tapings in terms of emergent narratives, linguistic structures, self reference, or any of the other themes that eventually came into focus. Tape recordings of crib speech were obtained through the cooperation of Emily's parents, who not only consented to taping their 21-month-old child's speech when she was alone at naptime and at night before falling asleep but, in addition, took responsibility for the taping, and in the mother's case, listened to each tape and (at the beginning) made a first transcription. This was an invaluable contribution because of the difficulty of interpreting infant speech, especially without the context or ongoing interpretive comments of other speakers.

On receipt of the first tapes, I realized that Emily's crib talk was not only advanced by normative standards but also unlike what was known about child language from child-parent talk—in both structure and apparent function. The evidence of independent construction by the child herself, unsupported by an immediate model, led to my decision to share the data with a small group of colleagues who were focused on the social origins of child language. The core of this group subsequently met together on a regular basis for more than 2 years, and individually produced the chapters in *Narratives*.[1] One of our major questions from the outset concerned the balance between adult input and child construction as the source of growth in child language. It was quite clear from the beginning that Emily received a very rich and complex array of linguistic input from her parents and other adults. But it was also very clear that she was intent on using language for herself, as well as in social interactions, and in her crib monologues she seemed to zoom ahead of her social speech in interesting ways.

A second focal question concerned the function of such speech. Was it simply language practice, as the major previous analysis of crib speech (Weir, 1963) had assumed? The linguistic focus seemed too restricted, for Emily's crib talk was very revealing of her private concerns. Was the function then a cognitive one, as Vygotsky's (1962) conception of private speech maintained? Vygotsky viewed children as engaging in private speech to regulate action, a function eventually internalized as inner speech, or verbal thought. But in the crib monologues, there was no action to be monitored or regulated; speech was the action. Eventually, at least some of us came to believe that the function of crib speech might be to explain the world and the self to the self, resulting in a mental model, or to represent in language the significant events of one's life, a function served by autobiographical memory in adults, for which the basic form is narrative.

The Child in the Monologues

Emily was the firstborn child of parents who held professorial positions in a major university.[2] Child care was shared among parents, grandmother, and a group caregiver for Emily's first 2½ years, with preschool beginning when she was 32 months old. Emily began talking early and was engaging in talk in her crib prior to sleep at naptime and bedtime by 14 or 15 months old. Taping of her crib talk began when she was 21 months old. Tape recordings were made intermittently over the succeeding months by her parents, including a good sample of parental talk prior to bedtime as well as the child's monologues after they left her alone. At the time of the first recordings, Emily's language development was very advanced for her age in terms of grammatical constructions, vocabulary, and the pragmatics of discourse (see details in *Narratives*; Nelson, 1989c). She typically produced long strings of related clauses around a topic, interspersed with isolated comments, long pauses, song fragments, and talk directed to or about the play objects (dolls, stuffed animals, etc.) in her crib.[3] A noticeable shift occurred around Emily's second birthday, when some of her monologues became more organized around an event theme. The fact that Emily's language was so advanced implies that we cannot make normative age comparisons in terms of her development of concepts of self, or its relation to narrative, but it does not necessarily imply a difference in process of development.

Identification and Segmentation of Crib Talk

In the first recordings, Emily made reference to different everyday events, as is evident in the following monologue:

Example 1   1. That Daddy brings down basement washing,

2. I can hold Emmy,

3. so, Daddy brings down the,

4. the washing on the basement,

5. washing,

6. so my can,

7. so why, the, the, the

8. na- daddy brings washing.

9. And not down, um, um, um . . .

10. Emmy, Emmy, Emmy da- and the (?) in the (?).

11. So, so Emmy change right there, baby,

12. then my daddy bring them that time.

13. So, naptime go to sleep.

This segment illustrates the many decisions made about how to go about transcribing and analyzing the child's productions.[4] In child language analysis, the basic unit is the utterance, which is usually identified in terms of speaking turns and, secondarily, in terms of pauses and prosody. From this unitization it is possible to construct a measure of the development of the child's language in terms of the mean length of utterance (MLU), a measure introduced by Brown (1973). MLU is based on the number of morphemes or words in each utterance produced in dyadic speech, typically in 50 to 100 child utterances. In a stream of monologic child speech where there is no turn-taking to mark boundaries, the decision as to what counts as an utterance is ambiguous.

An obvious method for segmenting crib talk into analyzable parts is to group together all talk that was produced in a single, unbroken prosodic stream. Chafe (1986) described methods for identifying continuity of thought units across utterances in adult oral narratives, characterized by rising or flat intonation at the end of clauses, indicating that the following segments are continuous with the previous ones, allowing the speaker to hold the floor until the account is completed. These segments are referred to as paragraphs. When we viewed Emily's productions in this way (Nelson & Levy, 1987), we found that she utilized a similar prosodic pattern to hold a long sequence of phrases together, although, as in Example 1, her thoughts did not seem necessarily unified and there was no interlocutor to interrupt her. However, these sequences usually contained a common theme—in the present example, the theme of Daddy's activities. Thus the segments within a prosodic sequence of this kind seemed to belong together. Contrary to what most of us would have expected from a 21-month-old, given evidence from prior studies of dyadic speech, there were many portions like Example 1 that were sustained without significant pauses over an extended period of time.

Although the group did not formalize rules for marking, the method used for segmenting the monologues emerged as illustrated in Example 1. Three dots (. . .) at the end of a line indicate a flat or slightly rising intonation, a comma (,) indicates a falling tone and brief pause, and a period (.) indicates a completed thought segment with a definite falling tone and a longer pause. A question mark (?) is used conventionally to indicate a grammatical question or a definite question intonation (rising or rising and falling). (Question marks were also used internally in parentheses to indicate segments of speech that were uninterpretable.) Often the segment following a comma retains the theme of the overall product, while the segment that follows a period introduces a new topic, although the theme may be returned to in subsequent phrases. Then within these larger frames or paragraphs, each separate "utterance" was identified in terms of a following pause, however brief, and regardless of the final tone. This method of segmentation is consistent with Chafe's "thought unit" system. One of the remarkable discoveries of the study of Emily's private speech productions was the similarity of her intonation patterns to those of adult discourse, including storytelling, as discussed later.

A problem that is especially evident in child monologues lacking either discourse or activity content is the existence of unclear or ambiguous words that are not interpretable even with the best available equipment. In our study, for the most part, we were primarily interested in what Emily was attempting to say rather than the specifics of how she said it. Thus her exact wording sometimes remained ambiguous, but the content of the majority of Emily's monologues was usually quite clear. The group analysis focused more on themes and meaning than on details of transcription and coding, and the members of the group each undertook an analysis of the data from a particular perspective consistent with their own interests. Different transcription practices and interpretations emerged therefrom, and these differences served to illustrate both methodological and conceptual problems evoked by different analytical goals.

Originally, none of the group was focused on the narrative quality of Emily's talk. However, her extended speech productions from the beginning suggested that she might be trying to build some sort of story, albeit without a sequence or clear action frame. This was especially evident in the fact that even when she was 21 to 24 months old, Emily was producing extended discourse using adultlike prosodic frames. Some members of the group (see, in *Narratives*, Bruner & Lucariello, 1989; Feldman, 1989) immediately identified these as narratives, while others searched for further evidence that Emily was developing narrative forms. I now address this evidence.

Narrative Analysis

The independent analyses carried out by group members and reported in *Narratives* relied on different analytic schemes. Some (Dore, 1989; Bruner & Lucariello, 1989; Stern, 1989) adapted analyses from literary or dynamic theory. Others (Gerhardt, 1989; Levy, 1989) located emergent child categories in Emily's monologue that departed from standard grammatical or semantic analyses but appeared to be precursors to adult categories. Feldman isolated functional cognitive uses in the child's monologic topics that raised new issues for the relation of language and thought. My analyses were drawn primarily from prior cognitive developmental work. In the following descriptions, I am combining several of these analytic approaches—using narrative analyses from Labov and Waletsky (1967), together with Bruner's conception (partially realized in his chapter in *Narratives*; Bruner & Lucariello, 1989)—but I am also identifying early child forms that precede their functional use. The emphasis here is on building toward the fully realized narrative scheme conceptualized in narrative theory, while keeping fully in view the child's own themes and early modes of expression.

According to Labov and Waletsky (1967), a simple narrative about a personal event consists of connecting two related actions from the past, plus an evaluation. If Emily was producing narratives, then we should have observed in the monologues, at minimum, a sequence of actions describing a specific episode located in (past) time, and an evaluation of the happening. Temporal marking is important, and it is generally expected to be with regard to the past, but present and future narrations have also been observed. In Bruner's (1990) view, narratives consist of a "landscape of action" organized around a theme and a problem or "trouble" with respect to the way that things are expected to be, as well as a "landscape of consciousness" that specifies the goals, motivations, emotions, and beliefs of the actors that instigate the action (see also, in *Narratives*, Bruner & Lucariello, 1989). Bruner's narrative stance was just coming into focus at the time of our group meetings and had an obvious influence on our thinking and subsequent analyses (e.g., see the difference between my Chapter 1 and 8 in *Narratives*; Nelson, 1989a, 1989b). Subsequent scholarship has emphasized that although narrative is universal across human societies, it has also been observed—at least since Bartlett (1932)—that the structure and content of narratives vary by specific historical periods and cultural traditions (Eakin, 1985; Freeman, 1998; Watt, 2001). Telling stories may be a natural function of our capacity for using language to communicate with each other; nonetheless, children may acquire the forms for expressing the function in culture-specific ways, and they may develop facility with different aspects of narrative in individual patterns. In other words, the narrative genre of a culture is acquired by children from the models they are exposed to (Nelson, 2003c).

With this in mind, we would expect that the beginnings of narrative would consist of sequentially and causally related actions. In addition, there should be a reason for construing the sequence as a narrative and not just an event sequence: a specific episode or series of episodes, an unusual event, a *high point,* a problem that arose with or without a solution, and a *resolution or evaluation.* Statements about *emotion, motivation, goals,* thoughts, and beliefs would indicate inclusion of the landscape of consciousness. In addition, the teller of the tale should employ the speech register of storytelling, including quoted voices, exaggeration, emphasis, markers of suspense, and so on. Separate parts of the narrative may be demarcated by the kinds of prosody and tonality that Chafe (1986) identified in natural storytelling. The following sections examine the ways in which the narrative features identified here—temporal/causal sequence, specific (past) episode, point/problem/reso-lution/evaluation, landscape of consciousness, and prosodic speech register—appeared in Emily's monologues, with a particular view to the relation between content and form.

A First Look: Sequencing

Some of Emily's early monologues could be considered incomplete or proto-narratives, containing action only. For example, one of the first tapes included "MommyDaddy [pronounced as one word] cocktail party. So Mormor babysit Emily." This could be a past account, but given evidence from later dialogue-monologue comparisons, it seems probable that it was simply modeled on a parental report. Quite typical was the monologue in Example 1, a portion of an extended sequence (see, in *Narratives*, Nelson, 1989c, pp. 70–71) in which Emily strings together activities of Daddy and herself, without either a clear theme or sequence. These early productions consist of rather loosely affiliated clauses, some of which represent actions but lack even simple sequencing. They appear to be associated "factoids" extracted from everyday experience, memories of a kind, but mostly not spe-cific memories, rather, generalizations of experience. Nonetheless, it can be noted that in Example 1 Emily had already begun to acquire the lexical markings of reasons and causes (e.g., "why" and "so"), although there is no causal or even temporal relation apparent among the clauses so connected.[5]

Because of prior work on young children's memory, I was prepared to see these productions not as proto-narratives but as scraps of scripts from everyday life. From one cognitive perspective (Schank & Abelson, 1977), scripts for familiar repeated events form the background of our interpreta-tion of our everyday experiences, as well as of personal memories and fic-tional stories. For example, when we hear someone tell about going to a restaurant, we do not need all of the details to be spelled out (standing in line, being seated, getting a menu, etc.) in order to appreciate the point of the story being told. These details form the restaurant script that is taken for granted when we hear about, remember, or act within such an activity. It seems to be functional for young children to build up a great deal of back-ground knowledge of a script sort (Mandler, 1983; Nelson, 1986), and research suggests that children 3 years old or younger remember events in terms of general scripts and not in terms of specific memories (Nelson, Fivush, Hudson, & Lucariello, 1983). By the time children are 3 years old, their verbal scripts for familiar events typically have a sequential order of actions, but they are produced in a general tenseless form, just as Emily's early monologues were.

Verbalizing daily routines draws on memory to predict what can be expected to happen in everyday encounters. Although the evidence from Emily's earliest monologues was not conclusive, much of her later talk concerned representations of general happenings—the way things are and should be. Here is a striking example from Emily's early monologues.

Example 2   1. I can't go down the basement with jamas on.

2. I sleep with jamas.

3. Okay sleep with jamas.

4. In the night time my only put big girl pants on.

5. But in the morning we put jamas on.

6. But, and the morning gets up . . . of the room.

7. But, afternoon my wake up and play.

8. Play with Mommy Daddy . . .

Note that the specification of what happens when Emily is this age (24 months old), although presumably modeled on a stricture of her parents ("can't go down the basement with jamas on"), is slightly askew, possibly because the temporal markers (night, morning, afternoon) are misplaced, just as the causal markers in the previous monologue were. It is becoming clear in this look at different narrative components that, in general, forms are acquired before their functions are mastered.

Emily's recitals of how things go increased in length and precision over the course of the year, culminating in the following extended monologue from when she was 2¾ years old:[6]

Example 3   1. Tomorrow, when we wake up from bed,

2. first me and Daddy and Mommy,

3. you, eat breakfast . . .

4. eat breakfast,

5. like we *usually* do,

6. and then we're going to p-l-a-y,

7. and then soon as Daddy comes,

8. Carl's going to come over,

9. and then we're going to play a little while,

10. and then Carl and Emily are both going down the car with somebody,

11. and we're going to ride to nursery school,

12. and then we when we get there,

13. we're all going to get out of the car,

14. go in to nursery school,

15. and Daddy's going to give us kisses,

16. then go,

17. and then say,

18. and then we will say goodbye,

19. then he's going to work,

20. and we're going to play at nursery school.

21. Won't that be funny?

22. Because sometimes I go to nursery school cause it's a nursery school day.

23. Sometimes I stay with Tanta all week,

24. and sometimes we play mom and dad.

25. But usually,

26. sometimes I um,

27. oh go to nursery school.

This long monologue continues for another 35 lines, repeating the sequence. She reports this "precount" of what happens on a nursery school day with all the flourishes of a narrative, although it is a detailed script and not an account of a specific experience. Scripts encode a sequence of actions, the most essential requirement of narrative, and if scripts are the cores around which narratives are formed, as argued by Bruner and Lucariello (1989, in *Narratives*), they may pave the way toward story understanding and telling.

But even elaborate scripts like the one in Example 3 are not themselves narratives. A narrative is about a particular episode in which the action sequence frequently departs from the expected script, and children's first stories usually focus on this aspect of the narrative—the action itself (Nelson & Gruendel, 1986; Seidman, Nelson, & Gruendel, 1986). In a narrative, something happens to provide the "trouble" that disrupts the normal expectation of the script and requires attempting to set things right, overcoming obstacles, and in the end evaluating the result. However, many specific memories and made-up stories by young children are organized around the generalities of script structures, with only an added bit to indicate a violation of the expected "default" conditions.

The relevance of background event knowledge to full narrative should not be underestimated. It provides a format for achieving the first requirement of narrative, the sequence of action, connected by causal and temporal terms. Further, it supplies the background that can be assumed in recounting a memory or story, such that the specific details and highlight—the point of the narrative—stand out, without needing to articulate the structural framework supplied by shared cultural knowledge of the event or scene. Thus, Emily's early acquisition of and focus in her monologues on the everyday expectations about how her world is organized can be seen as a very important move toward acquiring the cultural tools for narrative making.

It is not until the early school years that children focus on the "landscape of consciousness" that provides the motivations and emotions that accompany the action (Henseler, 2000). Evaluation in a narrative does not need to be explicitly stated, but may be incorporated in the language used to describe the action or in extralinguistic expressions (Daiute & Nelson, 1997). Similarly, it may be that the "landscape of consciousness" is apparent in implicit forms prior to explicit expression, as the following sections suggest.

The Storytelling Register

A very important characteristic of the monologue in Example 3 that is not apparent in the "cold" transcript and is very difficult to incorporate in verbal codes, even those including intonation, is the expressive quality of the production. Indeed, one of the first qualities apparent to those listening to the recordings of Emily's talk was her capacity for deploying different voices and rhetorical registers, that is, supra-intonational expressiveness. Within the first monologues were "quotations" from her parents, produced in a high-tone "parent" voice, which contrasted with her raised tone "soliloquy" voice and with her low "talk to the dolls" play voice. Dore

(1989; in *Narratives*) viewed these expressive characteristics as revealing parental "voices in the mind" along lines set forth by Bakhtin (1986), but to my ear they seemed specific to the genre of storytelling.

Sometimes Emily's production of a monologue took on a sing-song rhythm, as in the first four lines of Example 3, which are then broken with the line "like we USUALLy do" where the portion capitalized was produced more loudly. The following line draws out the word "play," providing emphasis. The subsequent lines were produced with "normal" intonation and emphasis, followed at line 21 by "Won't that be funny?" This line punctuates the action, but its reference is odd, as there is nothing funny about what has been said—it is a simple normative statement. Yet, the (emerging) narrative form seems to require a questionlike comment, which is often used in storytelling to mark the end of an episode or to point up something worthy of attention. The next 6 lines summarize the "usual" happenings. Then follow 35 lines that recapitulate and add to the first account, this time with added intonational expression and emphasis.

Emily had had a great deal of experience with story reading and story-telling by expert adults, as well as experience of adult narrativising of every-day events. These characteristics of the monologues imply that she had picked up the appropriate rhetorical forms of storytellers. In this respect, her productions were characterized by the surface features of the oral narrative form *before* they incorporated the full content or structure of the narrative genre. Together with her cumulated background of script knowledge, this early acquisition of the prosody of storytelling provides a basis for moving on to the more specific, novel, and self-significant tellings about her life.

Specific Episodes: The Landscape of Action

Although there were some suggestions in the earliest monologues that Emily was attempting to recount a specific happening in the past, the attempts were at best fragmented. Recounting of specific episodes from everyday life that are definitely situated in the past is a more explicit move toward the construction of narrative than are reports of expected event routines. The following is the first clear example in the recordings of Emily (at 23 months, 8 days old) that appeared to be an effort to reconstruct verbally what had happened on a particular occasion.

Example 4   1. When Mormor get me,

2. when Mormor make pretty,

3. Mommy had a help,

4. my sleep,

5. Mommy came

6. and Mommy get,

7. get up, time to go home.

8. When my slep and,

9. and, Mormor came.

10. Then Mommy coming then get up,

11. time to go ho-o-me.

12. Time to go home.

13. Drink p-water [Perrier].

14. Yesterday did that.

15. Now Emmy sleeping in regular bed.

Emily's mother indicated that this excerpt referred to what had happened on the morning of the day when Emily recounted it at bedtime. The child attempts to locate the episode through lexical markers—"yesterday" in contrast to "now"—which indicates an early sensitivity to the relative times referred to in language. However, the semantics of these markers is still vague; "yesterday" seems to refer to any preceding time, as it does for many young children. Note that without the mother's identification, it would not be possible to locate the account with respect to a particular occasion, nor with respect to its temporal location. The mother's review of the tapes within a few days of their recording made it possible to discriminate this specific account from a general script with some certainty, as well as to locate it in time.

The version in Example 4 is one of five different sub-versions, each starting at a point of sleeping at Tanta's (Emily's day care provider) but including different details, different beginnings and endings, and even different people (mommy, daddy, and Mormor, her grandmother). This series of productions suggests that Emily was making an effort to construct a coherent organized account of something that she remembered—replacing bits, adding bits, and ending with a variation at odds with what had come before. For example, the last segment goes as follows:

Example 4 (continued)   32. when, when I sleeping Tanta house . . .

33. Mommy came wake my up because to go home,

34. drink p-water.

35. And then Mormor came and Mormor said

36. time to drink p-water . . .

37. Daddy, Mommy, Daddy put my into bed,

38. in my regular bed.

39. Actually, actually Mommy did it.

The entire monologue presents a dilemma to the analyst: Which version is "right"? It seems likely that in the course of constructing this account, Emily was finding it difficult to coordinate the specific episode with the general script from which it varied. This suggestion implicates the complex process of reconstructing an episodic memory within the background of general event knowledge, sometimes merging parts that are actually conflicting.

From the point of view of narrative construction, this example has three points to be noted: It is of a single episode rather than general happenings, it incorporates at least one high point, and it has a finalized, evaluated endpoint. The high point is clearly Mother's saying "get up, time to go ho-o-me." This line is produced in Emily's "adult voice" with a distinct emphasis—"time to go *ho-o-me*"—in a somewhat sing-song intonation at the beginning, although in the later versions it is produced softly and/or with no specific emphasis. Drinking "p-water [Perrier]" is an obviously important detail, part of the bedtime routine, not unusual. The endpoint resolution is clearly sleeping in her regular bed.

Completing the Narrative: The Landscape of Consciousness

The final point to be noted with regard to Example 4 is the large number of connective terms used throughout—"when," "then," "now," "and then," "but," and "because," as well as the truth marker "actually." These clearly reveal that this is meant as a sequential narrative. Emily had used connectives, particularly "when," and "and then" in previous monologues, but not to the degree and with the variety found here. Thus it seems likely that she was reaching for a new mode of discourse formulation, one appropriate to the recounting of a temporally sequenced "story." At this very young age then (23 months old), Emily was able to deploy, at least on occasion, the major constituents of narrative: sequence, temporal location, episode, high points, and evaluations, as well as the rhetoric of story in terms of paragraph structure, tonality, prosody, and emphasis. However, at this point she was not able to capitalize on this to the extent of producing a complete "true" episode or to express the subjective perspective of the landscape of consciousness.

A more mature example of a specific episode from 10 months later was formulated quite precisely on the first try (after a bit of "mind-clearing" in lines 2 to 4).

Example 5   1. We *bought* a baby,

2. cause,

3. the, well because,

4. when she, well,

5. we *thought* it was for Christmas,

6. but *when* we went to the s-s-store we didn't have our jacket on,

7. but I saw some dolly,

8. and I *yelled* at my mother and said

9. I want one of those dolly.

10. So *af*ter we were finished with the store,

11. we went over to the dolly and she *bought* me one.

12. So I have one.

This monologue has all of the narrative components that were specified earlier: temporal and causal sequencing with appropriate lexical markers, a specific past episode, high point, and resolution, the rhetoric and tonality of storytelling, and it includes the language of consciousness (e.g., "thought" and "want"). Thus, by the time she was 33 months old Emily had acquired both the forms and the functions of personal narratives. Practice with hearing and producing narrative forms over the previous 10 months no doubt facilitated the concise formulation evident in this example. Perhaps also the lack of conflicting familiar script content (present in the bedtime scene) aided her in its construction. In any event, it is evident here that although Emily was not yet 3 years old, she had consolidated her narrative skills for producing a personal story.

The one factor that was most obviously missing from Example 4 is the articulation of aspects of the landscape of consciousness as well as the landscape of action. Scattered bits of "mental state" language appear throughout the transcripts (e.g., "I don't know why" and "maybe") and such terms began to appear in sequences that indicated reflection on reasons and motivations a month or two before Example 5. In the beginning, however, they usually appeared disconnected from the action, suggesting that, as with causal and temporal language and prosody, Emily was acquiring the forms before the functions (Levy & Nelson, 1994).

Sources of Narrative Skill

Two contributions to the origin of narratives in Emily's talk have been identified as script structures and prosodic contours of extended speech productions. While scripts emerge from personal experience in social activities, prosody is modeled in adult discourse either in recounting events or in reading or telling stories. In searching for models of parental discourse in prebed talk, we were struck by the large proportion of parental talk devoted to future events, happenings expected on the next morning, afternoon, day, or weekend. Subsequent research has indicated that Emily's parents were by no means unique in this regard; such practices are quite general (Benson, 1994; Presler, 2000). Future talk by parents or children is based on routine everyday knowledge of events, together with suppositions about unknown or unexpected portions and inferences from present or past states of the world. These precounts were of great interest to Emily; she frequently requested that her father repeat them many times, and she attempted to reproduce them verbatim in her subsequent monologues (see examples of this in *Narratives*; Dore, 1989; Nelson 1989c). My original supposition was that Emily's repetitions of her parents' precounts were attempts to understand what would happen in the future and that they might affect her experience of the event, perhaps leading to a revision of the account after it had taken place. No evidence of such a function was ever found in the monologues or dialogues; no recapitulation after the fact of some event earlier precounted was ever located.

However, experiences with precounting added to Emily's store of narrative skills, as is evident in the monologues modeled on those of her father's prebed dialogues. Consider the monologue that followed her father's precounting of their coming excursion to visit friends at the shore at least three times (to save space this is transcribed as a continuous text):

Example 6   We are gonna . . . at the ocean. Ocean is a little far away. I think it's . . . couple blocks . . . away. Maybe it's down, downtown, and across the ocean, and down the river, and maybe it's in, the hot dogs will be in a fridge, and the fridge would be in the water over by a shore, and then we could go in, and get a hot dog and bring it out to the river and then sharks go in the river and bite me, in the ocean, we go in the ocean, and ocean be over by . . . I think a couple of blocks away. But we could be, and we could find any hot dogs, um the hot dogs gonna be fore the fore the beach. Then the bridge is gonna, we'll have to go in the green car, cause that's where the car seats are. Um, I can be in the red car, but, see, I be in the green car. But you know who's going to be in the green car . . . both children . . . I'm going to be in the green car in my car seat, he's gonna be . . . and nobody's gonna be, just . . . you know, these people, we don't know, and too far away from the beach, and two things.

Emily's precount contains many bits that were not provided by her father, including the speculation about how far the beach is (actually many miles), where the hot dogs will be, and which car the family will go in. According to her mother, Emily's speculation about the car was wrong, but it was based on a logical inference about the car seats. These inclusions clearly implicate Emily's growing general knowledge and her capacity for bringing known facts into conjunction with a predicted novel experience based on the linguistic representation presented by someone else. Emily's attention to the precounts of her parents and attempts to reproduce them verbally while alone highlight an important transition in the acquisition of complex language functions—the ability to take in a verbal representation from someone else about something not experienced by the self and re-present it to the self in a verbal form partially modeled on the presentation of the other but reconstructed and transformed for the self (Nelson, 1996).

Note that the monologue in Example 6 has many of the characteristics of a narrative, in terms of the topic (we are going at the ocean), the location of the event (a little far away), the sequence of actions, and the specification of how things are found to be (in the fridge). However, in contrast to Emily's memory narratives, the main connective she uses in this monologue is "and." The sequence lacks the variety of the temporal and causality markers of even the earliest experientially based sequences, suggesting a loose string of events that are not connected through the firm temporal-causal relations of personal experience. Revealingly, in the last section of the monologue, when Emily switches to explain the choice of cars on the basis of her own knowledge, the markers include "cause" and "but" in addition to "and." The monologue in Example 6 suggests that the two sources of information are merged, and perhaps not differentiated, although the evidence from the use of varying connectives and the assurance (not "maybe," but "cause") of the latter half suggest a firmer grasp on the story that comes from her own experience of "reality." Thus, although the monologue reveals a sophisticated use of linguistic representation and the interweaving of Emily's heard account with personal experience, the resulting product lacks the coherence of one of her episodic narratives.

Stories as a Source of Cultural Narratives

Emily was an avid listener to stories, and she often took books that had been read to her into her crib at naptime or bedtime. An important question is what young children absorb from stories about characters and situations that are foreign to their experience. One clue from Emily's monologues was the appearance of story characters (e.g., Babar) in the midst of an account of her own activities, even as the story character is reported to be engaged in his own and different actions ("babar doing exercises"). A long monologue from when Emily was 25 months old was organized around retelling the story from one of her books, as she looked at the pictures (reported in Nelson, 1991). There she re-envoiced parts of the story line, but in the process she inserted pieces from her own experience, as well as reordering the parts from the way they had been presented in the book. These practices are similar in many ways to those reported by Miller, Hoogstra, Mintz, Fung, and Williams (1993) in which a child repeats the story of Peter Rabbit many times with transformations that fit his own understanding of gardens, prohibitions, and family relations. It appears that during the early period when children are beginning to be able to absorb narratives from story reading or from retold experiences of others—with or without their own participation—they may tend to merge the accounts with their own knowledge base, which is based on their personal experience. This is understandable from the perspective that, at the beginning, the only resource children have for interpreting stories is the platform of personal experience, which is the same resource they use for interpreting novel experiences in real life. This event-based schematic knowledge structure enables the retention of sequential accounts found in narrative, but it may bias which aspects of content are retained and the way in which they become interpreted and amalgamated with personal experience. Too little is known at this point about how story content and form are retained by very young children (2 to 4 years old) to elaborate or test this account.

Conclusion: The Role of Narrative in the Cultural Construction of the Self

A major outcome of this reexamination of child monologues is the observation that the mastery of the forms for the construction of narrative and other discourse genres—grammatical, lexical, prosodic, pragmatic, rhetorical—precedes their fully functional use. For example, Emily acquired causal and temporal terms, mental state language, and the prosodic contours appropriate to oral narrative—and used them in varying ways—long before they acquired the functional roles that they serve within representational speech such as narrative. Such a process has been observed previously for word meanings (Levy & Nelson, 1994; Nelson & Shaw, 2002). Although some of these asymmetries had been previously noted (in *Narratives*; Levy, 1989), together they suggest a more general process, one with important implications for both linguistic and cognitive development.

A major focus of the earlier group discussions of this data set focused on the child's development of self, with some speculating that language itself was serving as a "substitute object" in Winnicott's (1971) sense. My first attempt to trace the emerging self through linguistic forms was reported in Chapter 8 of *Narratives* (Nelson, 1989b). This new close look at Emily's asynchronous acquisition of the forms and functions of narrative in personal memory tellings has provided new insight into the early development of her conception of herself. This conception is growing in complexity—from its relation to the people in her present family surround, extending outward to the wider cultural world of nursery school and friends at the beach, to the intricacies of cultural institutions such as buying things in stores for Christmas. There is much more that could be filled in on these issues. What is of interest is the way in which Emily uses language to delineate the significant events, routines, specific episodes, and anticipated happenings, as well as to locate herself within them. Memory of personal experience is intertwined with the development of self and the emergence of levels of consciousness, involving the child's reflective understanding of her own experience of events in the light of parental representations of these events and, concomitantly, her new sense of a unique self in relation to the unique selves of other persons (Nelson, 2003a). In this view, the memories and other narratives that Emily shares with her parents and other adults or peers are central to these developments.

Emily's concept of self is expanding from one that is wrapped within a cozy family milieu, where routines are memorized as they are told or experienced (Example 2) and the relational roles to the self may be variously played by the different members (Example 4). As viewed in Example 6, she has become an active participant with expectations and inferences derived from previous experience, as well as from the representations in language provided by her parents. In Example 4, she takes on almost a directive role in articulating the scenario for how the morning will go and, in Example 5, she reports her success in directing the activity of buying a doll at the store. Thus, we see her moving from the experiencing status of the 2-year-old to the active agent status of the 3-year-old. The same move takes her from a focus on the immediate action of the "experiencing I" to the past and future awareness of the "continuing me" (Nelson, 2001).

The development of a "cultural self" (as promised in the title of this chapter is founded in the fact that Emily's view of reality is that of a historically and culturally specific reality. The cultural world of the child is a storied world of many kinds. As such, it contains a vast amount of information that does not derive from direct experience of the child. However, at the end of the period examined here, Emily's knowledge of the cultural world around her was still very restricted. She had begun to branch out, largely through storybooks and parental discussions, and some of this larger view had begun to seep into her accounts of how things are and should be in her world. However, to be fully a "cultural person" in our society is to understand one's role within a variety of culturally determined institutions and milieus, thus broadening one's view of oneself in terms of a complex or hierarchy of identities (family, school, religion, ethnicity, nation, etc.). This is partly accomplished through mastery of cultural tools such as writing and reading. From this perspective, Emily had not advanced beyond the first step toward becoming a cultural person. However, her experiences with narratives of all kinds, and her growing capacities to view herself within a narrative framework, had provided her with both the tools and the knowledge that formed a platform from which to launch into the next phase.

Notes

1. The regular participants included Jerome Bruner (a social-cognitive-developmental psychologist then in the process of writing a book on child talk), John Dore (a linguist focused on child language), Carol Feldman (a psychologist and linguist focused on pragmatics), Dan Stern (a psychiatrist and psychoanalyst focused on mother-infant communication), Rita Watson (a postdoctoral fellow, with Bruner, with an interest in semantics), and myself (a cognitive developmental psychologist with interest in early child language). Julie Gerhardt, Elena Levy, and Joan Lucariello, postdoctoral fellows, joined the group later.

2. Contrary to general inference, Emily is no relation to the author of this chapter or to any of the authors of the chapters in the book reporting on the data analyses (Nelson, 1989c).

3. Actually, one form of Emily's crib speech that we did not analyze was that accompanying her play with the dolls and stuffed toys in her crib. Two reasons for this decision were that this talk was carried on at such a low volume that it was difficult to understand and that its content was of lesser interest than was Emily's talk about herself and her world.

4. When the project began, the Childes data base and transcription conventions had not yet been established. We relied on prior transcription systems for most of our decisions. Also, we worked with a variety of different and noncompatible

computer operating systems, which made sharing data quite difficult. The world of text analysis has changed radically over the past 20 years, yet theoretical and analytical decisions remain similar.

5. See Levy and Nelson (1994) for a detailed analysis of causal forms in these data.

References

Bakhtin, M. (1986). *Speech genres and other late essays.* Austin: University of Texas Press.

Bamberg, M., & Moissinac, L. (2003). Discourse development. In A. Graesser (Ed.), *Handbook of discourse processes* (pp. 395–437). Mahwah NJ: Lawrence Erlbaum.

Bartlett, F. C. (1932). *Remembering: A study in experimental and social psychology.* Cambridge, UK: Cambridge University Press.

Benson, J. B. (1994). The origins of future-orientation in the everyday lives of 9- to 36-mo-old infants. In M. M. Haith, J. B. Benson, R. J. Roberts, & B. Pennington (Eds.), *The development of future-oriented processes* (pp. 375–408). Chicago: University of Chicago Press.

Brown, R. (1973). *A first language: The early stages.* Cambridge, MA: Harvard University Press.

Bruner, J. S. (1990). *Acts of meaning.* Cambridge MA: Harvard University Press.

Bruner, J. S., & Lucariello, J. (1989). Monologue as a narrative recreation of the world. In K. Nelson (Ed.), *Narratives from the crib.* Cambridge MA: Harvard University Press.

Chafe, W. L. (1986). Cognitive constraints on information flow. In R. Tomlin (Ed.), *Coherence and grounding in discourse.* Amsterdam: John Benjamins.

Daiute, C., & Nelson, K. (1997). Making sense of the sense-making function of narrative evaluation. In M. Bamberg (Ed.), Oral versions of personal experience: Three decades of narrative analysis [Special issue]. *Journal of Narrative and Life History, 7,* 207–216.

Donald, M. (1991). *Origins of the modern mind.* Cambridge, MA: Harvard University Press.

Dore, J. (1989). Monologue as reenvoicement of dialogue. In K. Nelson (Ed.), *Narratives from the crib* (pp. 231–260). Cambridge, MA: Harvard University Press.

Eakin, P. J. (1985). *Fictions in autobiography: Studies in the art of self-invention.* Princeton, NJ: Princeton University Press.

Feldman, C. F. (1989). Monologue as problem-solving narrative. In K. Nelson (Ed.), *Narratives from the crib* (pp. 98–122). Cambridge, MA: Harvard University Press.

Fivush, R., & Haden, C. A. (Eds.). (2003). *Autobiographical memory and the construction of a narrative self: Developmental and cultural perspectives.* Mahwah, NJ: Lawrence Erlbaum.

Freeman, M. (1998). Mythical time, historical time, and the narrative fabric of the self. *Narrative Inquiry, 8,* 37–50.

Gerhardt, J. (1989). Monologue as a speech genre. In K. Nelson (Ed.), *Narratives from the crib* (pp. 171–230). Cambridge, MA: Harvard University Press.

Henseler, S. (2000). *Young children's developing theory of mind: Person reference, psychological understanding and narrative skill.* Unpublished doctoral dissertation, City University of New York Graduate Center.

Labov, W., & Waletzky, J. (1967). Narrative analysis. In J. Helm (Ed.), *Essays on the verbal and visual arts* (pp. 12–44). Seattle: University of Washington Press.

Levy, E. (1989). Monologue as development of the text-forming function of language. In K. Nelson (Ed.), *Narratives from the crib* (pp. 123–170). Cambridge, MA: Harvard University Press.

Levy, E., & Nelson, K. (1994). Words in discourse: a dialectical approach to the acquisition of meaning and use. *Journal of Child Language, 21,* 367–390.

Mandler, J. M. (1983). Representation. In J. H. Flavell & E. M. Markman (Eds.), *Cognitive development* (4th ed., Vol. III, pp. 420–494). New York: John Wiley.

Miller, P. J., Hoogstra, L., Mintz, J., Fung, H., & Williams, K. (1993). Troubles in the garden and how they get resolved: A young child's transformation of his favorite story. In C. A. Nelson (Ed.), *Memory and affect in development* (Vol. 26, pp. 87–114). Hillsdale, NJ: Lawrence Erlbaum.

Nelson, K. (1986). *Event knowledge: Structure and function in development.* Hillsdale NJ: Lawrence Erlbaum.

Nelson, K. (1989a). Monologue as representation of real-life experience. In K. Nelson (Ed.), *Narratives from the crib* (pp. 27–72). Cambridge, MA: Harvard University Press.

Nelson, K. (1989b). Monologue as the linguistic construction of self in time. In K. Nelson (Ed.), *Narratives from the crib* (pp. 284–308). Cambridge, MA: Harvard University Press.

Nelson, K. (Ed.). (1989c). *Narratives from the crib.* Cambridge, MA: Harvard University Press.

Nelson, K. (1991). Remembering and telling: A developmental story. *Journal of Narrative and Life History, 1,* 109–127.

Nelson, K. (1996). *Language in cognitive development: The emergence of the mediated mind.* New York: Cambridge University Press.

Nelson, K. (2001). Language and the self: From the "experiencing I" to the "continuing me." In C. Moore & K. Lemmon (Eds.), *The self in time: Developmental issues* (pp. 15–34). Mahwah, NJ: Lawrence Erlbaum.

Nelson, K. (2003a). Narrative and self, myth and memory: Emergence of the cultural self. In R. Fivush & C. A. Haden (Eds.), *Autobiographical memory and the construction of a narrative self (pp. 3–28).* Mahwah, NJ: Lawrence Erlbaum.

Nelson, K. (2003b). Narrative and the emergence of a consciousness of self. In G. D. Fireman, T. E. McVay, Jr.,& O. Flanagan (Eds.), *Narrative and consciousness: Literature, psychology, and the brain (pp. 17–36).* New York: Oxford University Press.

Nelson, K. (2003c). Self and social functions: Individual autobiographical memory and collective narrative. In S. Bluck (Ed.), Autobiographical memory: Exploring its functions in everyday life [Special issue]. *Memory, 11, 125–136.*

Nelson, K., & Fivush, R. (2000). Socialization of memory. In E. Tulving & F. Craik (Eds.), *Handbook of memory* (pp. 283–295). New York: Oxford University Press.

Nelson, K., Fivush, R., Hudson, J., & Lucariello, J. (1983). Scripts and the development of memory. In M. T. H. Chi (Ed.), *Trends in memory development research* (Vol. 9, pp. 52–70). Basel, Switzerland: S. Karger, A.G.

Nelson, K., & Gruendel, J. (1986). Children's scripts. In K. Nelson (Ed.), *Event knowledge: Structure and function in development* (pp. 21–46). Hillsdale, NJ: Lawrence Erlbaum.

Nelson, K., & Levy, E. (1987). Development of referential cohesion in a child's monologues. In R. Steele & T. Threadgold (Eds.), *Language topics*. Amsterdam: John Benjamins.

Nelson, K., & Shaw, L. K. (2002). Developing a socially shared symbolic system. In E. Amsel & J. Byrnes (Eds.), *Language, literacy and cognitive development* (pp. 27–58). Mahwah, NJ: Lawrence Erlbaum.

Nicolopoulou, A., & Weintraub, J. (1998). Individual and collective representations in social context: A modest contribution to resuming the interrupted project of a sociocultural developmental psychology. *Human Development, 41, 215–235.*

Presler, N. (2000). *Pre-writing memories: From anticipatory discourse to children's personal narratives.* Unpublished doctoral dissertation, City University of New York Graduate School.

Schank, R. C., & Abelson, R. P. (1977). *Scripts, plans, goals, and understanding.* Hillsdale, NJ: Lawrence Erlbaum.

Seidman, S., Nelson, K., & Gruendel, J. (1986). Make believe scripts: The transformation of ERs in Fantasy. In K. Nelson (Ed.), *Event knowledge: Structure and function in development.* Hillsdale, NJ: Lawrence Erlbaum.

Stern, D. N. (1989). Crib monologues from a psychoanalytic perspective. In K. Nelson (Ed.), *Narratives from the crib* (pp. 309–320). Cambridge, MA: Harvard University Press.

Vygotsky, L. (1962). *Thought and language* (E. Hanfmann & G. Vakar, Trans.). Cambridge: MIT Press.

Watt, I. (2001). *The rise of the novel: Studies in Defoe, Richardson and Fielding.* Berkeley: University of California Press. (Original work published 1957)

Weir, R. M. (1963). *Language in the crib.* The Hague: Mouton.

Winnicott, D. W. (1971). *Playing and reality.* New York: Routledge.

2.2

Creative Uses
of Cultural Genres

Colette Daiute

Telling—or writing—a story about an event in your life is telling a social story. Autobiographical narrations are also, to be sure, personal and unique, but the social nature of narrating is often overlooked in research and education. In particular, to appreciate what young people are doing when we ask them to share their personal experiences in public institutions like school, we need a theory to guide our reading of narratives as conversations.

This chapter focuses on how young narrators juggle the demanding yet potentially rewarding activity of narrating in public settings, and it offers insights for research and educational designs sensitive to the tensions children feel between fitting in and expressing some of their personal diversity. I draw on data from a study of 7- through 10-year-old children's auto-biographical and fictional narrating in a multiyear study about discrimination conflicts in the context of a violence prevention program (Walker, 1998). Autobiographical and fictional narrating proved to be valuable developmental media for children's analysis of social issues, and children's narrating practices in this context taught me a lot about the nature of narrating as an adaptive and subversive process. The results of the study suggest that as researchers and educators we should redefine narrating to account for issues of power and creativity.

Narrating Social Development

Scholars have argued that, beyond mere reporting, narrating is a medium of identity development, healing, learning, and planning for the future (Bamberg, 1997; Daiute & Griffin, 1993; Lightfoot, 1997; Polkinghorne, 1991; Spence, 1982). Theories of narrative development explain that telling one's story creates one's self-concept—an idea that has evolved over time in psychology.[1] This important insight that narrating a life creates its meaning should not, however, obsure the social nature of that process.

Sociohistorical theory explains, for example, that human development is a social process (Vygotsky, 1978). Sociohistorical theories propose several mechanisms for the socialization of cognitive, affective, and social skills, including internalization (Vygotsky, 1978), procedural facilitation (Rogoff, 1990), activity (Arievitch, & Stetsenko, 2000), and dialogic processes (Bakhtin, 1986). As one sociohistorical theorist explains, personality

> originally arises in society . . . and [one] becomes a personality only as a subject of social relations. . . . The method of . . . dialectics requires that we go further and investigate the development as a process of "self-movement," that is, investigate its internal moving relations, contradictions, and mutual transitions. (Leont'ev, 1978, p. 105)

Many scholars have focused on narrating as a site of development because it is an activity of social cohesion entailing interactions among individuals' values and actions, which relate dynamically in culturally heterogeneous societies.

Psychodynamic theories envision narrating as a means for eliciting subconscious or unconscious memories and feelings about interpersonal processes (Freud, 1909). Freud (1909) noted the importance of verbalizing dreams, fantasies, and other psychological events as a talking cure which could offer temporary relief by "sweeping the mind clean" and "bring[ing] about the disappearance of painful symptoms of . . . illness" (p. 8). In this view, language is a vehicle for raising repressed feelings to consciousness. Later psychoanalytic theorists extended the role of the narrative, defining it as an "aptly chosen reconstruction [that] can fill the gap between two apparently unrelated events and, in the process, make sense out of nonsense" (Spence, 1982, p. 21). That explanation posits a more integrative function for narrating in the developmental process. Recently, the narrative therapy movement has acknowledged that change occurs in narrating via processes such as valuation, involving "anything people identify as a relevant meaning unit when telling their life narrative . . . including . . . a precious memory, a difficult problem, a beloved person, an unreachable goal, an unanticipated death of a significant other, and so forth" (Hermans & Hermans-Jansen, 1995, p. 15). "Through the process of self-reflection, in dialogue with oneself or another person, valuations are organized into a single narratively structured system." (Hermans & Hermans-Jansen, 1995, p. 15).

This project of "how a human being turns him- or herself into a subject" (Foucault, 1988, p. 3) acknowledges tensions between cultural prescriptions and people's lived experiences: "How had the subject been compelled to decipher himself [or herself] in regard to what was forbidden?" (Foucault, 1988, p. 17). Literary scholars explain life processes with discourse analyses of narrative structure, imagery, and myriad other cultural devices as they embody mores and practices that become perceptions defining human connections like love and distances like racism (Gates, 1992; Gergen & Gergen, 1995; Morrison, 1992). Telling one's story is, also, very much about presenting one's self in ways that conform to cultural ideals (Harré, & van Langenhoeve, 1999). On the other hand, in Western cultures, narrating one's "best self" (Oliviera, 1999) or heroic self (Freeman, 1998) is also a means for identifying personal subjectivities and goals that distinguish one's self from other selves. Narrating is a form of social positioning (Bamberg, this volume; Stanley & Billig, this volume), even in writing (Nystrand, Gamoran, Kachur, & Prendergast, 1997) where, according to dialogic theory, the audience looms large, although its presense is usually tacit.

Dialogic theory offers insights for defining narrative texts as social interactions. "Any speaker is . . . a respondent . . . not, after all, the first speaker, the one who disturbs the eternal silence of the universe" (Bakhtin, 1986, p. 69). Conceptualizing oral and written discourse as "speech genres," this insight extends to written works: "The work is a link in the chain of speech communication. Like the rejoinder in a dialogue, it is related to other work-utterances: both those to which it responds and those that respond to it" (Bakhtin, 1986, p. 75).

Narrative texts are, thus, intersubjective—belonging to the context as well as to the author. Physical circumstances of life contexts—a salient word, glance, movement, physical arrangement—are embedded in the dialogue among narrator, audiences, and self-subject. Past interactions, such as those in our native cultures, become relatively stable organizational frames (also referred to as "cultural scripts" by Nelson, this volume), such as when children who identify as European American consistently describe conflicts as fights, while children who identify as African American describe conflicts as mutual problems for participants acting in broader social systems (Daiute & Jones, 2003). Narrators are thus social agents, but even young children transform the social worlds in which they live. On the basis of this dialogic theory of writing, we can redefine narrative genres as they serve important functions in public institutions.

Autobiographical narrating is the genre of choice in research and practice because it is usually assumed to be the quintessential identity medium. Researchers, educators, and clinicians mention the naturalness, authenticity, cultural relevance, and psychosocial richness of personal narration. Qualitative research methods have involved collecting and analyzing narrative discourse in participant observations, ethnographies, and interview studies (Denzin & Lincoln, 2000). Psychological research, in particular, has a history of eliciting narratives of different kinds for different purposes. Narratives have, for example, been elicited as projective tools to assess personality (Smith, Feld, & Franz, 1992), health (Baerger & McAdams, 1999), community relations (Mishler, 1986), law, and beliefs about a whole range of phenomena from life choices to diverse ways of interpreting people and events in the world. Narrative writing is also a popular genre in U.S. schools, especially during the elementary years and, increasingly, up through high school (Graves, 1983; Greenwald, Persky, Campbell, & Mazzeo, 1999).

In contrast, fiction is not typically included as a medium of knowledge or identity development. Although reading fiction is sometimes the basis for literacy instruction in the elementary grades, fiction writing is not a prominent activity in the typical curriculum. In the primary grades, developmentalists and educators value fiction for its role as a medium akin to play and, sometimes, emotional release—but not as a medium of identity development or learning. Fiction writing is not, after all, a first-person medium. Fiction is also presumed to be detached from reality and thus not authentic or related to scientific subject matter. This exclusion of fiction writing from elementary and even secondary school contexts is curious indeed given the recent emphasis on literature in the curriculum. The distinction between reading and writing fiction underscores the place of literature as a domain of others rather than self and of art rather than development.

When defining narrative writing as dialogical, we pose questions about familiar narrative genres. If narrative writing is a conversation, is self-reporting always personal and true? Is fiction always other-worldly? I propose the concept "sociobiographical activity" to blur such distinctions between autobiography and fiction in ways that account for dynamic uses of these genres as developmental media. I will draw on a study of children's writing to illustrate how autobiographies are social and how fictional accounts are highly subjective. As a theory-based unit of analysis, sociobiography integrates the forces of social reproduction, which play a major role in children's self-representations and, at the same time, children's subjective experiences, which they express by exploiting relatively unclaimed genres, like fiction.

Given the public nature of autobiographical narrating in the face of institutional values and pressures, it would be no surprise if narrators performed personal experiences in ways that conform to the context. Children's writing, like their oral interactions, responds to the demands of the context, such that autobiographical writing "about conflicts with peers" in a classroom studying conflict might be oriented more to satisfying the audience than to recalling feelings about a personal conflict experience. Even when children are free to generate their own topics out of journal entries, as is common practice in contemporary elementary education, what they are doing is embedded in a web of explicit and implicit rules (e.g., writing a grabber opening and writing about endearing interactions).

Fiction is rooted in play and virtual reality, which allow people to imagine themselves as they would like to be, fear to be, or have repressed. Freed to some extent from the burdens of verisimilitude, individuals spinning fictional narratives engage their interpretive processes, transforming known contexts to suit desires, needs, and goals. A youngster can for a moment establish some distance from the pressures of institutional values and manipulate them with subjective means like imagination and exaggeration. Fiction thus offers qualities especially adapted to psychosocial development—imagining (also discussed by Sarbin, this volume), expressing a best self, idealized circumstances, and creating alternative scenarios, including ones that are taboo.

Sociobiographical Activities

Sociobiographical activities are analytic tools for moving beyond assumptions about the distinctions between autobiography and fiction in terms of truth. The concept of sociobiography situates development in institutional practices, in this case education, but it could also apply to work (Hollway, 1998), clinical contexts (Hermans & Hermans-Jansen, 1995), community organizations (Solis, this volume), and law.

The sociobiographical activities "performing self," "contesting self," and "centering self" are units of analysis answering this challenge to investigate children's development as a complex social system of "moving relations, contradictions, and mutual transitions" (Leonte'v, 1978, p. 105).

Although a text may be written by an individual child, a narrative, according to this theory, is a conversation embodying social context. Each narrative text represents an intersection of dialogues or "moving relations," and sociobiographical activities capture tensions among cultural imperatives and responses to those imperatives. Autobiographical and fictional narrative tasks are thus cultural forms carrying a range of previous and potential experiences with which a child must contend. By comparing two similar genres that differ primarily in the nature and stakes of self-exposure, we begin an inquiry into the sociopolitical nature of genres. Information about the context sets the scene for discussing this analysis.

Writing About Social Conflict in a Violence Prevention Program

A curriculum invokes institutional values that children as young as 7 years old can read, as they read their teacher's likes and dislikes of the official rules and their own need to present a self-image in the educational context. To the extent that the classroom provides opportunities for self-expression, participants have the chance to be complex subjects rather than rigid performances in relation to the institutional demands they perceive and practice. For this discussion of narrative genres as developmental media, I draw on data from an ethics and violence prevention curriculum involving narrative writing about social conflict as a means for socializing conflict resolution strategies (Walker, 1998).

The violence prevention curriculum involved teachers and students in the analysis of social conflicts of ethnic discrimination and strategies for dealing with such conflicts in peaceful ways (Walker, 1998). Curriculum activities toward these ends involved reading and discussing high quality children's literature about peer conflicts. Literature with a range of culturally embedded examples of discrimination conflicts provided a context for discussing conflicts and individuals' roles in these conflicts. The selection for third grade classes was *Angel Child, Dragon Child* (Surat, 1983), a story about a recently immigrated Vietnamese girl named Hoa who was the object of discriminatory teasing, and for fifth grade classes the selection was *Mayfield Crossing* (Nelson, 1993), a story about a group of African American children in the South in the 1960s, and the White children in the neighboring town where Black children must attend school after theirs closes. A teacher's guide for working with each literary selection suggested discussion questions, activities for analyzing and role-playing conflict negotiation strategies, and a variety of writing activities.

Narrative writing activities were designed as opportunities for children to analyze social problems raised in the literary selections, to consider how such problems had occurred in their own lives, and to imagine effective and healthy ways of dealing with such conflicts. The writing activities included autobiography and fiction, to provide young narrators with different types of exposure to implicit and explicit audiences, including the institution represented in the curriculum and the teacher's implementation of the curriculum, as well as the children's peers and parents—in the background but audiences nonetheless. The research rationale for analyzing autobiographical and fictional narratives was that autobiography is a highly public and judgmental forum in which to report conflict experiences, while fiction could provide a more private space.

The following two narratives written by 7-year-old Eudora, in the fall of third grade when she began participating in the curriculum, illustrate how young people narrate personal and fictional accounts of social conflicts.[2] When asked to write about "a conflict or argument you or someone you know had," Eudora, who identified as African American, wrote:

Me and Lerissa

Me and Lerissa (my friend) had a disagreement because I wanted to do dolls and some thing else but she wanted to play on her computer but I said "why can't we just do dolls and she said" no. Fine I will do the computer.

Compare that narrative to one Eudora wrote around the same time, responding to a prompt for a fictional narrative potentially about conflict.[3]

One day when Jama saw Max and Pat jama felt very sad because she was alone. When it was getting late Jama was going home then when she was eating dinner she was thinking about her friends so after dinner she went to bed when she was going to bed she had a dream about her friend. On the next day she saw Pat and Max again

---

The dialogic theory of writing is a resource for reading Eudora's narratives as they speak to the context where she wrote them, as well as for reading how Eudora represents herself and others as subjects. Eudora is the narrator of "Me and Lerissa," and she is also the subject, "me." Lerissa and the objects and events involved in the conflict are also explicit subjects in the narrative. Implicitly, the various audiences in the classroom context (the curriculum, the teacher, peers) and beyond the classroom (those with whom Eudora interacts outside of school) are also present.

The entire narrative "Me and Lerissa" is a response to an invitation to write about a time when she or someone she knew had a conflict or disagreement, and each phase echoes interactions in the classroom about analyzing how conflicts get started, progress, and must be resolved. "Fine I will do the computer" conforms, for example, to the teacher's emphasis on resolving conflicts.

In the fictional account about Jama, Max, and Pat, the dialogic interactions also occur among the narrator, characters, and audiences, but, in this story, Eudora is not explicitly the subject and thus, as narrator, she can be a ventriloquist voicing her point of view through her characters. And so she does. Like many children in the nine classes whose narrative writing my colleagues and I have studied, Eudora represented conflict differently in her autobiographical and fictional narratives (Daiute, Buteau, & Rawlins, 2001).

Eudora's fictional narrative provides a foil for reading "Me and Lerissa." Notably different in the fictional narrative is the emotional orientation to the task, which reveals a personal perspective by reporting the psychological states of Jama, who emerges as the protagonist. There is a whisper of curriculum values expressed in Jama's individual reflection, yet more prominent is the alternative to curriculum values with the lack of resolution. The emotional expression embodies a subjective voice that is silent in Eudora's more explicitly autobiographical piece.

Reading these narratives in the light of the curriculum context makes clear just how much public scrutiny the children felt when writing about personal experiences and how salient fiction had become in the classroom. A violence prevention program, like any curriculum, conveys a particular version of social relations. The literary selection, the discussion questions, the conflict negotiation skills taught, and feedback to students' talk and writing all convey values about social relationships, what can go wrong in them, and what can be done to address social relational problems. In particular, the emphasis on analyzing conflict as the escalation of interpersonal tensions and on writing peaceful resolutions influenced how children narrated their personal experiences (Daiute, & Jones, 2003; Daiute, Stern, & Lelutiu-Weinberger, 2003).

To examine the nature and extent of this impact, I analyzed autobiographical and fictional narrating by four children whose writing we collected as part of a larger study of the violence prevention curriculum from third through fifth grades. The four children completed eight individually written narratives (among other texts) in classrooms where we had recorded and analyzed teacher-led discussions for all lessons related to the curriculum (Daiute, Stern, & Lelutiu-Weinberger, 2003). This group includes two girls and two boys, two identifying as African American and two as Latino (the two major identifications among children in the school). Referring to the children with pseudonyms (similar to their names), I will describe how Eudora and Jackson (who identify as African American), Caterina (who identifies as Dominican), and John (who identifies as Puerto Rican) used narrative genres.

Redefining Narrative Genres

Performing, contesting, and centering self are all social interactions, yet they differ in their dialogic emphasis. In performing self activities, the social context is the predominant influence—with narrators reproducing context values. Contesting self activities, in contrast, express ambivalence in the narrator's stance toward social pressures, acknowledging them in a self-interested way by justifying, defending, or aggrandizing a personal perspective that seems at odds with the context values. Centering self activities express a more subjective point of view.

When *performing self,* an author orients to the social context, expressing the values and expectations of the audience. In this case, performance-dominated narrating expresses curriculum values, in particular those emphasizing conflict escalation, de-escalation, conflict negotiation strategies, and resolution, especially peaceful resolution. Performing activities thus highlight specific sociocultural aspects of the narrator's self-presentation. Performing is a predominant activity in the following narrative by Caterina:

A Fight with my Friend

One day me and my friend named: Mary were fighting by mouth. We tesesing each others. She called me a pig and I called her a stup girl So we satring beieng Friends because it's bad.

In addition to performing conflict escalation as it had been examined in class, "She called me a pig and I called her a stup girl," Caterina made it clear that she had been involved in verbal conflict, "[we] were fighting by mouth," the form of conflict that had been presented in class as more tolerable than physical conflict. Caterina also wrote that her conflict with Mary was resolved, albeit abruptly, "So we satring beieng Friends," and she offered an evaluative coda demonstrating her understanding that "it's bad" to have conflicts.

As we saw in the narrative "Me and Lerissa" above, Eudora also performed an abrupt and somewhat grudging resolution, "Fine I will do the computer," to the conflict she described over a disagreement about play activities. Eudora's appeal to Lerissa, "why can't we just do dolls," mirrors the conflict negotiation strategy of "talking it out" when there's a disagreement, which her teacher had emphasized in curriculum activities.

John, who identified as Puerto Rican, also performed a conflict escalating from calumny to physical fighting, followed by a common resolution of antagonists becoming friends.

> *When Angel was talking about me. I a talk about him. And we start fighting and hiting each other. We started punching each other every where we went when we were fight we started getting other people to fight then we became friends.*

In the following narrative, Jackson also resolved a conflict in which he tried to satisfy two friends.

> **Friends Fight**
>
> *one day in music I was working with Alex. Tyrone got Mad a[t] Me Because I did not work with him. But then we came Friends. So I worked with Tyrone. But then Alex got mad at me. But then I with both of them. We all became friends.*

"But then I with both of them" expresses the highly valued strategy of compromise (Daiute, Stern, & Lelutiu-Weinberger, 2003).

The following narrative by Jackson performs curriculum values by modeling them in a narration of Martin Luther King, Jr.'s peaceful resistance to conflict (e.g., "turned his cheek," boy cotted the buses"). In some ways, this was an unusual approach because the narrative does not play out the conflict, but it does conform to the predominant value—peace. This was also an unusual response to the autobiographical prompt, as it presented another person as the main character—strategy consistent, I believe, with the idea that the autobiographical narrative had become a genre for performing curriculum values.

M.L.K. J.R.

Hes not a real in-person friend or my age but we celibrate his birth day he is a crist beliver a strong black man and will always be a man to his word Martin Luther King Jr. was a man for our rights, a man that turned his cheek to get hit, who boy cotted the buses to help us, who made this world a better lace, I can't say thank you enough. Thank you so much Maybe God put me in this world to be a man like you were. If I'm the first black president and if I am I'll think of you. Thank you.

Differing from performing activities that orient to social norms, contesting self is a sociobiographical activity that distinguishes, often subtly, a personal stance from a cultural norm. Contesting involves presenting a best self by explaining, justifying, defending, and/or aggrandizing self-representations that ignore or implicitly critique norms. This form of contesting reveals, through narrative organization and inflection, responses about cultural norms not performed. Like performing self, contesting self is socially oriented, but it opens a realm to explain identity and conflict processes that are less-than-ideal, less-than-complete, especially worthy of praise given the difficulty of the situation, or apparently unique in some other way. This analysis is not, however, explicitly marked with reference to the curriculum, or the need to save face, and depends on the background information.

Just as the performed narrative is conformity and normality, contesting self is a claim and justification for uniqueness. An implicit subtext of contesting self is "What else could I do?!"—an appeal recognizing that a personal act might not have been desirable, but that there were justifying circumstances (which may only be alluded to in the narrative). Such explicit (the exclamation point and question mark) and implicit (the evaluative emphasis in "what else") moral illocutionary acts suggest the author's perception of a need to explain his or her actions. Contesting moves also include heroic descriptions implying "I saved the day!" The contesting self might also hide things "We just won't mention *that!*" Self-contesting might also be expressed in shifting the focus to nonself characters, especially to attribute blame for moral infractions. Caterina uses several techniques to complicate her image in this story about a conflict.

> *In afterschool me and my friend and I had a desagreement, her name is Chantell. One day went to after school together We seat down then she said to me "just because you won the contest of the singing the Monica song, dosen't mean you look like her." I asked her what's borthering you girl said "Nothiing!" In a mean vioce. How come you didn't congurats? Me, In a sweet voice. "Because I was busy you know" She asked me If she look like Monica I said "NO" Boy I knew she was mad because her face got red. I said to her I look like Monica she said "No you don't I said "what" "What has gotten into you." Ever since you I mean I win the contest you got mad. "Caterina" "OK." . . .*

Caterina characterizes her side of the interaction as reasonable by reaching out with questions that characterize Chantell as rigid (e.g., "what's bothering you girl," "What has gotten in to you"). Caterina also uses the colloquial "girl," implying solidarity, and contrasts Chantell's "mean voice" with her own "sweet voice." Caterina uses these and other techniques to place responsibility for the conflict with Chantell and the reasonable stance with herself.

Contesting self activities also occurred in the fictional narratives, as in Eudora's text below. In this story, Eudora characterized Jama as a flexible and creative victim of rejection—with Jama explaining why she was sad, then trying several approaches to Max and Pat doing something together and other persistent moves that transform conflict resolution into something more heroic.

> *When Jama saw Max and Pat laughing she turn back around. She was mad that Max and pat were together. The next day jama did not bother with Max and Pat She knew that they were happy with out her. So instead of Jama staying home she went to the park. After 15 minutes Jama wanted an Ice cream so she walked in the Ice Cream shop. She saw Max and Pat together. Max said" hi to Jama Jama said" Hi back. Max asked Jama were was you the other Day. So she lied to Max and said" I was not feeling well. Pat ask her If she was feeling ok. Jama said" Yes. So max invented Jama to the movies to go see*

(Continued)

> (Continued)
>
> *Monster. Jama said"ok. Jama ask what time Max said" 7:00. Pat and Max said" see you there. Jama said" Bye. At 7:00 Jama met Pat Max and went in the movie theater and Brought Popcorn, soda, and candy. They was a Little Late one minute Later. 2 hours Past the movie was over. And Jama yelled to Max Jama said" Sorry. Max said" why because I lied. I was julious of you and Pat. Jama said" I was your best friend. Max said" we all are friends Jama said" OK. They were all friends later.*

Still social, *centering self* emphasizes subjective experience via sensual representations such as expressing emotions, cognitions, and interpretations. Centering activities occur in descriptions of psychological states, multiple author perspectives stated as narrator and as character, and literary devices that enhance the reflectiveness of the presentation. The following fictional narrative by Jackson packs in a range of emotions and senses: "jealous," "so sad," "cried," "saw Max and Pat," "ready to tell," "took a deep breath."

> *Jama was jealous of Max and Pat. She was so sad she cried on the way home She went out sade again. She saw Max and Pat she was ready to tell Max the news. Ran up to them he took a deep breath.*

The character Jama, offered in the fictional narrative prompt, was consistently cast by the young authors as the focal character, indicated by Jama's being mentioned most often, being mentioned first, expressing the central point of view monitoring and evaluating story events, and merging most frequently with the narrator voice; Jama was occasionally represented as "I."

There may be other sociobiographical activities, but performing, contesting, and centering accounted for the self-representational moves appearing in this data set.

What's Going On With Autobiographical and Fictional Writing About Conflict?

Analyses of performing, contesting, and centering activities in the narratives by Eudora, Caterina, Jackson, and John demonstrate the dynamic nature of self-representation. Table 2.2.1 summarizes the patterning of these activities across 16 autobiographical and 16 fictional narratives. After an activity is identified for each meaning unit (defined as a clause with all its dependent clauses), the combination of assignments is the basis for determining the dominant orientation in a text. As shown in Table 2.2.1, some texts are characterized predominantly by one sociobiographical activity but may also include some of another. A few narratives balanced three sociobiographical activities.

Analyses revealed interesting patterns across context and time, illustrating the dialogic nature of self-representations in the narratives as the children used the public face of autobiography and the mask of fiction to perform, critique, defend against, or personalize the values promoted in the curriculum.

Autobiography as Performance

As shown in Table 2.2.1, many of the autobiographical narratives were predominantly involved with performing curriculum values, while a few balanced performing with centering and to a lesser extent with contesting. Especially interesting, considering that autobiography is supposed to be an explicitly self-representational medium, is that centering was never the predominant activity in the autobiographical narratives. The children described very few character psychological states across the autobiographical narratives, depicting mostly "wanting" and "need" as the basis of conflicts in the third grade and eventually "knowledge" and belief in the fifth grade.

The relatively limited range of performing activities in the autobiographical narratives also indicates context sensitivity. While the specific conflict issues across the 16 autobiographical texts included conflicts over play activities, relationships, identity issues (respect, status, etc.), possessions, and others issues, several common conflict values predominated—conflict escalation, conflict negotiation, and resolution. In short, the ways of representing conflicts were limited to the curriculum strategies.

Given differences across African American and Latino cultures, there might have been a broader range of conflict values expressed. African American

Table 2.2.1   Patterning of Sociobiographical Activities Across Narrative Genres in Four Cases

Child	Autobiographical Narrating			Fictional Narrating		
	Performing	Contesting	Centering	Performing	Contesting	Centering
Eudora						
3rd grade, Fall	Predom.	—		—	—	Predom.
3rd grade, Spring	Predom.	Some	Some	—	Some	Predom.
5th grade, Fall	Predom.	—	Some	Some	Some	Predom.
5th grade, Spring	Predom.	—	Some	Some	—	Predom.
Caterina						
3rd grade, Fall	Predom.	—	—	Some	—	Predom.
3rd grade, Spring	Predom.	—	—	Some	—	Predom.
5th grade, Fall	Some	Predom.	Some	—	Some	Predom.
5th grade, Spring	Some	Predom.	Some	Some	Predom.	Some
Jackson						
3rd grade, Fall	Some	Some	Some	Some	Some	Some
3rd grade, Spring	Some	Some	Some	Some	—	Predom.
5th grade, Fall	Predom.	—	—	Some	Some	Predom.
5th grade, Spring	Predom.	—	—	Some	Some	Predom.
John						
3rd grade, Fall	Predom.	—	—	—	—	Predom.
3rd grade, Spring	Predom.	—	—	—	—	Some
5th grade, Fall	Predom.	Some	Some	Some	—	Predom.
5th grade, Spring	Predom.	—	—	Some	—	Predom.

Note: "Predom." = the predominant strategy used across the sentences in the text; "Some" = the strategy used some of the time, usually in one or two sentences in the text; "—" = no occurrence of the strategy in the text.

culture is often expressed in explicitly social ways, such as embedding interpersonal interactions in broader social systems and referring to broader powers (like God in Jackson's narrative "M.L.K.J.R.") (Daiute & Jones, 2003; Gates, 1992; Lee, Rosenfeld, Mendenhall, Rivers, & Tynes, this volume; Morrison, 1992). Latino culture often appeals to spirituality, family, and nature (Fine, Roberts, & Weis, 2000; Hurtado, in press).

The performance of these conflict values in the autobiographical narratives could, of course, be interpreted as an internalization of the values and thus as the success of the conflict resolution program. The relative lack of subjectivity around conflict processes in autobiographical narratives, however, and the children's reliance on fictional narratives, as discussed below, suggests a much more complicated situation.

Fiction as Subjectivity

As shown in Table 2.2.1, the children used the fictional narrating context predominantly to express subjectivity in the form of centering. Often behind the veil of Jama, the children expressed emotions, other subjective states, dramatic relationships, and values counter to the curriculum, such as violence.

As we see in Table 2.2.1, sociobiographical activities are more likely to co-occur in the narratives the children wrote in fifth grade than in those they wrote in third grade, suggesting that young people eventually learn to use genres like autobiography and fiction in expected ways, an observation supported in another study, which included writing by college students (Daiute & Stern, 2003).

Performing for Different Audiences

Guided by dialogic theory and previous analyses of institutional values promoted in the curriculum, we have read narrative texts as social interactions and observed how the children responded to different demands in autobiographical and fictional narratives. A brief comparison of the values the children performed in autobiographical narrating across classes illustrates their sensitivity to specific values.

Mrs. Smith, a third grade teacher who identified herself as White, emphasized a different subset of the curriculum values than did Mrs. Morales, a third grade teacher who identified as Puerto Rican. Analyses of teacher-led class discussions devoted to the violence prevention curriculum units in the fall and spring in nine third and fifth grade classes identified the percentage of teacher and student talk turns expressing the 21 curriculum values (Daiute, Stern, & Lelutiu-Weinberger, 2003). This analysis offered information about different teachers' implementations of the curriculum, which we then related to their students' narrative representations of social conflict across the year. Although Mrs. Smith and Mrs. Morales focused on pedagogical issues in similar ways, they differed in their emphasis on many other values. The differences between Mrs. Smith's and Mrs. Morales's implementations are relevant here because these differences add detail to the notion of performing in narrative writing. This comparison also highlights how teachers interact differently with institutions—as they do with the mainstream educational values in a curriculum.

Mrs. Smith emphasized the values of self-determination (such as the need for all the participants in conflicts to take responsibility for resolving them), understanding the causes of conflict escalation, and the importance and feasibility of resolving conflicts. For example, guiding her students to understand individuals' responsibilities in conflicts, Mrs. Smith said "What could Hoa [the little girl from Vietnam in the novel *Angel Child, Dragon Child*] have done so things wouldn't have gotten so intense? What could the teacher have done so things between Raymond [the red-haired boy who teased Hoa because she wore "pajamas" and talked funny] and Hoa shouldn't have gotten so intense? What should Raymond have done so things wouldn't get so intense?"

Another excerpt of the class discussion several weeks later shows how Mrs. Smith applied this emphasis on conflict resolution to the children's collaboratively written endings to *Angel Child, Dragon Child*. "What we're gonna do is, in the group, if you would like to [you may] share your ending with us, and hopefully many people will. John, the rest of us are going to figure out what they did to solve the conflict. Okay? And I'm going to keep notes. Tomorrow, I'll get this on chart paper. . . . Toni, will you talk about what ways you used to solve the conflict?"

Several excerpts from transcripts of Mrs. Morales's class discussions about *Angel Child, Dragon Child* highlight her very different emphases when guiding class discussion about the same novel. Mrs. Morales emphasized interdependence in conflicts (compared to self-determination), focused on the strategy of appealing to adults to assist in children's conflicts with peers, and qualified conflict resolution, in particular by addressing issues of justice, such as determining responsibility for resolution initiatives based on who was in the wrong. Mrs. Morales also devoted considerable time to discussing how interpersonal conflicts relate to broader problems like discrimination and to helping children understand that conflicts aren't always resolved easily or at all.

In the following excerpt, Mrs. Morales engages one of her students, Kenny, in analyzing Raymond's part in the conflict with Hoa and over time, this teacher points to an injustice.

Mrs. Morales: Why does Raymond tease Hoa? Why do you think that happens, Kenny? Your opinion, you, your thinking. . . .

Kenny: Raymond, he thought it was not right for them to come into the country and spoil the country with their closing.

Mrs. Morales: Spoil the country with their clothing?

Kenny: I don't know.

Mrs. Morales: That's a strong statement. You think that people that dress differently spoil?

Kenny: Wasn't right for the country.

Mrs. Morales: Why wasn't it right?

Kenny: 'Cause it wasn't what they wanted.

On another day, Mrs. Morales encouraged another student to think critically about conflict resolution. The excerpt begins with Jessie summarizing a narrative her classmate Christine had written.

Jessie: Christine went to the boys' and girls' club . . . where there's like a hockey field, and Christine is waiting on line and the girl said that her friend was first, so the girl's cousin went in and he said to her, she got kicked out.

Mrs. Morales: How did you feel about that, Christine?

Christine: I felt bad 'cause I had next and she said that her friend had next when he was at the end of the line, waiting.

Mrs. Morales: How did you think this made the girl feel? How do you think she was feeling at her end?

Christine: I thought she had felt mad and sad because she got kicked out.

Mrs. Morales: Why do you think she felt mad?

Christine: 'Cause her friend didn't get his way, I got my way.

Mrs. Morales: Would you have done anything differently?

Christine: I would have apologized.

Mrs. Morales: You would have apologized to the girl? Why would you apologize to her?

Christine: I would have said sorry.

Mrs. Morales: But who was in the wrong? Who was doing something that they shouldn't have been?

Students across these classes performed curriculum values in their autobiographical writings, as discussed above, but the specific values performed across classes conformed to ones their teachers had emphasized. Analyses of changes in students' values expressed in their autobiographical narratives at the beginning and end of the school year indicate, for example, that students in Mrs. Smith's class tended to increase conflict resolution in their autobiographical narratives across the school year, while students in Mrs. Morales's class tended to increase the number of resolution strategies but *not* resolutions in their narratives over the school year. This brief description provides some breadth to the idea of performing self-representations.

Significance for Research

Researchers who invite participants to share their understandings, feelings, and opinions by narrating personal experiences are tapping into a rich mode of human discourse, but I have argued here that it is important to acknowledge the intensely social nature of narrating when designing research. I have focused on autobiographical and fictional narrating in an educational context not because narrating in school is uniquely subjected to social forces but for several other reasons. First, failing to recognize that narrators perform often means equating narrative texts with the persons who wrote them. What I suggest here instead is that we read young authors' autobiographical narratives as responses to what they perceive to be requests or imperatives. Reading them as mostly personal or cultural may involve falsely judging students or their cultural backgrounds rather than judging the situation where the narrative was produced. In short, I am arguing that there is no individually authentic narrative. The implication of this argument is, moreover, that research designs could provide ways of exposing the dialogue within and around narrative data. Employing dialogic theory is one way to do this, and making the audience explicit in the narrative task or interview is another.

Second, narratives are everywhere (as Freeman points out elsewhere in this volume) and are ripe for analysis. The prevalence of narratives in human discourse is certainly another reason why narrative inquiry is so important, but narratives must also be considered as merged with the contexts where they are produced, which may mean acknowledging specific aspects of the context or using theory to guide observation and analysis of the context. I have argued here, for example, that reading autobiographical and fictional narratives with their contexts provides a fuller and more accurate picture of how young people perceive the world around them than about their personal thoughts and beliefs. Any narrative text points elsewhere, so we researchers can gain insights from identifying those distributed points and including them in our analyses.

Finally, personhood is complex, so in studying the development of persons, we must cast broadly across cultural symbols. Sharing personal experience is an important life skill, as well as a research activity, but we have seen here how children find clever—even subversive—ways of expressing their experiences. Examples from children's autobiographical and fictional writing suggest that the imaginative activities required by the latter may be the more important process for personality development up through adolescence and beyond, as other scholars have also argued (Lightfoot, 1997; this volume; Sarbin, this volume). As demonstrated here, fiction in particular, with its anonymity, can hold psychosocial secrets, experiments, and desires, while the public quality of autobiography ensnares the narrator in psychosocial obligations, and those patterns can be further complicated by shifting the proscenium. Understanding how fiction, in particular, can elicit intersubjective themes connected to historical issues that may be censored in public spaces is essential for those of us who work with young people from a range of ethnic and social class backgrounds. School-aged children's creative manipulation of genres designed as autobiographical and fictional suggests that they have the right to a range of different curriculum activities in a range of modes.

Complexity and variation also emerge as important in this study. Coherence is often noted as characteristic of healthy development, but patterns of sociobiographical activities suggest that variability is an indicator of health because it reflects social orientation. If healthy development means, at least in part, orienting to one's environment, then identifying variability or even incoherence spawned of context sensitivity is a measure of health worth further inquiry. Being able to make flexible use of educational media, as did the children who distributed personal expression to fiction, is also a skill. Issues of power related to these skills are, moreover, appropriate for classroom discussion, and this study suggests children are ready for that.

The potential of the public school context to socialize young people is enormous, so it's important to provide media allowing them diverse representations of self and knowledge. The significance of the idea that the discursive circumstances of everyday life become people, their problems, and their possibilities is that many children grow up involved in activities that limit their physical, symbolic, and emotional lives. A range of approaches is needed to provide children with equitable opportunities, and understanding the developmental power of narrating is central to identifying resources for children in public schools.

Notes

1. Across the recent history of inquiry into narrating, the way of referring to persons and personality has likewise evolved from "personality," to "identity," "self," and "subject position."

2. Although children's punctuation, grammatical constructions, and spelling are not consistently in standard written English, previous research has shown that beginning writers can use writing for complex sociocognitive functions (Dyson, 1989; Teale & Sulzby, 1986). Written forms are inventions (Ferreiro & Teborosky, 1979; Graves, 1982) based on native speech dialects such as Black English. Thus, children's writings are presented here in their original form.

3. The task was as follows: Imagine this scene in a story called "Three." Jama and Max were best friends. Pat moved in next to Max, and they began to spend lots of time together. One day, Jama saw Max and Pat walking together and laughing. What happened next? Continue this story about how the friends got along. What happened? How did they all think and feel about the events? How did it all turn out?

References

Arievitch, I. M., & Stetsenko, A. (2000). The quality of cultural tools and cognitive development: Gal'perin's perspective and its implications. *Human Development, 43*, 69–92.

Baerger, D. R., & McAdams, D. P. (1999). Life story coherence and its relation to psychological well-being. *Narrative Inquiry, 9*, 69–96.

Bakhtin, J. J. (1986). *Speech genres and other late essays*. Austin: University of Texas Press.

Bamberg, M. G. W. (1997). Positioning between structure and performance. *Journal of Narrative and Life History, 7,* 335–342.

Daiute, C., Buteau, E., & Rawlins, C. (2001). Social relational wisdom: Developmental diversity in children's written narratives about social conflict. *Narrative Inquiry, 11*(2), 1–30.

Daiute, C., & Griffin, T. M. (1993). The social construction of written narrative. In C. Daiute (Ed.), *The development of literacy through social interaction* (pp. 97–120). San Francisco: Jossey-Bass.

Daiute, C., & Jones, J. (2003). Diversity discourses: Reading race and ethnicity in children's writing. In S. Greene & D. Abt-Perkins (Eds.), *Talking, reading, writing, and race: Contributions to racial understanding by literacy research.* New York: Teachers College Press.

Daiute, C., & Stern, R. (2003, April). *Self performances in writing.* Paper presented at the Society for Research on Child Development (Panel on Writing and the Composition of Self) Tampa, FL.

Daiute, C., Stern, R., & Lelutiu-Weinberger, C. (2003). Contradictions in a violence prevention program. *Journal of Social Issues, 59*(1), 83–101.

Denzin, N. K., & Lincoln, Y. S. (2000). *Handbook of qualitative research.* Thousand Oaks, CA: Sage.

Dyson, A. H. (1989). *Multiple worlds of child writers: Friends learning to write.* New York: Teachers College Press.

Ferriero, E., & Teberosky, A. (1979). *Literacy before schooling.* Exeter, NH: Heinemann Educational Books.

Fine, M., Roberts, R. A., & Weis, L. (2000). Refusing the betrayal: Latinas redefining gender, sexuality, family & home. *Review of Education/Pedagogy/Cultural Studies 22,* 87–119.

Foucault, M. (1988). Technologies of the self. In L. H. Martin, H. Gutman, & P. H. Hutton (Eds.), *Technologies of the self: A seminar with Michel Foucault.* (pp. 16–49). Amherst: University of Massachusetts Press.

Freeman, M. (1998). Mythical time, historical time, and the narrative fabric of the self. *Narrative Inquiry, 8,* 27–50.

Freud, S. (1909). *Five lectures on psycho-analysis.* New York: W.W. Norton.

Gates, H. L. (1992). *Loose canons: Notes on the culture wars.* New York: Oxford University Press.

Gergen, M. M., & Gergen, K. J. (1995). What is this thing called love?: Emotional scenarios in historical perspective. *Journal of Narrative and Life History, 5,* 221–237.

Graves, D. (1983). *Writing: Teachers and children at work.* Portsmouth, NH: Heinemann.

Greenwald, E. A., Persky, H. R., Campbell, J. R., & Mazzeo, J. (1999). *NAEP 1998 Writing report card for the nation and the states.* Washington, DC: National Center for Education Statistics.

Harré, R., & van Langenhove, L. (1999). Reflexive positioning: Autobiography. In R. Harré & L. van Langenhove (Eds.), *Positioning theory* (pp. 60–73). Malden, MA: Blackwell.

Hermans, H. J. M., & Hermans-Jansen, E. (1995). *Self-narratives: The construction of meaning in psychotherapy.* New York: Guilford.

Hollway, W. (1998). Fitting work: Psychological assessment in organization. In J. Henriques, W. Hollway, C. Urwin, C. Venn, & V. Walkerdine (Eds.), *Changing the subject: Psychology, social regulation, and subjectivity* (pp. 22–59). London: Routledge.

Hurtado, A. (in press). Theory in the flesh: Toward an endarkened epistemology. *International Journal of Qualitative Studies in Education.*

Leont'ev, A. N. (1978). *Activity, consciousness, and personality.* Englewood Cliffs, NJ: Prentice Hall.

Lightfoot, C. (1997). *The culture of adolescent risk-taking.* New York: Guilford.

Mishler, E. G. (1986). *Research interviewing: Context and narrative.* Cambridge, MA: Harvard University Press.

Morrison, T. (1992). *Playing in the dark: Whiteness and the literary imagination.* Cambridge, MA: Harvard University Press.

Nelson, V. M. (1993). *Mayfield crossing.* New York: Avon.

Nystrand, M., Gamoran, A., Kachur, R., & Prendergast, C. (1997). *Opening dialogue: Understanding the dynamics of language and learning in the classroom.* New York: Teachers College Press.

Oliveira, M. (1999). The function of self-aggrandizement in storytelling. *Narrative Inquiry, 9,* 25–48.

Polkinghorne, D. (1991). Narrative and self-concept. *Journal of Narrative and Life History, 1,* 135–153.

Rogoff, B. (1990). *Apprenticeship in thinking.* New York: Oxford University Press.

Smith, C. P., Feld, S. C., & Franz, C. E. (1992). Methodological considerations: Steps in employing research content analysis systems. In C. P. Smith, J. W. Atkinson, D. C. McClelland, & V. Joseph (Eds.), *Motivation and personality: Handbook of thematic content analysis.* New York: Cambridge University Press.

Spence, D. P. (1982). *Narrative truth and historical truth: Meaning and interpretation in psychoanalysis.* New York: W.W. Norton.

Surat, M. M. (1983). *Angel child, dragon child.* New York: Scholastic.

Teale, W. H., & Sulzby, E. (Eds.). (1986). *Emergent literacy: Writing and reading.* Norwood, NJ: Ablex.

Vygotsky, L. S. (1978). *Mind in society.* Cambridge, MA: Harvard University Press.

Walker, P. (1998). *Voices of love and freedom: A literacy-based ethics and prevention program.* Iowa City, IA: Prescription Learning.

2.3

Positioning With Davie Hogan

Stories, Tellings, and Identities

Michael Bamberg

L et me begin with something that is simple and (I hope) common sense: When we speak, we usually speak *to* others and we speak *about* something (or *about* others)—and we do both at the same time and by use of discursive means (such as lexical devices, syntax, suprasegmentational devices, and gestures). When we tell stories, we do a little more; we signal to others that we are entering, maintaining or handing over the floor to "do" a story, and we order aspects of what the story is about (particularly the *characters* in the story) in space (*there*) and time (*then*) into a plot; again, by use of the same discursive devices. In other words, time, space, and characters inside the story world gain their existence in story performance; they are creations or constructions, and so is the self (in its role as storyteller) as well as the audience (in their role as participants and listeners). Taking off from this very simple but basic orientation as my starting point, I will lay out and demonstrate with an example how we can use the concept of "positioning" to link not only the creative act of storytelling with the construction of story content but both in a fuller and more productive way to the act of constructing identities, that is, identities of the speaking (storytelling) *subject*.

In the following, I will briefly introduce the notion of positioning as a way to conceptualize the subject's identity as impinged on by two opposing forces, one with a person-to-world and the other with a world-to-person direction of fit—the first relying on a notion of the unitary subject as ground, the latter on a subject as determined by outside (mainly social and biological) forces. Making the interactive site of story*telling* the empirical ground, where identities come into existence and are interactively displayed, I will present *positioning analysis* as the tool for analyzing the (identity) question "Who am I?"—and with a brief film clip in which four 12-year-olds sit around a campfire and engage in storytelling, I will demonstrate how this type of analysis operates.

Positioning, Identities, and Positioning Analysis

Current discussions of the concept of positioning draw on two rather different interpretations. The more traditional view, which was very influential for the development of this concept and its current relevance in theorizing identity and subjectivity, explains positions as grounded in "discourses" (also variably called "master narratives," "plot lines," "master plots," "dominant discourses," or simply "cultural texts") that are viewed as providing the meanings and values within which subjects are "positioned" (Davies & Harré, 1990; Harré & van Langenhove, 1999; Hollway, 1984). The problem of agency is addressed by giving the subject a semi-agentive status inasmuch as discourses are construed as inherently contradictive and in competition with one another, so that subjects are forced to choose: They agentively pick a position among those available. Thus, positions are resources that subjects can choose and that when practiced for a while become repertoires that can be drawn on.

Elaborating Butler's (1990, 1995) view of performing identities in acts of "self-marking," a view that is concerned with self-reflection, self-criticism, and agency (all ultimately oriented toward self-revision), I suggest that a line be drawn between the "being positioned" orientation, with its relatively strong determining underpinning, and a more agentive notion of the subject as "positioning itself," in which the discursive resources or repertoires are not always and already given but, rather, are constructed. As a matter of fact, I have argued (Bamberg, 2000, in press) that "being positioned" and "positioning itself" are metaphoric constructs of two very different agent-world relationships: the former with a world-to-agent direction of fit, the latter with an agent-to-world direction of fit. Of course, one way to overcome this rift is to argue that both operate simultaneously and concurrently when subjects engage in talk-in-interaction and make sense of self and others in their stories. However, the interaction between these two direction-of-fit metaphors may be a lot more complex than is suggested by notions of relatively ready-made resources or repertoires that are employed in talk-in-interaction. Actually, if positions themselves are viewed as constructed in talk by lexical, grammatical, and interactive means (and not just "expressed" through them), we may be better off analyzing the process of how such positions come into existence and how they assist the construction of a sense of self and identities.

Taking this orientation, the (identity) question "Who am I?" no longer needs to originate from a notion of a unitary subject as the ground for its investigation. Rather, the agentive subject is the point of departure for its own empirical instantiation (Butler, 1995, p. 446); however, as a subject that is constantly seeking to legitimate itself, situated in language practices and interactively accomplished, where "world- and person-making take place simultaneously" (Bamberg, 2000, p. 763). Thus, the pluralization of identities "disrupts the social ontology of the subject itself . . . as the internal impossibility of the subject as a discrete and unitary kind of being" (Butler, 1995, p. 446) and, simultaneously, this pluralization opens a new empirical territory for where and how subjects come to existence, that is, sites where positions are actively and interactively taken (and explored) for the purpose of self and world construction.

The type of analysis undertaken here of how speakers actively and agentively position themselves in talk—in particular with and in their stories—starts from the assumption that the orderliness of story talk is situationally and interactively accomplished. However, since this orderliness is the result of what is being achieved, and therefore inherently oriented to, the actual analytic process begins with the story as original unit, and we work from the story outward toward its interactional embedding. In other words, although we assume that stories gain their structure and content from their situatedness in interactional settings, we begin by analyzing the means that contribute to their inherent order as discourse units (i.e., we scrutinize first how characters are designed in time and space inside story worlds, in order to get an initial hold of the "identity claims" of the teller (Positioning Analysis Level 1). Thereafter, we scrutinize the interactional means employed for getting the story accomplished (Positioning Analysis Level 2), and finally we will be better situated to see how speakers and audiences establish and display particular notions of selves (Positioning Analysis Level 3). The analysis of the first two positioning levels is intended to progressively lead to a differentiation of how speakers work up—often jointly—the construction of normative discourses. It is at this juncture that we come full circle in observing how subjects position themselves in relation to the discourses by which they are positioned. In other words, analyzing stories in interaction enables us to circumvent the aporia of two opposing subject theories—one in which the subject is determined by existing discourses, the other in which the subject is the ground from where discourses are constructed.

Story Data

The data I will use to demonstrate positioning analysis come from *Stand By Me* (1986), a film about four 12-year-old friends who set off into the woods in search of a missing boy's dead body. At some point, the four are sitting around the campfire and one of them entices Gordie, who is also the narrator in this film, to tell a story.[1] Gordie begins, and at the point where the plot is about to unravel, the camera angle switches into the "real" fictive world of the story, replacing the narrator's focalization with the story characters who speak "for themselves." In the transcription (see the Appendix), I have replaced this part with two narratives written by two students who were asked to fill in this piece of the story as part of an assignment in my narrative workshop.[2] The narratives (Story A and Story B) tell the sequence of events from Gordie's (the story's principal narrator's) perspective.

It is important to note that both the story and the campfire setting in which this story is shared are fictional and do not thematize any of the participants in the campfire conversation. While we have an author and a director behind the film, we also have three tellers (Gordie and two students), a narrator who focalizes the story world,[3] and a number of story characters (i.e., those who are acting their parts in the Davie Hogan story). So, what looks rather complex at first ultimately simplifies the analysis of positioning strategies: We can focus solely on the written texts of Story A and Story B for Positioning Analysis 1, and since both are available as written texts, we have no clues to any interactive orientations apart from the verbal material. Subsequently, Positioning Analysis 2 can focus on the situational embedding of what has become the written story, leading up to Positioning Analysis Level 3, where we will be in a more empirically grounded position to tackle the identity question (i.e., how the four interactants employ the story and display in this setting a sense of who they are).

Positioning Analysis Level 1: The Davie Hogan Story

As previously mentioned, I transformed the contents of the filmed part of the Davie Hogan story into a told (i.e., written) story, one that incorporated a narrator's focalization in its telling. Since the filmed part of the story did not reveal its focalization point, and as our interest in this first part of the analysis is in how the characters are ordered (focalized) in space and time,

I needed to transform it into a spoken or written equivalent. In order to be even better able to show the discursive construction of focalization strategies, I chose two contrasting strategies for Positioning Analysis Level 1. After his prenegotiation of the story's possible plot, and having secured his storytelling rights, Gordie launches in turn 17 into an elaborate preface to the story, which culminates in the revelation that the story is not only about a fat kid called Lardass and a pie-eating contest (as he had announced earlier on) but, and more important, about "the greatest revenge a kid ever had" (consisting of Davie causing himself to throw up and, in doing so, causing the watching crowd to throw up over one another—"a complete and total barf-o-rama"). At this point, we start our level 1 analysis with the written excerpt of Story A.[4]

Story A: Davie and the Others—Flat or Shallow Characters?

A–1   Davie went out to buy a bottle of castor oil and a dozen eggs. Then he went on to enroll for the pie-eating contest at the local summer fair. On his way he secretively swallowed these raw eggs and drank up the whole bottle of castor oil. At the fair he registered together with five other guys and entered the contest. In front of the watching crowd, he was introduced by the mayor, who presided over the contest as judge and empire.

Story A continues the strand laid out before by Gordie by use of his first name for the protagonist in the subject and sentence initial position and marking the event in the past tense: The narrator is on a first-name basis with Davie and sets up a past-temporal perspective. (This is in stark contrast to Story B, where the narrator continues with the third-person pronoun "he" in the present tense.) The use of the full name versus the use of the pronoun is typical for shifting to a new character in the subject position (which actually does not seem to apply in this situation, because the referent remains the same), or it signals a new topical unit, such as a paragraph. If this procedure is in operation, this new paragraph-like unit of Story A(A-1) can be argued to hold as long as there is no new fully named character introduced, that is, the topical unit consists of the subsequent eight clausal structures of Story A, all keeping the protagonist in the subject slot, mostly as pronoun, with the exception of one null form. The first two activities that Davie is reported to have engaged in are sequentially ordered: first he buys oil and eggs, then he enrolls in the contest. At this point, however, the narrator jumps back in time[5]: Swallowing the castor oil and egg reportedly took place before he got to the contest. It is mentioned further that he does this "secretively," that is, he tried not to be observed by anyone around. Then the focalization perspective resumes and catches up with the sequence of actions at the place of the contest: Davie registers and enters the contest. In "front of the watching crowd" and "he was introduced by the mayor" are linguistically configured by use of a passive construction, thereby keeping Davie in the subject slot and guaranteeing the thematic flow—and by use of a nominalization ("the watching crowd"), avoiding moving "the crowd" into the subject position of a semantic agentive role. Both constructions serve the function of keeping the mayor and the crowd, although both acting as agents, in background positions. The last clause of this topical unit, a subordinate relative clause, is the only clause in which another character (the mayor) occupies the subject slot (as presiding over the contest).

A–2   Davie, together with the other contestants started to gobble the pies down, with their hands on their back[s], and their mouths in the pies.

The next topical paragraph in Story A (A-2) is very short and only consists of one sentence, although it assembles at least four different pieces of simultaneous action and state-of-affairs descriptions: (1) Davie, with the other contestants, (2) started to gobble down some pies (the narrator's use of the inceptive aspect marker "started to" focalizes the continuous duration), (3) with his hands behind his back, and (4) his mouth in the pie. All the descriptions hold true for all the contestants, not just Davie.

A–3   Davie, who was clearly ahead of his contestants, and cheered by the crowd, stuffed himself with these pies like crazy and . . . .

The third and last topical unit of Story A (A-3) again starts out with a reference to the main character by first name, establishing a narrator's perspective that focalizes on all contestants in this contest, concluding and summing up that Davie was ahead and relating his standing in the contest to the crowd's reactive assessment: They were cheering him on. Again, the passive construction manages to keep "the crowd" out of subject position, preserving the thematic flow with Davie in the thematic subject position. He is reported as simultaneously continuing to eat pies, though from a narrator's perspective that attempts to highlight his eating behavior as doing something to himself, using the self-reflexive verb "stuffed himself."

In sum, the linguistic forms chosen to generate an action sequence leading up to the accomplishment of a revenge plot create a main character who is focalized as positioned within a pie-eating contest vis-à-vis four other contestants, a mayor, and a crowd. The actions are viewed as brought about by Davie himself, except for the mayor's introduction and presiding over the contest. However, the mayor's actions remain unfocused or, better, they are moved into the background, underscoring the importance of the main character's action orientation. Nevertheless, we as readers are never fully brought into the main character's decision-making process. Only on two occasions are we given a glimpse of what is on Davie Hogan's mind, and then only minimally: One time, we hear that Davie *wanted* to go unnoticed (the presentation of this event coincides with the only temporal break in the story, which comes in the form of a minimal flashback); the other time, the narrator gives us an evaluative glimpse of Davie's eating behavior. But, in general, we just follow the character the way the narrator moves him through the event sequence. It is clear that the narrator knows more but does not seem to be willing to reveal it. The narrative perspective laid out for the reader is straightforward; there is no moving around from narrator to one character to another character. The choice of the simple past assists in keeping us minimally involved. There is little tension, the character remains relatively simple. Davie clearly is the main character, but his role as protagonist (i.e., his relationship and position vis-à-vis the others as antagonists) is underdeveloped. Why this was a revenge and what was motivating Davie are not accentuated. We walk with him, but why we move along and why we should feel for and identify with him is not convincingly or fully laid out. It is a singular perspective or orientation that is laid out by the narrator. All this quite dramatically shifts when Story A is compared with Story B, the second and contrasting (written) excerpt we analyze as part of Positioning Analysis Level 1.

Story B: Lardass–the Round Protagonist

B–1   . . . he enters this pie-eating contest. They have it every year. It's like a parade, everyone is there, all the kids from school and all of their parents, The Women's Auxiliary and Benevolent Order of Antelopes, the school principal, everyone. And all the women in town had baked pies.

As already mentioned, the written account of the event sequence in Story B continues by use of the present-tense marker and by use of the personal pronoun, the way Gordie had started his turn in the film. This marks the transition from Gordie's oral performance to the narrator's written account as a continuation rather than a new unit (as in Story A). The first topical unit (B-1) starts with a clear shift into the background: The people who are involved in organizing the fair are moved into the center, however, not as actors but, rather, as having had a hand in setting the scene for something else to happen. The narrator clearly steps out into the time before the reported event sequence (note the use of the timeless present "have it every year" and the plu-perfect "had baked"), presenting a focalization perspective from where all this information is assembled as knowing, authoritative, and detailed.

B–2   So one by one the mayor calls the pie eaters up on stage and introduces them. The crowd cheers, especially for Bill Travis, who has won this contest 4 years in a row. But when the mayor calls up Lardass, they snicker and try to insult him. Bill Travis trips him and everyone laughs.

The next topical paragraph consists of seven clauses as information units, all seven shifting back and forth between different agents in the subject position: (1) the mayor, (2) the crowd, (3) Bill Travis, (4) the mayor, (5) the crowd, (6) Bill Travis, and (7) the crowd. Davie Hogan is mentioned three times, though only in the object position, and more relevant, by the name he was given by his tormentors, "Lardass." Thus, the narrator has crafted a constellation of characters in which Lardass is positioned as the undergoer and the others as perpetrators who are having fun. It should be noted that thus far the audience or readership does not have a clear grasp of either of the two parties as pro- or antagonistic; all we are confronted with is an antagonistic relationship between two character constellations, Lardass and all others.

B–3   But Lardass will be the only one laughing in the end, because—what the crowd didn't know—before the contest, he had made a plan: He drank a whole bottle of castor oil, and if that wasn't enough, he ate a half a dozen raw eggs. Lardass could hardly keep his lunch down.

However, this changes quite drastically with the shift to Lardass as the thematic subject in the next topical unit (B-3): "But" signals this contrast not only between who is laughing (in segment B-2) and in what the narrator foreshadows will happen at the end of the story but also, and more pointedly, between the two character constellations. It is at this point that the narrator moves into the future and then, immediately thereafter, into the recent past in order to back up and give evidence for the prophecy. The narrator's prophecy is constructed as if it is based on some intimate knowledge of Lardass's revenge scheme, and this knowledge has been held back thus far. As a consequence of the crowd's misdemeanor, it looks like the narrator is willing to step out of a more neutral space and take sides with the main character of the story. Revealing the sequence of events that happened before the pie-eating contest, the narrator steps back in time and elaborates. Note that this paragraph starts in the future tense, but it ends in the past tense: As a consequence of his having downed the castor oil and raw eggs, he "could hardly keep his lunch down." By this point, the narrator has moved in and become acquainted with Lardass, having intimate knowledge of how Lardass feels inside his body.

B–4   So when they placed that first pie in front of him, he was ready. Gobbling down one pie after another, he let the excitement build up waiting for the perfect moment. As he bit into his 5th pie, he couldn't hold back any longer. . . .

This paragraph (B-4) moves the focalization point back from where it was in the previous paragraph (B-3) to the here and now of the contest. This is where the narrator had left the scene in B-2 before flashing forth and back in B-3. It is noteworthy that this is accomplished in keeping the simple past tense, just as in B-3. In other words, the narrator does not shift back to using the present tense as it was used for focalizing the narrative here and now in B-2. The use of the shifter "so" signals this temporal or topical shift to the here and now of the contest. The anonymous "they" as the subject in the temporal subordinate clause (in "when they placed that first pie in front of him") only serves to provide the background against which "he" becomes even more prominent as the thematic subject, newly focalized in terms for his readiness for what is going to happen next. Again, the linguistic devices used clearly orient the listener or reader forward to some high point of the developing action sequence. Commenting on Lardass's intentions to "let the excitement build up" and wait "for the perfect moment" further signals the narrator's proximity to the main character and, at the same time, the narrator's distance from the crowd, which, at this point in the telling of the story, has been stripped of its original active and agentive characterization as Lardass's tormentor, receiving instead the brunt of the action sequence.

Reflecting on the overall structure of Story B, we see a very different character development from that in Story A. The narrator begins to present Lardass, but the choice of referential devices focalizes him from the perspective of his tormentors. Lardass, placed in the syntactic object position, is the object of mockery and others' insults, without exception. There is no clear index as to where the narrator stands, on Lardass's side or on the side of those who are just having a little fun (at the expense of others). The axis of good versus evil has not been demarcated yet. This, however, changes with paragraph B-3. Here, the narrator draws the line between the protagonist of the story and his antagonists. Shifting perspective away from the antagonists and promoting the internal viewpoint of the protagonist results in a narrator or reader alignment and positive identification with Davie

Hogan, alias Lardass. The secondary characters in this story have been provided with a face, although an ugly one, resulting in the recognition of Davie's actions as motivated by, and in service of, the revenge plot that was announced early on by Gordie in his preface to the story.

In Sum

Having worked in a somewhat detailed fashion through the written excerpts of Story A and Story B as two versions of the same sequence of events (the way they were presented in the filmed Davie Hogan story), it becomes apparent how characters are linguistically constructed and become positioned across time and space vis-à-vis one another as protagonists and antagonists, as flat or full, as good, bad, or ugly. Furthermore, and more important, the perspective from which these values are inserted into the story order can be from a more or less authoritative position of the (fictional) truth. Signs of a narrator's reliability and accountability are woven into the relationships that the characters are said to enter into in the story; the characters are invested with the perspective from which they are positioned.

At this point, it does not seem to make much of a difference whether the author has this perspective in mind (of what is good and what is evil or of whether the characters referred to *are*—or exist in "real" life as—round or flat), and invests the narrator with the authority to carry this into the narrator's focalization, or whether we assume that this perspective comes into existence (i.e., emerges) in the linguistic realization of the text. However, for purposes of doing positioning analysis, we deal with the wording and grammar of the text as our starting point. How the story is bound into a thematic unit and how it unfolds from the characters' point of view (here in both cases Davie's)[6] is a matter of its language (i.e., the discursive devices operating to bring into existence what we are calling the focalizer or narrator).

At the end of both Story A and Story B, the story writers hand back their narrators' focalizing powers to Gordie, who, back at the campfire, continues to tell the story.

| 17 (continued) | Gordie: | Slowly, a sound started to build in Lardass's stomach. A strange and scary sound like a log truck coming at you at a hundred miles an hour. Suddenly, Lardass opened his mouth. And before Bill Travis knew it, he was covered with five pies worth of used blueberries. The women in the audience screamed. Boss man Bob |

Cormier took one look at Bill Travis and barfed on
Principal Wiggins. Principal Wiggins barfed on the
lumberjack that was sitting next to him. Mayor Grundy
barfed on his wife's tits. But when the smell hit the
crowd, that's when Lardass's plan really started to
work. Girlfriends barfed on boyfriends. Kids barfed on
their parents. A fat lady barfed in her purse. The
Donnelly twins barfed on each other. And the Women's
Auxiliary barfed all over the Benevolent Order of
Antelopes. And Lardass just sat back and enjoyed what
he created. A complete and total barf-o-rama.

The rest of the narrative (turn 17 above) resembles a listing of the same
kind of events performed by a number of different characters on other characters, whereby it is relevant that the chain reaction originated in and
through Davie's action; he barfed first and so caused this chain of reactions.
The extent and level of detail in which Gordie paints these events displays
very nicely what Mechling (1980, p. 50) calls "a preoccupation with the
disgusting" that runs through campfire texts, particularly in the age bracket
of young teenagers.

Positioning Analysis Level 2: Storytelling as Co-Construction

Having analyzed in some more detail the linguistic means that contribute to
the emergence of a narrator's perspective or orientation (actually, in this
case, two different orientations), we will turn next to the analysis of the
interactional setting of the four boys around the campfire, within which this
particular orientation was made possible. At this point, we will work
through the sequence of turns first as they result in the story told (turns
1–17) and then as the story is picked up and renegotiated after it has been
accomplished (turns 18–33).

"Hey Gordoe, why don't you tell us a story?" (turns 1–17)

The opening scene finds four 12- to 13-year-olds sitting around a campfire, smoking cigarettes. Turns 1 and 2, by Vern and Teddy, respectively,

are evaluation tokens that employ an adult scenario, in which fathers typically relax by smoking after having finished their meal. The act of cherishing a smoke after meals is a token that invokes the image that this is a standard ritual, something they engage in at home with other (male?) adults. Chris's laughter in turn 3 can be interpreted as challenging this attempt at positioning themselves as habitual smokers. This is shown in Teddy's response—"What did I say?"—which indexes that he would like a clarification of Chris's challenge.

1	Vern:	Nothing like a smoke after a meal.
2	Teddy:	Yeah. I cherish these moments.
3	Chris:	(laugh)
4	Teddy:	What? What did I say?
5	Chris:	Hey, Gordoe, why don't you tell us a story?
6	Gordie:	I - I don't know.
7	Chris:	Oh come on.
8	Vern:	Yeah, come on, Gordoe. But not one of your horror stories, okay? I don't wanna hear no horror stories. I'm not up for that, man.
9	Teddy:	Why don't you tell us one about Sergeant Stone and his battling leathernecks?

Instead of answering Teddy's question and explicating his own position vis-à-vis smoking and being adult, Chris changes the topic by inciting Gordie to tell a story, which is followed by Gordie's hesitation to engage in this activity. Chris, Teddy, and Vern (turns 7–9) all seem to interpret this hesitation as an invitation for further pressing, whereupon Gordie takes the floor with what can be seen as a story opening (turn 10): He picks up "story" as the referent that has been floated about in the last five turns and elaborates what his story is going to be about. He states that the main character is a "fat kid that nobody likes" and that the story is going to be about "this pie-eating contest."

Gordie's vouching for his kind of story is a response to the suggestions of Vern (turn 8) and Teddy (turn 9) regarding a potential story topic—a horror and a war or battle story, respectively. In contrast to these options, Gordie's suggestion may come across as very mundane and potentially boring. Vern's bid for Gordie to elaborate on some specifics of the given character description (turn 11) challenges Gordie's bid for a story, but it is secured by Chris's uptake (turn 12). Gordie's elaboration of the character description is overridden again by Vern (turn 14), who seems to orient to his own story, only to be cut off by Chris, this time abruptly ("Shut up, Vern"). Consequently, Vern yields to Gordie's right to continue his story and hands over the floor to Gordie—"it's a swell story" (turn 16).

10	Gordie:	Well the one I've been thinking about is kind of different. It's about this pie-eating contest. And the main guy of the story is this fat kid that nobody likes named Davie Hogan.
11	Vern:	Like Charlie Hogan's brother. If he had one.
12	Chris:	Good Vern. Go on, Gordie.
13	Gordie:	Well, this kid is our age, but he's fat, real fat. He weighs close to 180. But you know it's not his fault, it's his glands.
14	Vern:	Oh yeah, my cousin's like that, sincerely. She weighs over 300 pounds. Supposed to be hyboid gland or something. Well, I don't know about any hyboid glands, but what a blimp. No shit. She looks like a Thanksgiving turkey. And, you know, this one time—
15	Chris:	Shut up, Vern.
16	Vern:	Yeah, yeah, right. Go on, Gordie, it's a swell story.
17	Gordie:	Well, all the kids instead of calling him Davie, they call him Lardass. Lardass Hogan. Even his little brother and sister call him Lardass. A-at school they put a sticker on his back that says "wide load," and they rank him out and beat him up whenever they get a chance. But one day he gets an idea. The greatest revenge idea a kid ever had.

In sum, in the first 16 turns, we catch a glimpse of the local procedures that are called into place to occasion a story: Two of the boys attempt to draw up some adult space, placing themselves as experienced smokers. They are challenged by one of their peers who, instead of turning this into the object of controversy, incites the fourth participant to share a story. After some initial negotiation with regard to what the story should be about, and after two brief challenges to his storytelling rights, Gordie comes out as the teller and works up a preface to his story. Up to this point, the audience has received some details of a description of the main character of the story and is informed that the upcoming story is about a pie-eating contest. In turn 17, Gordie continues to draw out the character as a kid who is like them but different: Davie Hogan is a defenseless outcast, who is not at fault but is ranked out and beaten up at every possible occasion by the young and old in his community. At the end of this preface, the teller foreshadows an important frame for the plot to come, namely, not only that the sequence of events will follow a sequence typical for a pie-eating contest (where competitors enroll then compete in a usually gross eating contest, resulting in winners and losers) but also that the revenge plot (and it promises to be an exciting revenge) is over-arching the pie-eating plot. At this point, the camera angle changes, and the campfire scenario, with Gordie as the teller and animator of the characters in the story, is transformed into the story world, in which the characters are not animated any longer by a narrator but, rather, seem to animate themselves.

"It's a good story, Gordie, I just didn't like the ending" (turns 18–29)

In turns 18 to 20, all three story recipients express their appreciation for the story. However, in turn 21, Teddy challenges an important component of the story—its ending. If the revenge plot was central to Gordie's story, the por-trayal of the main character at the end resembles a perfect ending: Davie enjoys his accomplishments. In addition, the fact that Davie was portrayed as not wanting to win the contest but, rather, as striving for revenge gives the revenge plot absolute priority over the contest plot. Thus, within the revenge plot, Davie's enrolling and participating in the contest was on the pretext of turn-ing the contest into a "barf-o-rama," that is, to embarrass and humiliate those who had been persistently embarrassing and humiliating him.

18	Chris, Teddy, Vern:	Yeah!
19	Chris:	Now that was the best, just the best.
20	Vern:	Yeah.
21	Teddy:	Then what happened?
22	Gordie:	What do you mean?
23	Teddy:	I mean, what happened?
24	Gordie:	What do you mean what happened, that's the end.
25	Teddy:	How can that be the end, what kind of an ending is that? What happened to Lardass?
26	Gordie:	I don't know. Maybe he went home and celebrated with a couple of cheeseburgers.
27	Teddy:	Geez. That ending sucks. Why don't you make it so that—so that Lardass goes home, an' he shoots his father. An' he runs away. An'- an' he joins the Texas Rangers. How about that?
28	Gordie:	I - I don't know.
29	Teddy:	Something good like that.

Teddy, in turn 25, requests an ending in which we hear more about Lardass, that is, what happened after the contest. He had had his revenge, but what then? Lardass couldn't just go back home and continue life as usual. Although Lardass comes out in Gordie's version of the story as repositioned, this doesn't seem to be enough for Teddy. Teddy pushes for a broader or more radical reposition: He wants Lardass to go home but not to continue as usual. He wants him to shoot his father, then run away to join the Texas Rangers. But why did Teddy suggest that Lardass kill his father and run away from home to join the Texas Rangers?

There are two possible answers, one that seeks (and constructs) some form of coherence between Teddy's turns, his life, and his subjectivity, and a second that simply declares him as crazy or a "loony" (as he was called by others in the film). In an attempt to follow the first option, the killing of Lardass's father would only make sense if his father had been to blame for the misery that he is suffering (i.e., if his father had been the reason for all the teasing, ranking out, and beating that Lardass suffered)—as Teddy's father, who once held Teddy's ear to a lit stove and later was institutionalized, could potentially be held responsible for the teasing Teddy had suffered. Only from this focalization point is the revenge scheme potentially incomplete, requiring to be followed through with additional actions. Although winning the contest repositioned Lardass for the moment (note that the crowd dropped their all-time favorite, Bill Travis, and cheered for Lardass), Gordie and Teddy agree that this would not suffice to reposition him in the story world. Thus the radical solution Teddy asks for—killing the real tormentor and seeking a new life by joining the Texas Rangers, where he is totally repositioned—appears consequent and coherent.

However, Gordie, the creator of Lardass, doesn't want to follow this route. He wants Lardass to return home, eat a couple of cheeseburgers, and celebrate his triumph. It is interesting here that Gordie not only positions Lardass back where he was before but also moves him into a slot as a big eater, a position he previously had carefully circumnavigated: "it's not his fault [that he's fat], it's his glands" (turn 13).

In sum, then, Teddy's challenge to the principal narrator's version represents an attempt to position the characters in the story world so that Lardass as the main character could develop in his alternative plot as a new character—someone who had left his (miserable) life behind and had advanced through his own actions into a newly ordered life world. And it makes sense, from this perspective, to qualify Gordie's story as a "good story" but express dissatisfaction with its ending.

"Did Lardass have to pay to get into the contest?" (turns 30–33)

Vern follows up on the exchange between Teddy and Gordie and, in contrast to Teddy, he aligns himself with Gordie by giving preference to the original ending.

30	Vern:	I like the ending. The barfing was really good. But there is one thing I didn't understand. Did Lardass have to pay to get into the contest?
31	Gordie:	No, Vern, they just let him in.
32	Vern:	Oh! Oh great. Great story.
33	Teddy:	Yeah, it's a good story, Gordie, I just didn't like the ending.

However, when he makes explicit his reasons (because "the barfing was really good"), Vern does not focus on the revenge theme but, rather, picks a detail that was not one of the aboutness choices laid out in Gordie's preface to the story. He picks a new element, one that seems to appear relevant to him personally and individually. Obviously, it is possible to like a story or a story's ending because of details that are not central to everyone within one's own community or culture. Other details the story was said to be about, as offered by the narrator in his preface, were the story's central character, Davie Hogan, and the blueberry pie-eating contest. However, Vern chooses to make the barfing the central focus of his evaluative stance. Vern's focus on what was disgusting, which was not necessarily most central to the narrator's perspective, matches up nicely with his preoccupation with the concrete details of extreme body size when Gordie was orienting the boys to the story's topic during the preface negotiations (Vern's turns 11 and 14).

In Sum

In spite of the fact that there appear to be competing bids en route to the final choice of the principal teller and the aboutness of the story, all four settle on Gordie as the storyteller and on his right to determine what the story is about. The joint appreciation they show after Gordie completes *his* story, in the form of laughter in turn 18, and in turns 19 and 20 as evaluation tokens by Chris and Vern, indexes a high degree of affiliation with the main character as well as the narrator's focalization point, from which the sequence of events came across as ordered.

However, as the subsequent negotiation over the story's ending signals, there is more going on: In spite of the fact that I have inserted two written stories for comparative purposes, and that there is only one "text" of the Davie Hogan story—that presented by Gordie as the principal narrator and displayed in the film sequence from the angle of the characters, a closer look at the negotiation of the four interactants before and after the storytelling reveals that we are dealing with (at least) three different versions: Two of the versions are typical revenge stories, one is challenged by Teddy as incomplete and defended by Gordie as complete, a second is promoted by Teddy as more complete but is not acceptable to Gordie, and a third is complete but belongs more to the genre of barfing stories, with revenge as a subordinate component. From the way we hear Chris inciting Gordie to claim and subsequently maintain the floor for his story, and then not making explicit which elements of Gordie's story stand out for him personally or individually, we can conclude that he is principally aligned with Gordie in favor of Gordie's version.

Thus, what is revealed by a closer look at how the particular story is challenged and secured in the conversational bids that are surrounding it (Positioning Analysis Level 2) may be extremely relevant for what the particular story actually means to the teller and his audience. The interactional accomplishment of identity work of the four boys seems to function as the embedding and ground for the construction of the story and its personal meanings—not only for the person who is elevated into the teller role but for all the participants involved in this elevation in the true sense of what it means to *co-construct*.

Positioning Analysis Level 3: Who Are *We*?

Pulling together what we have thus far, and irrespective of whether we take the round or the flat version of Davie's character development, Gordie, the teller of the Davie Hogan story, constructed a narrator's focalization through which Davie became positioned as an adolescent male outcast, who was harassed by old and young alike and contrived to pay them back in the form of a grand "barf-o-rama." The adults, who at the beginning of the story are positioned as agentive characters hostile to Davie, are repositioned at the end of the story as incompetent laughingstocks, stooped by a 12-year-old. Davie, the representative of a childhood full of heartbreak and hostility, of growing up as an outcast and unloved, is empowered through the narrator's lens with a repositioned identity.

Taking this to be the central theme brought into focus by Gordie's narrative orientation, all four participants in the campfire narrative event can be said to be drawn into the same basic alignment with this orientation, creating a sense of an elevated self that undermines adult authority and struggles to assert its independence.

While the barfing theme is only a subtheme of the revenge plot of the story, it nevertheless contributes significantly to the general understanding of the story (i.e., for its tellability and its appreciation by boys). Smoking cigarettes and indulging in disgusting topics are manly campfire activities, partly because they help construct maleness as unruly and uncivilized but also assist in presenting adolescent selves as rebellious and independent. Thus, the four boys, in their alignment with the story content and in their activities with each other, draw up positions that align them with discourse positions that are out there, on the shelf, used and marketed in genres of kids' and adolescent films.

While all four boys position themselves and each other in relation to the story, and enter into a bond with one another around themes of adolescent independence and manly unruliness, they also draw up their individual territories that help to differentiate between their own identities: Gordie as the one who sensitizes the others to themes of harassment and injustice; Chris as the one who leads them through interactive struggles; Teddy as the one who strives hard for a strong sense of independence, flirting with disaster and borderline disturbed; and Vern as the one who is the scaredy-cat, obsessed with details and insignificant trivialities. In sum, four male adolescent identities have emerged in front of the viewers who followed this 5-minute film clip. And although it is possible to argue that they all brought these identities with them to this specific campfire storytelling encounter, it is clear that the boys created the sense of how they wanted to come across to each other (and to us as overviewing audience) as empirical subjects in their (storytelling) actions. In their interactions they positioned themselves vis-à-vis the characters in the story and vis-à-vis one another and, in doing exactly that, they formed a sense of who they are.

Narratives and Positioning Analysis

The situated story analyzed in this chapter is by no means a spontaneous, everyday segment of interaction. The film clip in which this fictive story is shared by a few 12- and 13-year-olds was created in the service of the nostalgic characterizations of four film characters and their friendship and coming of age. Consequently, the analysis of adolescent and male identity formation is unsuitable to be generalized in these directions. The use of a film clip, nevertheless, also has advantages. First of all, the clip is commonly available and can be used to develop a transcript from visual material (see the first endnote to this chapter). Second, it nicely exemplifies how stories and story genres are open to negotiations in actual storytelling situations. Third, it removes narrative analysis from the realm of personal stories and self-thematizations that, unfortunately, have become the privileged site for identity analysis, and it opens up the territory of narrative analysis to third-person thematizations and generalized accounts. And last, but not least, it attempts to make narrative analysis open to deeper empirical scrutiny by moving traditional narrative analysis and conversation-analytic techniques closer together.

To summarize, positioning analysis starts from the assumption that narratives are situated actions, that is, they are co-constructed in interactive settings, and their main function is to reveal how what is said—and behind this the "I" and performer of the story—ought to be understood. In other words, narratives, whether they are primarily about the self of the speaker or not at all, are always indexical with regard to the speaker's subjectivity. Consequently, narratives have to be analyzed as (performed) situated actions that are interactively accomplished, and not transparent windows into speakers' minds, their subjectivities, or their lived experience. From this vantage point, it simply is not enough to analyze narratives as units of analysis for their structure and content, though it is a good starting point.

Positioning analysis is designed as an empirically grounded analysis of how subjects construct themselves by analyzing the positions that are actively and agentively taken in their narratives vis-à-vis normative discourses. Thus, positioning analysis avoids the view of subjects as simply acting out their preestablished selves and identities. It also escapes from viewing selves and identities as taken off the shelf of preexisting normative discourses. Rather, subjects are argued to agentively construct their situated positions, and in this process both normative discourses as well as their individual sense of self are called into existence. Again, this is not meant to imply the negation of the existence of normative discourses outside of subjects and their interactions; and neither is it meant to imply that subjects do not act on previous experiences or practices and always have to start from scratch in their self and identity formation processes. However, in order to empirically analyze narratives and what they mean to those who are in the process of creating them, it seems to be highly advantageous to bracket assertions encouraged by speculations with regard to both what we think the world is that impinges on the subject and his/her sense-making activities, or what we think the subject is, as someone who is bringing a stock of individual uniqueness to narrative tellings and world making.

Appendix

Transcript of the Davie Hogan Story

1	Vern:	Nothing like a smoke after a meal.
2	Teddy:	Yeah. I cherish these moments.
3	Chris:	(laugh)
4	Teddy:	What? What did I say?
5	Chris:	Hey, Gordoe, why don't you tell us a story?
6	Gordie:	I - I don't know.
7	Chris:	Oh come on.
8	Vern:	Yeah, come on, Gordoe. But not one of your horror stories, okay? I don't wanna hear no horror stories. I'm not up for that, man.
9	Teddy:	Why don't you tell us one about Sergeant Stone and his battling leathernecks?
10	Gordie:	Well the one I've been thinking about is kind of different. It's about this pie-eating contest. And the main guy of the story is this fat kid that nobody likes named Davie Hogan.
11	Vern:	Like Charlie Hogan's brother. If he had one.
12	Chris:	Good Vern. Go on, Gordie.
13	Gordie:	Well, this kid is our age, but he's fat, real fat. He weighs close to 180. But you know it's not his fault, it's his glands.
14	Vern:	Oh yeah, my cousin's like that, sincerely. She weighs over 300 pounds. Supposed to be hyboid gland or something. Well, I don't know about any hyboid glands, but what a blimp. No shit. She looks like a Thanksgiving turkey. And, you know, this one time—
15	Chris:	Shut up, Vern.
16	Vern:	Yeah, yeah, right. Go on, Gordie, it's a swell story.
17	Gordie:	Well, all the kids instead of calling him Davie, they call him Lardass. Lardass Hogan. Even his little brother and sister call him Lardass. A-at school they put a sticker on his back that says "wide load," and they rank him out and beat him up whenever they get a chance. But one day he gets an idea. The greatest revenge idea a kid ever had.

STORY A		STORY B
A-1	Davie went out to buy a bottle of castor oil and a dozen eggs. Then he went on to enroll for the pie-eating contest at the local summer fair. On his way	B-1	. . . he enters this pie-eating contest. They have it every year. It's like a parade, everyone is there, all the kids from school and all of their parents, The Women's

he secretively swallowed these raw eggs and drank up the whole bottle of castor oil. At the fair he registered together with five other guys and entered the contest. In front of the watching crowd, he was introduced by the mayor, who presided over the contest as judge and empire.

A-2   Davie, together with the other contestants started to gobble the pies down, with their hands on their back, and their mouths in the pies.

A-3   Davie, who was clearly ahead of his contestants, and cheered by the crowd, stuffed himself with these pies like crazy and. . . .

Auxiliary and Benevolent Order of Antelopes, the school principal, everyone. And all the women in town had baked pies.

B-2   So one by one the mayor calls the pie eaters up on stage and introduces them. The crowd cheers, especially for Bill Travis, who has won this contest 4 years in a row. But when the mayor calls up Lardass, they snicker and try to insult him. Bill Travis trips him and everyone laughs.

B-3   But Lardass will be the only one laughing in the end, because—what the crowd didn't know—before the contest, he had made a plan: He drank a whole bottle of castor oil, and if that wasn't enough, he ate a half a dozen raw eggs. Lardass could hardly keep his lunch down.

B-4   So when they placed that first pie in front of him, he was ready. Gobbling down one pie after another, he let the excitement build up waiting for the perfect moment. As he bit into his 5th pie, he couldn't hold back any longer. . . .

17
(continued)

Slowly, a sound started to build in Lardass's stomach. A strange and scary sound like a log truck coming at you at a hundred miles an hour. Suddenly, Lardass opened his mouth. And before Bill Travis knew it he was covered with five pies worth of used blueberries. The women in the audience screamed. Boss man Bob Cormier took one look at Bill Travis and barfed on Principal Wiggins. Principal Wiggins barfed on the lumberjack that was sitting next to him. Mayor Grundy barfed on his wife's tits. But when the smell hit the crowd, that's when Lardass' plan really started to work. Girlfriends barfed on boyfriends. Kids barfed on their parents. A fat lady barfed in her purse. The Donnelly twins barfed on each other. And the Women's Auxiliary barfed all over the Benevolent Order of Antelopes. And Lardass just sat back and enjoyed what he created. A complete and total barf-o-rama.

18	Chris, Teddy, Vern:	Yeah!
19	Chris:	Now that was the best, just the best.
20	Vern:	Yeah.
21	Teddy:	Then what happened?
22	Gordie:	What do you mean?
23	Teddy:	I mean, what happened?
24	Gordie:	What do you mean what happened, that's the end.
25	Teddy:	How can that be the end, what kind of an ending is that? What happened to Lardass?
26	Gordie:	I don't know. Maybe he went home and celebrated with a couple of cheeseburgers.
27	Teddy:	Geez. That ending sucks. Why don't you make it so that—so that Lardass goes home, an' he shoots his father. An' he runs away. An'- an' he joins the Texas Rangers. How about that?
28	Gordie:	I - I don't know.
29	Teddy:	Something good like that.
30	Vern:	I like the ending. The barfing was really good. But there is one thing I didn't understand. Did Lardass have to pay to get into the contest?
31	Gordie:	No, Vern, they just let him in.
32	Vern:	Oh! Oh great. Great story.
33	Teddy:	Yeah, it's a good story, Gordie, I just didn't like the ending.

Notes

1. The film clip can be viewed @ http://www.clarku.edu/~mbamberg/Stand_by_Me.htm

2. As an assignment in the narrative workshop I am teaching, the participants were given the transcript of the interactions among the four boys around the campfire that is reproduced in the appendix to this chapter (with turn 1 to turn 17 followed by a blank in the middle and then the continuation of turn 17 to turn 33). Then, after watching the whole clip, they were asked to tell (in writing, and from Gordie's perspective) what happened between turn 17 and the continuation of turn 17, that is, in the filmed sequence of events in which Davie Hogan enacted the plot during the pie-eating contest.

3. I am following Toolan (2001) and use the terms "narrator," "focalization," and "orientation" interchangeably.

4. The two written texts were segmented into units resembling paragraph structures in order to assist the sequential procedure of the analysis. The Appendix displays the structure of the segments in the form of a concordance so that the reader can easily compare and contrast how the two narrator orientations have been put together.

5. Another way to interpret the order of events would be that the narrator actually does not let Davie reach the contest scene. Rather, the narrator takes a somewhat more internal focalization point: "He went on to enroll" only means that Davie intends to go to the pie-eating contest, so that his food consumption actually develops subsequent to this intention. Whichever way we decide, it is the choice of linguistic devices that forces us to relate what is presented in the clauses in one or the other way. Note that the narrator had a myriad of other possibilities but happened to choose what we have in the present text.

6. It is noteworthy that the story does not need to be told from a particular character's point of view. It would have been perfectly possible to present it from a number of characters' points of view, shifting back and forth, or from everybody's point of view—which ultimately is nobody's. In that case, however, it might have been more difficult to bring out the particularities of the revenge theme.

References

Bamberg, M. (2000). Critical personalism, language, and development. *Theory & Psychology, 10,* 749–767.

Bamberg, M. (in press). I know it may sound mean to say this, but we couldn't really care less about her anyway. Form and functions of "slut-bashing" in male identity constructions in 15-year-olds. *Human Development.*

Butler, J. (1990). Performative acts and gender constitution: An essay in phenomenology and feminist theory. In S-E. Case (Ed.), *Performing feminisms: Feminist critical theory and theatre* (pp. 270–282). Baltimore, MD: Johns Hopkins University Press.

Butler, J. (1995). Collected and fractured: Responses to Identities. In K. A. Appiah & H. L. Gates (Eds.), *Identities* (pp. 439–447). Chicago: University of Chicago Press.

Davies, B., & Harré, R. (1990). Positioning: The social construction of selves. *Journal for the Theory of Social Behaviour, 20,* 43–63.

Harré, R., & van Langenhove, L. (1999). Introducing positioning theory. In R. Harré & L. van Langenhove (Eds.), *Positioning theory: Moral contexts of intentional action* (pp. 14–31). Oxford, UK: Basil Blackwell.

Hollway, W. (1984). Gender difference and the production of subjectivity. In J. Henriques, W. Hollway, C. Urwin, C. Venn, & V. Walkerdine (Eds.), *Changing the subject: Psychology, social regulation and subjectivity* (pp. 227–263). London: Methuen.

Mechling, J. (1980). The magic of the boy scout campfire. *Journal of American Folklore, 93,* 35–56.

Evans, B., Gideon, R., & Scheinman, A. (Producers), & Reiner, R. (Director). (1986). *Stand By Me* [Motion picture]. United States: Columbia Pictures.

Toolan, M. J. (2001). *Narrative: A critical linguistic introduction.* (2nd ed.). London: Routledge.

2.4

Dilemmas of Storytelling and Identity

Steven Stanley and Michael Billig

The present chapter presents an approach to the study of narrative that is based in the perspective of discursive psychology. Over the past 15 years, discursive psychology has established a distinctive theoretical position, as well as a wide body of empirical research that has developed methodologies from conversation analysis, discourse analysis, and rhetoric. The discursive position follows the later philosophy of Wittgenstein by claiming psychologists often have been seeking the topics of psychology in the wrong place. Instead of assuming that memories, beliefs, and so on are internal mental structures, psychologists should be examining how in ordinary talk, people use terms such as "memory" and "belief" and other lay psychological language (for statements of the discursive position and its methodology, see, for instance, Antaki, 1994; Billig, 1991, 1996; Edwards & Potter, 1992; Harré & Gillett, 1994; Potter, 1996; Potter & Wetherell, 1987; Wetherell, Taylor, & Yates, 2001). Accordingly, the detailed analysis of talk, especially talk involving what Wittgenstein called "psychological language" has been an important empirical focus of discursive psychology.

There are broad similarities between discursive psychology and theories of social construction in the sense that narration is understood as a "discursive resource" (Gergen, 1994, p. 207). Discursive psychologists have shown that when people tell stories they are performing social actions within particular social contexts. Edwards (1997) points out that the "analysis of narratives in the human and social sciences has mostly ignored the interactional business that people might be doing in telling them" (p. 265). The study of discourse has shown that narrative versions are "highly patterned in their detail for the performance of action" (Potter, 1996, p. 174). A narrative analysis based on the perspective of discursive psychology will therefore be attentive to "the specifics of actual stories and tellings" (Edwards, 1997, p. 188). To do this, it is important to acknowledge the social context of storytelling, including both the immediate social context and, in certain cases, the broader ideological context.

The research to be reported concerns the broad issue of "identity." Identity claims can be part of narrative stories, for in making claims about the self speakers will often tell stories. The discursive position warns against treating identity as an internal state. Tajfel (1981) claims that identities depend on the use of categories, for a social identity is a form of categorization. Discursive psychologists take this point further by emphasizing that if categories are part of language, then identities should be considered as discursive constructs. That means that the topic of identity should be studied by examining what people are doing when they make claims about their own and others' identity.

It has been argued that common sense contains contrary ideological values. These values are frequently brought into argumentative conflict with each other, constituting what can be termed as "ideological dilemmas" (Billig et al., 1988). In an ideological dilemma, two sets of commonly shared values will appear to be in rhetorical conflict. However, speakers will try to manage both sets rather than siding with one or the other. For instance, politicians will deplore poverty, expressing sympathy with the poor, while at the same time criticising the poor for their failures (Edelman, 1977). In the course of talk, speakers might show flexibility, emphasizing first one side and then another of such dilemmas, depending on the flow of the conversation. If one side is emphasized, then other speakers might make countercriticisms using the opposing value, and vice versa (see Billig, 1992). The point about such dilemmas is that they are not resolvable, because they are framed within a wider, contradictory ideology. When narrating past events, people can be attempting to negotiate such dilemmas of ideology.

The talk and the telling of stories always takes place in specific rhetorical contexts. In consequence, the wider themes of ideology are revealed not just in the small words of talk but also in the complexity of interactional business that is being conducted. This is why the analyst needs to maintain a double focus: The wider processes of ideology have to be caught within the observable and hearable detail of talk and text.

Dilemmas of Doctoral Education

The narrative analysis to be reported is taken from a research project concerning the dilemmas of social science doctoral education. In an early discourse study, Edwards and Mercer (1987; see also Billig et al., 1988, Chapter 4) analyzed the activities of teachers working according to a progressive or child-centered model of teaching.[1] One of the central tenets of this model is that pupils are expected to "learn for themselves" by making independent educational discoveries. The teacher is merely to act as a facilitator, assisting pupils on their "voyage of discovery." In this respect, the progressive classroom appears to be democratic or egalitarian in nature. However, Edwards and Mercer show that, in practice, the progressive teachers who took part in their study did not act according to "democratic" principles alone. Rather, they attempted to negotiate a balance between the contrary themes of "democracy" and "authoritarianism." Thus, the ideology of progressive teaching was found to be dilemmatic, being composed of contrary themes and demands. The progressive teachers negotiated these themes as they taught and as they told stories about their teaching in conversational interviews.

In the United States, Tracy and her graduate student colleagues have investigated intellectual discussion seminars involving academic faculty members and graduate students (see Tracy, 1997). In particular, they have analyzed how discussion participants balance the themes of "equality" and "expertise" when they do their presentations (Tracy & Carjuzáa, 1993; Tracy & Muller, 1994). The authors argue that while discussants are expected to evaluate ideas according to their own merits, the institutional inequality of the university and the differing status positions of "graduate student" and "faculty member," which connote differences in expertise and experience, mean that it is neither possible nor desirable to treat everyone's ideas equally.

From the perspective of sociological ambivalence, the role of the doctoral postgraduate can be seen to be ambivalent, being composed of conflicting and contradictory tensions (Merton & Barber, 1976). For example, Becher, Henkel, and Kogan (1994) ask whether doctoral postgraduates are students or academic members of staff. This ambivalent status of the doctoral postgraduate becomes especially apparent when we come to consider the supervisory relationship. British doctoral students in the social sciences are generally supervised by one or more academic members of staff (Hockey, 1994; Lindén, 1999). In being "supervised," doctoral postgraduates appear to resemble subordinate students rather than academic faculty members. While in many ways doctoral postgraduates are dependent on their supervisors (Parry, Atkinson, & Delamont, 1997), at the same time, they are also expected to be autonomous scholars or researchers (Austin, 2002; Henschen, 1993; Johnson, Lee, & Green, 2000; Smith, 2000). This "doctoral dilemma" becomes ideological within the context of the supervisory relationship because it is a relationship of power, characterised by inequality between the participants (Hewson, 1999; Stina Lyon, 1995). Within discursive psychology, however, any claims about ambivalence and dilemmas are to be instantiated in the detailed analysis of doctoral student discourse. Here the emphasis will be on a single case study taken from this wider project.

Narrative Analysis of a Single Case

This analysis concerns an interview sequence taken from a corpus of "semi-structured" or "conversational" interviews with doctoral students at universities in the North West and East Midlands of the United Kingdom. The first author of this chapter, Steven Stanley, carried out 15 in-depth discussions with 11 female and 4 male doctoral students in various social science and psychology departments. The respondents were asked about their experiences of doing doctoral work, whether they considered themselves to be academics, their views on academia, and so on. Audio recordings of the interactions were transcribed using a simplified and modified version of the notation used for conversation analysis (see the Appendix). The particular extract presented is taken from an interview with "Hanako." Hanako was a Japanese mature student of psychology in the final year of her doctoral study. The sequence was chosen because Hanako tells a story about attempting to publish a book chapter with her supervisor, "Pete." Pseudonyms have been used for the student and her supervisor but not for the interviewer.

Extract

1	Steven	**have you published anything from the thesis?**
2		(0.7)
3	Hanako	mmmmmmm no- not yet

4	Steven	**Right**
5	Hanako	I've written some (.) draft chapter (.) (mm) of erm (0.6) a book
6		chapter that my supervisor and I decided to do (mm) but (.) ahh (.)
7		draft came back with comments (.) and we need to woHHrk on (.)
8		a lot of things (a- riHHght) so (.) I decided to focus on my thesis
9		first (.) (yes) and then (.) after (1.0) the (0.7) thesis then (0.6)
10		I can (0.7) take the chapter (.) and then in- (1.5) (mm) ahm
11		made into a (0.6) journal aHHrticle hopefully
12	Steven	**right (0.9) how did that draft (.) chapter come about?**
13		(0.6)
14	Hanako	MMMMM (2.4) THE DRAFT CHAPTER (0.7) of the book (.)
15		(mmm) (0.8) aahhm (2.5) I (.) I DID IT (1.0) with the momentum
16		of the conference (.) I did in Australia this this past summer (.)
17		(right) and er a way of finishing the conference (.) (mm) paper
18		(mm) (0.9) and also I was planning to do that- (.) ahh (.) do a
19		chapter (.) based on the conference paper so (m) it wa- a- e-
20		(0.6) FOR ME IT'S ALWAYS (1.0) related (.) like I use
21		something (.) that I did (.) as a small project (yes) and then (.)
22		making it bigger and deeper (.) in terms of (ye-) analysis (yes)
23		is always (.) practical way of getting myself motivated (.) (yeah)
24		and seeing the realistic (.) goal (.) (yeah) so (0.6) from that (0.6)
25		conference paper chapter ((smiley voice)) (mm) and then (.)
26		Pete suggested that it- we should do a book chapter on
27		somebody's ahm edit- edited (.) book (yes) so I just use (.) the
28		Australia paperHH (uhuhm yHHeah) and get some more (0.6)
29		ahm (mm) (0.9) ahm (0.8) adjustment (mm) to the orientation
30		to the book (right) (.) and Pete put some touch ups (.) ahm to
31		make it (.) work (mm) and he said 'okayt- you don't have to
32		do much just do this and this and this' and then I did what he
33		suggested to do ((smiley voice)) (yes) and he just submitted it
34		and then we received commen- a lot of comments (.) ahh saying
35		(1.0) BASICALLY I FEEL HHHUH THEY DIDN'T
36		UNDERSTAND THIS (.) cognitive (.) perspective (right)
37		(.) the kind of analytical take (.) (yes) that (0.6) we had
38		(0.6)
39	Steven	**so you submitted it TWICE then (.) is that right?**
40		(.)
41	Hanako	ahm (1.4) I- we submitted it once and then we received the
42		comments (oh) yah (I see)

In discursive psychology, if a story is told within the context of an interview, then it is important to acknowledge this social context by transcribing and analyzing what the interviewer says along with what the interviewee says (see, e.g., Widdicombe & Wooffitt, 1995). To understand what Hanako is doing when she tells the first story of the draft chapter (line 5 onwards), we need to look back to see what happened in the preceding lines. By asking the question "have you published anything from the thesis?" (line 1), Steven establishes a subtle frame of accountability. He implies that Hanako might have, or should have, published something from her thesis. When Hanako answers with "mmmmmmm no- not yet" (line 3), she shows her awareness of this social accountability. While she might not have published anything from it "yet," she implies that she expects to publish from it in the future. It is only after giving this reply that Hanako then proceeds to tell the first story of the draft book chapter (lines 5 to 11). As Buttny (1993) points out, speakers often use narratives to "re-present past events in such a way to defend their conduct" (p. 18). By telling her story, Hanako defends or justifies her "no- not yet" reply to the question. She implies that she has good reasons for not yet having published and that these reasons will be evident, based on the story she tells.

Identifying Patterns of Justification

Ideological dilemmas can be found in the patterns of rhetorical justification evident within particular sequences of discourse and narrative (Billig, 1991). Doctoral postgraduates are expected to publish to show that they are being productive researchers (Brewer, Douglas, Facer, & O'Toole, 1999; Rodgers & Maranto, 1989) and that they can secure academic jobs (Gaston, Lantz, & Snyder, 1975; for criticisms of this idea, see Fox, 1983, 1984). However, the concern expressed in the United Kingdom about the falling submission rates of social science doctorates has meant that doctoral postgraduates are expected to complete and submit their theses as quickly as possible (Winfield, 1987). The tension between completing the thesis and working on publications becomes ideological within the context of the supervisory relationship, for it directly relates to issues of power and the demands of the wider institutional and economic context.

Hanako strikes a balance between her autonomy and dependency by placing a rhetorical limit on her publishing activities. For example, she describes her attempt at publishing in such a way as to imply that it did not involve that much work. When she is asked how the draft chapter came about, she says that she did it as a way of finishing the conference paper (lines 15 to 17). By saying this, Hanako implies that the conference paper was nearly finished already, and therefore that most of the work on the draft chapter had been done previously. Similarly, when she says that the draft was the Australia paper with adjustments to fit the orientation of the book (lines 28 to 30), she is implying that the publication involved minimal work.

When Hanako says that she was planning to do a thesis chapter based on the conference paper (lines 18 to 19), she is again justifying doing the publication. This description of a plan is what discursive psychologists have called a "stake inoculation," because Hanako is protecting herself against the possible accusation that the book chapter was topically unrelated to her thesis (on stake and interest, see Edwards & Potter, 1992).

While Hanako implies that this attempted publication did *not* involve that much work, she also implies that it *might* have involved a lot of work, had it been pursued any further. For example, she says that the draft book chapter came back from the editors with comments and that her supervisor and she need to work on "a lot of things" (line 8). The description "a lot of things" is rhetorical in the sense that it is used to justify why the publication was abandoned. After all, to work on "a lot of things" might involve a lot of work: possibly too much work for a thesis publication during the period of doctoral study.

Hanako identifies her thesis as the reason for the publication being abandoned. She says that she decided to focus on her thesis first, and that after the thesis, she hopes to take the chapter and make it into a journal article (lines 8 to 11). By saying that she decided to focus on her thesis first (lines 8 to 9), Hanako gives priority to her thesis and thereby presents herself as a dependent thesis student. However, there is also the subtle implication that publishing in the future is expected. This is implied by her addition of the word "first." While she presents herself as dependent by claiming to focus on her thesis, Hanako does not dismiss publishing and the corresponding identity of the independent research academic.

Positioning and Ideological Dilemmas

The doctoral student's pushing and pulling alternation between autonomy and dependency with regard to the supervisor can be appreciated more explicitly when Hanako describes the work that went into the draft book chapter. This is because she negotiates a balance between crediting herself and crediting her supervisor for the work done on the draft chapter. Van Langenhove and Harré (1999) point out that conversations "have story lines and the positions people take in a conversation will be linked to these story lines" (p. 17) and go on to claim that "whenever there are story lines, there are positionings" (p. 30). But what is positioning? "Positioning . . . is the discursive process whereby people are located in conversations as observably and subjectively coherent participants in jointly produced story lines" (Davies & Harré, 1999, p. 37).

In the present extract, there are variations in the positionings that are made in the story of the book chapter. At the beginning of the extract, Hanako says that she and her supervisor decided to do the book chapter (lines 5 to 6). However, when she is asked how the book chapter came about (line 12), she says that she did it with the momentum of the conference she did in Australia during the previous summer (lines 15 to 16). It could be suggested that variation in this story is to be expected, because any coauthorship is going to involve an element of negotiation (Fox & Faver, 1982). However, collaborative publications of doctoral postgraduates and their supervisors are ideological because the negotiation itself is not egalitarian (see Heffner, 1979). The variation in this particular story is therefore argued to reflect the contrary themes of ideology (Billig et al., 1988).

The ideological tension between "autonomy" and "dependency" in the doctoral student-supervisor relationship unfolds in a subtle manner as soon as the sequence begins. Edwards (1997) argues that where to start a story is "a major, and rhetorically potent, way of managing causality and accountability" (p. 277). By starting the story by saying "I've written some (.) draft chapter . . . of a book chapter" (lines 5 to 6), Hanako prioritizes her own agency and takes sole credit for the writing of the chapter. Her statement also reveals the importance of little words such as pronouns. Discursive analysts have paid particular attention to the subtle and easily overlooked rhetorical role that pronouns can play (Billig, 1995, 1999).

Hanako's appearance as a singularity is "achieved grammatically through the use of the first person singular" (van Langenhove & Harré, 1999, p. 24). So at this moment Hanako is presenting herself as an independent researcher or scholar. However, by going on to say that it was a book chapter that "my supervisor and I decided to do" (line 6), she gives the impression that the decision to do the book chapter was made jointly. The contradiction is that while the decision to write the book chapter might have been made mutually, Hanako is also claiming to have written the draft chapter all by herself.

Hanako goes on to say that the book chapter came back with comments and that "we" need to work on a lot of things (lines 6 to 8). In Hanako's use of the plural pronoun, "other persons are brought into an obligation pattern and the responsibility of the speaker is accordingly reduced" (Mühlhäusler & Harré, 1990, p. 178). So while she initially takes credit for the writing of the draft chapter, Hanako nevertheless goes on to bring her supervisor into an obligation pattern for the subsequent work that needs to be done on the draft. However, Hanako then goes on to say that she decided to focus on her thesis first, and that after the thesis she hopes to take the chapter and make it into a journal article (lines 8 to 11). She thereby imagines herself making the chapter into a journal article independently of her supervisor.

When Steven asks the question "how did that draft (.) chapter come about?" (line 12), he uses a formulation that does not ascribe agency to the action of how the draft chapter came about. The agency for the production of the draft chapter is obscured through this agentless formulation. The formulation allows him to "avoid endorsing a particular story about responsibility" (Potter, 1996, p. 182). Steven therefore leaves the question of agency for the production of the draft chapter to Hanako (on the ideological implications of agentless formulations, see Fowler, Hodge, Kress, & Trew, 1979). When Hanako says "I (.) I DID IT (1.0) with the momentum of the conference (.) I did in Australia this this past summer" (lines 15 to 16), she brings attention to, and emphasizes, that she was the one who did the draft chapter. She presents the chapter as something she did by herself. In fact, she does not even mention her supervisor until much later (line 26). This sequential ordering of the story has a rhetorical effect in the sense that Hanako is prioritizing her own part in the draft and minimizing the part played by her supervisor. A "we did it" form of accounting, which might have been expected based on what Hanako said earlier about the joint decision to do the book chapter (line 6), is absent from this telling.

By giving the impression that she has done most of the work on the chapter, Hanako presents herself as independent of her supervisor and as someone who is working autonomously. However, this semblance of autonomy is contradicted when Hanako introduces Pete into the story line (line 26). Earlier on in the extract, when she used the institutional identity category "supervisor" (line 6), Hanako gave the impression that this relationship was not a relationship of equals. By positioning her supervisor, Hanako implicitly positioned herself as a student or as someone who is supervised. When she comes to tell the story again, however, Hanako uses the shortened first name of her supervisor ("Pete" rather than "Peter") to position him in the story line (line 26). By saying "Pete," Hanako implies that she is on equal terms with her supervisor. By using the shortened form of his first name, Hanako gives the impression that she and her supervisor are friends or colleagues rather than supervisor and student.

The utterance "Pete suggested that it- we should do a book chapter on somebody's ahm edit- edited (.) book" (lines 26 to 27) comes across as a proposal for an egalitarian collaboration between equals. This is because Pete is reported as using the pronoun "we," which implies that the authorship of the book chapter will be a mutual, collaborative affair. However, within the context of the supervisory relationship, a "suggestion" like the one attributed to Pete is rarely a mere suggestion. Rather, such a suggestion can be a piece of advice, a recommendation, or even a command (Li, 2000). Pete's suggestion that "we" should do a book chapter should therefore not be taken at face value. The ambivalent or dilemmatic character of the proposed coauthorship becomes apparent when Hanako says "so I just use (.) the Australia paperHH" (lines 27 to 28) and when she uses the first person pronoun "I" to position herself as personally using the Australia paper. She does not suggest that "we" used the Australia paper, as might have been expected, based on what Pete is claimed to have said previously. As Hanako said that she did the conference herself (line 16), the Australia paper is implied to consist of her own work. By using the word "just," Hanako implies that her use of the Australia paper was simple or straightforward (on uses of the word "just," see Lee, 1987). She thereby mitigates the possibility that the book chapter involved a lot of difficult and time-consuming work.

Hanako proceeds to say that "Pete put some touch ups (.) ahm to make it (.) work" (lines 30 to 31). What Pete is described as doing is implied to be minimal both in terms of the amount of work he did ("some") and the type of his contribution ("touch ups"). Hanako gives the impression that what Pete did was superfluous, for "touch ups" might connote superficial changes to the document, such as changes in spelling or grammar, for example. Also, the amount of touch-ups ("some") implies a couple or a few (i.e., not that many). In this sense, the claim that "Pete put some touch ups" is a risky one. Hanako might be understood as undermining her supervisor's work or as criticizing him for not doing enough work. However, by carefully adding "ahm to make it (.) work," Hanako implicitly praises Pete by giving him the ability to make the paper work merely by making "some touch ups." He is given expertise and authority as a supervisor, and Hanako is implicitly presented as being dependent on his expert touching up. She implies that the paper did not work as it was and that it might not have worked, had it not been for Pete's supervisory touch-ups.

Hanako strikes a balance between presenting Pete's work as minimal or superficial on the one hand and as essential or vital on the other. By bringing attention to his expertise and authority, Hanako is positioning herself as a student and as someone who is dependent on her supervisor. However, as the role of the doctoral student is ambivalent, this presentation of dependency cannot be left unchecked. By minimizing her supervisor's contributions, Hanako lessens the apparent hold that her supervisor has over her and over her work, and thereby presents herself as somewhat more independent.

Ideological Naturalization

Eagleton (1991) brings attention to how ideology can "naturalize" forms of social life: "Successful ideologies are often thought to render their beliefs natural and self-evident—to identify them with the 'common sense' of a society that nobody could imagine how they might ever be different" (p. 58). The extract being analyzed can be understood as a general example of the naturalization of the ideology of supervision, because at no point is the supervisory relationship ever questioned or criticized. It is never implied that supervision might be a partial or contingent form of relationship. Along with this general sense of naturalization, however, there are specific moments in the sequence when the supervisory relationship is naturalized. One of these moments comes after Hanako credits Pete for making the touch-ups on the draft chapter: She says that "he said 'okayt- you don't have to do much just do this and this and this'" (lines 31 to 32).

At this point, Hanako changes her footing and uses direct reported speech to articulate what Pete is supposed to have said to her (on footing, see Goffman, 1983, Chapter 3; on reported speech, see Antaki & Leudar, 2001; Buttny, 1998; Vološinov, 1978). Hanako claims that Pete said "you don't have to do much just do this and this and this." The "this and this and this" is what conversation analysts call a "triple single" (Jefferson, 1990). Triple singles can sometimes be used in conversations to imply "muchness." The repetition of the same word three times can imply "many things." However, the earlier "you don't have to do much" and the use of the word "just" both work to contradict this meaning. The word "just," for example, places a rhetorical limit on the number of things that are to be done on the draft chapter. Pete's suggestion that Hanako has to "just do this and this and this" comes across as a suggestion that is specific in its scope. Hanako is not criticizing Pete for being a slave driver who orders her to do a great deal of work. She is only being told to do three specific things on the paper.

This implied specificity constructs Pete as someone who can make appropriate suggestions about what needs to be done. By going on to say that the draft chapter was then submitted (line 33), Hanako implies that the "touch ups" and the "this and this and this" were enough to complete the draft chapter sufficiently for submittal. Hanako thereby constitutes her supervisor's expertise and, at the same time, implicitly constitutes her own dependence on that expertise. Reliance on expertise, however, often comes at a price (see Billig et al., 1988, Chapter 5). After all, Hanako did not report Pete's saying that "he" doesn't have to do much, or even that "we" don't have to do much. His actual reported speech—"you don't have to do much"—gives the impression that it is obvious that Hanako is to do the work on the draft chapter. The inequality of this coauthorship, and of the supervisory relationship itself, is therefore presented as something self-evident or natural. After reporting Pete's suggestion, Hanako says "and then I did what he suggested to do" (lines 32 to 33).

Ambivalence in the Submittal

Hanako says that Pete "just submitted" the draft chapter to the editors (line 33). Here she is referring to the physical act of submitting, and she is attributing this act to Pete. When Hanako makes this attribution, she is subtly negotiating the themes of autonomy and dependency. By using the word "just," she gives the impression that her supervisor's act of submitting was simple or straightforward. Pete is said to have "just" posted the draft chapter off to the editors, for example. By implying that Pete's act was minimal or marginal, Hanako presents herself as somewhat autonomous (or potentially autonomous) from her supervisor. However, this suggestion of autonomy is undermined because the draft chapter would have had no chance of being published had it not been "submitted." In a way, the conference paper cannot become a proper paper unless it becomes a book chapter, that is, unless it is published. At an implicit level, Pete's act of submitting therefore comes across as vital or necessary, and Hanako's dependence on him becomes apparent.

When Steven asks Hanako for clarification about the submittal, the following exchange takes place. It is at this moment that the "doctoral dilemma" of autonomy and dependency appears to come to a head, albeit in a very subtle way.

Extract (continued)

39	Steven	**so you submitted it TWICE then (.) is that right?**
40		**(.)**
41	Hanako	ahm (1.4) I- we submitted it once and then we received the
42		comments (oh) yah (I see)

Earlier on, Hanako said that Pete submitted the draft chapter to the editors, and she thereby identified him as the sole submitting agent. When Steven asks for clarification about the submittal, however, he does not take into account this earlier description. He does not ask Hanako whether Pete submitted it twice, for example. Rather, he uses the pronoun "you" (line 39), which in this context refers to an ambiguous submitting agent. The agent denoted by "you" could be either Hanako or Hanako and her supervisor. Then Hanako herself shows her awareness of this ambiguity when she says "I- we" (line 41) and uses the first person singular but then abruptly cuts herself off and repairs with the first person plural (on conversational repairs, see Schegloff, Jefferson, & Sacks, 1977). The version that is left unrepaired is "we submitted it."

When Hanako said that Pete "just" submitted the draft chapter to the editors, she was referring to the physical activity of submitting. Pete was credited for sending it off to the editors, but in the clarification sequence, it is not necessarily the case that the physical act of submitting is being invoked. This is because to "submit" a paper can also mean to "author" a paper, in the sense that several authors can "submit a paper" without them all posting it off to the editors together. This double, or ambiguous, meaning of "submit" is being played on in this final sequence, and it is what allows Hanako to say "we submitted it" and leave it unrepaired.

But what of the "I" who submitted it? The ambiguity of the meaning of "submit" means that Hanako, had she said "I submitted it," might have given the impression that she was the sole author of the draft chapter. By using the plural "we," she takes partial credit for the authorship and avoids taking sole personal credit for the authorship. The use of the pronoun "we" seems to be a more persuasive taking of credit and responsibility (for more on the ideological aspects of pronouns, see Billig, 1995; Maitland & Wilson, 1987).

To summarize, the suggestion that Pete is said to have made to Hanako, that "we" should do a book chapter, came across as a proposal for an egalitarian collaboration between colleagues of equal status. However, this implied equality was contradicted by the details of the book chapter narration, in which a taken-for-granted inequality was articulated. The publication eventually came across not as a collaboration between colleagues but as a decidedly unequal affair.

Conclusion

This analysis has sought to show the value of examining the details of talk when stories are told. For example, the use of pronouns can be rhetorically significant for the narration that is unfolded, and it can also reveal the complexities of ideological dilemmas. The dilemmas identified stretch further than this individual student and her supervisor, however. For they are reflections of broader themes relating to the roles of doctoral students and their supervisors, the conflicting themes of autonomy and collaboration, and the institutional powers of British universities, which are funded directly by government. One of the functions of ideology is to soften or conceal the operations of power. This analysis implicitly points to the possible operation and hiding of power within the relations between graduate students and supervisors. In so doing, the analysis itself exemplifies and hides such power relations. Readers of this chapter may infer that one of its authors, Steven Stanley, conducted the interviews. They may correctly infer his status as graduate student. Because the chapter is presented as a coauthored chapter, there is no way of knowing whether or not Steven has done the bulk of the work, while the other author, Michael Billig, merely presented a few touch-ups to justify his name appearing as coauthor. The conventions of academic writing hide these matters of power. That is why academic work cannot escape the reach of ideology.

Appendix

The transcript notation used in the extract is a simplified and modified version of the system developed by Jefferson (1984) for conversation analysis. For a similar version to the one used in this chapter, and a brief discussion on the theory of transcription, see the appendix of Wetherell and Potter's (1992) *Mapping the Language of Racism*.

(0.7)	Pauses appear in rounded brackets and are measured in tenths
(.)	of seconds. Pauses which last for 0.5 seconds or less are marked with a (.)
(yes)	Minimal acknowledgment tokens by the interviewer also appear in rounded brackets
((smiley voice))	Commentary appears in double rounded bracket
I- we	The abrupt cutting off of a word is marked with a dash
TWICE	Speaker emphasis is indicated with capital letters
woHHrk	Within-speech or interpolated laughter is marked with capital aitches (see Jefferson, 1985)
?	Questioning intonation is indicated by a question mark

Note

1. Within discursive psychology, there has been a developmental interest in the ways that children acquire social competence through talk. Given the assumption of complex contradictory ideological values, this acquisition will not be straightforward. There have been attempts to reinterpret the Freudian concept of repression discursively and to examine how the roots of repression lie in the child becoming an accomplished conversationalist (Billig, 1998, 1999).

References

Antaki, C. (1994). *Explaining and arguing: The social organization of accounts.* London: Sage.

Antaki, C., & Leudar, I. (2001). Recruiting the record: Using opponents' exact words in parliamentary argumentation. *Text, 21*(4), 467–488.

Austin, A. E. (2002). Preparing the next generation of faculty: Graduate school as socialization to the academic career. *The Journal of Higher Education, 73*(1), 94–122.

Becher, T., Henkel, M., & Kogan, M. (1994). *Graduate education in Britain.* London: Jessica Kingsley.

Billig, M. (1991). *Ideology and opinions: Studies in rhetorical psychology*. London: Sage.

Billig, M. (1992). *Talking of the royal family*. London: Routledge.

Billig, M. (1995). *Banal nationalism*. London: Sage.

Billig, M. (1996). *Arguing and thinking: A rhetorical approach to social psychology* (2nd ed.). Cambridge, UK: Cambridge University Press.

Billig, M. (1998). Dialogic repression and the Oedipus complex: Reinterpreting the Little Hans case. *Culture and Psychology, 4,* 11–47.

Billig, M. (1999). *Freudian repression: Conversation creating the unconscious*. Cambridge, UK: Cambridge University Press.

Billig, M., Condor, S., Edwards, D., Gane, M., Middleton, D., & Radley, A. (1988). *Ideological dilemmas: A social psychology of everyday thinking*. London: Sage.

Brewer, G. A., Douglas, J. W., Facer, R. L., II, & O'Toole, L. J., Jr. (1999). Determinants of graduate research productivity in doctoral programs of public administration. *Public Administration Review, 59*(5), 373–382.

Buttny, R. (1993). *Social accountability in communication*. London: Sage.

Buttny, R. (1998). Putting prior talk into context: Reported speech and the reporting context. *Research on Language and Social Interaction, 31*(1), 45–58.

Davies, B., & Harré, R. (1999). Positioning and personhood. In R. Harré & L. van Langenhove (Eds.), *Positioning theory: Moral contexts of intentional action* (pp. 32–52). Oxford, UK: Basil Blackwell.

Eagleton, T. (1991). *Ideology: An introduction*. London: Verso.

Edelman, M. (1977). *Political language*. New York: Academic Press.

Edwards, D. (1997). *Discourse and cognition*. London: Sage.

Edwards, D., & Mercer, N. (1987). *Common knowledge: The development of understanding in the classroom*. London: Methuen.

Edwards, D., & Potter, J. (1992). *Discursive psychology*. London: Sage.

Fowler, R., Hodge, B., Kress, G., & Trew, T. (1979). *Language and control*. London: Routledge & Kegan Paul.

Fox, D. (1983). The pressure to publish: a graduate student's personal plea. *Teaching of Psychology, 10*(3), 177–178.

Fox, D. (1984). Alternative perspectives on the pressure to publish. *Teaching of Psychology, 11*(4), 239–241.

Fox, M. F., & Faver, C. A. (1982). The process of collaboration in scholarly research. *Scholarly Publishing, 13,* 327–329.

Gaston, J., Lantz, H. R., & Snyder, C. R. (1975). Publication criteria for promotion in Ph.D. graduate departments. *American Sociologist, 10*(4), 239–242.

Gergen, K. J. (1994). *Realities and relationships: Soundings in social construction*. London: Harvard University Press.

Goffman, E. (1983). *Forms of talk*. Philadelphia: University of Pennsylvania Press.

Harré, R., & Gillett, G. (1994). *The discursive mind*. London: Sage.

Heffner, A. G. (1979). Authorship recognition of subordinates in collaborative research. *Social Studies of Science, 9,* 377–384.

Henschen, B. M. (1993). Easing the transition: from doctoral student to academic professional. *Political Science and Politics, 26*(1), 80–81.

Hewson, D. (1999). Empowerment in supervision. *Feminism & Psychology, 9*(4), 406–409.

Hockey, J. (1994). Establishing boundaries: problems and solutions in managing the PhD supervisor's role. *Cambridge Journal of Education, 24*(2), 293–305.

Jefferson, G. (1984). Transcript notation. In J. M. Atkinson & J. Heritage (Eds.), *Structures of social action: Studies in conversation analysis* (pp. ix–xvi). Cambridge, UK: Cambridge University Press.

Jefferson, G. (1985). An exercise in the transcription and analysis of laughter. In T. A. Van Dijk (Ed.), *Handbook of discourse analysis: Vol. 3. Discourse and dialogue* (pp. 25–34). London: Academic Press.

Jefferson, G. (1990). List-construction as a task and resource. In G. Psathas (Ed.), *Interaction competence* (pp. 63–92). London: International Institute for Ethnomethodology and Conversation Analysis & University Press of America.

Johnson, L., Lee, A., & Green, B. (2000). The PhD and the autonomous self: Gender, rationality and postgraduate pedagogy. *Studies in Higher Education, 25*(2), 135–147.

Lee, D. (1987). The semantics of just. *Journal of Pragmatics, 11*, 377–398.

Li, Y. (2000). *The dynamics of power and politeness in cross-cultural supervision management: A pragmatic study of British and Chinese discourse strategies in an academic context*. Unpublished doctoral dissertation, Loughborough University.

Lindén, J. (1999). The contribution of narrative to the process of supervising PhD students. *Studies in Higher Education, 24*(3), 351–369.

Maitland, K., & Wilson, J. (1987). Pronominal selection and ideological conflict. *Journal of Pragmatics, 11*, 495–512.

Merton, R. K., & Barber, E. (1976). Sociological ambivalence. In R. K. Merton, *Sociological ambivalence and other essays* (pp. 3–31). London: Free Press.

Mühlhäusler, P., & Harré, R. (1990). *Pronouns and people: The linguistic construction of social and personal identity*. Oxford, UK: Basil Blackwell.

Parry, O., Atkinson, P., & Delamont, S. (1997). The structure of Ph.D. research. *Sociology, 31*(1), 121–129

Potter, J. (1996). *Representing reality: Discourse, rhetoric and social construction*. London: Sage.

Potter, J., & Wetherell, M. (1987). *Discourse and social psychology: Beyond attitudes and behaviour*. London: Sage.

Rodgers, R. C., & Maranto, C. L. (1989). Causal models of publishing productivity in psychology. *Journal of Applied Psychology, 74*(4), 636–649.

Schegloff, E. A., Jefferson, G., & Sacks, H. (1977). The preference for self-correction in the organization of repair in conversation. *Language, 53*(2), 361 - 382.

Smith, K. (2000). Academic supervision and the dysfunctional family: The problem of critical distance. *Research in Education, 64*, 12–19

Stina Lyon, E. (1995). Dilemmas of power in post-graduate practice: a comment on research training. *Sociology, 29*(3), 531–540.

Tajfel, H. (1981). *Human groups and social categories.* Cambridge, UK: Cambridge University Press.

Tracy, K. (1997). *Colloquium: Dilemmas of academic discourse.* Norwood, NJ: Ablex.

Tracy, K., & Carjuzáa, J. (1993). Identity enactment in intellectual discussion. *Journal of Language and Social Psychology, 12*(3), 171–194.

Tracy, K., & Muller, N. (1994). Talking about ideas: Academics' beliefs about appropriate communicative practices. *Research on Language and Social Interaction, 27*(4), 319–349.

van Langenhove, L., & Harré, R. (1999). Introducing positioning theory. In R. Harré & L. van Langenhove (Eds.), *Positioning theory: Moral contexts of intentional action* (pp. 14–31). Oxford, UK: Basil Blackwell.

Vološinov, V. N. (1978). Reported speech. In L. Matejka & K. Pomorska (Eds.), *Readings in Russian poetics: Formalist and structuralist views* (pp. 149–175). Ann Arbor, MI: Michigan Slavic Publications.

Wetherell, M., & Potter, J. (1992). *Mapping the language of racism: Discourse and the legitimation of exploitation.* Chichester, UK: Columbia University Press.

Wetherell, M., Taylor, S., & Yates, S. J. (2001). *Discourse theory and practice: A reader.* London: Sage.

Widdicombe, S., & Wooffitt, R. (1995). *The language of youth subcultures: Social identity in action.* London: Harvester Wheatsheaf.

Winfield, G. (1987). *The social science PhD: The ESRC enquiry on submission rates.* London: Economic and Social Research Council.

PART III

Reading Through
the Forces of History

To narrate a life is, at least in part, to undertake a process of locating oneself in time. This premise provides a launch pad for the chapters composing this third and final section. All are focused on material that is largely concerned with how individuals come to know themselves within the forces of history. For some (Carney, Chapter 3.2; Stewart & Malley, Chapter 3.3), history is sedimented into particular, well-defined moments—the Holocaust, World War II—that provide a backdrop for self-understanding. For others (Solis, Chapter 3.1; Chandler, Lalonde, & Teucher, Chapter 3.4), history is contained in and defines the present moment—the contemporary status of Mexican immigrants to the United States, the form of identity constructed by Western European compared to Native American youth. In yet another instance (Gergen, Chapter 3.5), history does not settle into the present but is defined and redefined by the particulars of the moment, the individual's goals and desires and interlocutors.

Similar to the work presented in the previous sections, the chapters in this section can be described in part as addressing the relationship between personal and cultural narratives. Here, however, a distinctive issue is the breaking down of or outright resistance to dominant culture narratives—of identity, gender, and mental health. But the relationship between personal agency and normalizing cultural forms is far from ambiguous; it is the driving force that orders a sense of self in relation to a historically emergent structure of power and authority.

Thus, several of the authors envision master narratives through which and, importantly, *against* which individuals compose the personal understandings of their lives. For example, in her analysis of narratives produced by individuals who survived the Holocaust, Carney (Chapter 3.2) identifies a narrative of transcendence that dominates the discourse of those professionals—clinicians and researchers alike—who aim to help and understand victims of trauma. According to the narrative, survivors who work through their trauma successfully do so by constructing and communicating an integrative, coherent interpretation that heroically transcends the horrors of their experiences. Contemporary culture valorizes Holocaust victims; so, too, must the victims see in themselves some evidence that confers meaning and even value on the events that constitute their histories. Carney's data, however, indicate that many Holocaust survivors, although aware of the expectation for heroic transcendence, defy this particular vision of mental health. Instead of framing their pasts as emotionally resolved and integrated—even as experiences of growth—many have constructed "counternarratives"—oppositional autobiographies that are fragmentary, emotionally conflicted, and speak of their suffering as a catalyst to their own aggression and callousness.

In her study of undocumented Mexican immigrants living in New York City, Solis (Chapter 3.1) identifies a dominant cultural narrative of illegality in which individuals by definition lack rights and means of self-empowerment and political action. Against this view is the identity—the counternarrative—constructed socially by the Mexicans in the course of their participation in a community organization that advocates and promotes the legal and human rights of Mexican immigrants and their families. Drawing broadly from oral, written, and graphic texts, Solis found evidence of "fairly stable products of the shared identity and culture" of the organization (p. 187) and a sense of identity in children and adults that both defined their social affiliation with other immigrants and set it apart from the dominant "other" in terms of class and language differences and inequalities. She argues that both narrative forms, the dominant and the counter, be understood as resources for the identity-seeking child whose own narrative, and developmental outcome, will ultimately reflect the diversity and complexity of the narrative forms present within the broader cultural milieu.

The presence of multiple cultural narratives—some dominant, others more marginalized—as potentialities for self-definition is also played out in Stewart and Malley's (Chapter 3.3) thematic analysis of young women's experiences in the United States during World War II. According to Stewart and Malley, the culturally valued narrative at this point in history belonged to the men who served in the war. Women's roles were more variable. They left school. Career and family plans were suspended. Many supported the war effort through their employment—Rosie the Riveter being an iconic example. Although women entered the workforce in unprecedented numbers, they left it just as abruptly when men returned home to pick up the pieces of their interrupted lives. While some feminist scholars have been quick to read this historic process as an unhappy path of women's increasing marginalization and consignment to the duties of home and family, Stewart and Malley's interviews suggest that when women reflect on their personal experiences, the sense of loss and sacrifice can be interpreted in more positive, historically relevant lights, and "marginalization" can be translated to mean autonomy from the dominant institution of making war.

The essay on comparative youth identity development in Western European and Native American cultures, by Chandler, Lalonde, and Teucher (Chapter 3.4), takes on the issue of self and time in two ways and challenges the assumption that all self-constructions are inherently narrative-like in form. Using a reference model to examine the relationship between the events of a life and the interpretive frame that gives them meaning, the authors ask their subjects to explain how they remain the same over time despite obvious change. They find that among Western European youth, accounts of self as continuous in time lean heavily on Western essentialist notions, by which some specifiable and enduring self-characteristic remains literally unchanged despite changing events and circumstances. One has the same set of fingerprints for example, or the same personality. Transformations thus become a distant and shifting ground over which a stable and enduring self reigns supreme. Native American youth, in contrast—and consistent with their own cultural heritage—view themselves as continuous in time to the extent that changing life events can be put into storied form. Change, in this case, provides the source material for fashioning an autobiography.

Saved for last is the chapter by Gergen (Chapter 3.5), an autobiography about autobiography. In it she traces her own intellectual journey as a participant in and witness to the emergence of narrative psychology, as well as the implications of assuming that we are each the bard of our own existence. Where others have set their caps on the influence of narrative content, form, and structure, Gergen elevates the issue of narrative dynamics. How rigid are our stories? How fluid? Stable stories, whether personal or cultural, provide ready-to-hand coherence and order. Master narratives, counternarratives, narratives of oppression and of redemption: We pull them off the shelf and use them to quicken our desires and our destinies. When narratives lose their coherence, they lose their authority, enabling self-reconstruction, cultural revision, and the creation of interdependent realities.

In this final section and, indeed, throughout the volume, the authors invite us into the world of challenge and intrigue that defines the context of their ongoing efforts to understand the creative possibilities engendered by narrative analysis. Applying a variety of methods across multiple domains of human action and experience, their work can be read as a collective testimony to the dynamic relations between developing individuals in changing societies and to our thankfully unfinished task of making sense of it all.

3.1

Narrating and Counternarrating Illegality as an Identity

Jocelyn Solis

The Association has helped us a lot to express ourselves. It's given us something—, made us realize by taking away the blindfold we had on our eyes when we would say that, because I'm illegal . . . I don't have any rights. It's taken away that blindfold from our eyes and made us realize that as human beings we're worth a lot. . . . We may not have documents, but we are worth a lot to ourselves.

— Mercedes, an undocumented immigrant, wife, mother, community organizer

This statement illustrates a major finding of a research project[1] I undertook between the years 1999 and 2000. For this project, I collected interviews and written texts as part of an ethnographic study of Asociación Tepeyac, a community-based organization in New York City that promotes, from the grassroots, the human and legal rights of Mexican immigrants and their families.[2] The finding, that undocumented immigrants can explain and defend their illegal status in terms of human rights and social justice, revealed an unusual developmental outcome in light of public animosity and federal regulations taken against them. The finding is especially significant considering the contradictions in which the undocumented live. Immigrants are said to be the foundation on which U.S. society is strengthened and to be key historical figures who add to the nation's prosperity, yet societal means often tell a different story about the country's discriminatory acceptance of foreigners. Such contradictions open the door for developmental diversity and variability.

In an attempt to protect the confidentiality and security of my informants, I approached Asociación Tepeyac, which had recently begun working closely with this population. There, I became a participant observer, providing voluntary service on a range of tasks in which I worked closely with the association's staff and met its members and nonmembers who were involved in a range of planning and/or service-seeking activities. While collecting Tepeyac's written documentation (including press releases, public informational documents, and grant proposals), I also conducted a writing project with children and teenagers and later interviewed their mothers. In this chapter, I will illustrate how my analysis of oral, written, and graphic narratives of illegality was conducted and led me to argue that immigrants' involvement in Tepeyac served as a means of intervention in their identities. That is, once individuals became active participants in their social, cultural, and political environments and became conscious of various external forces that promote illegality beyond the individual's own intention, they became vocal, visible advocates of their own human and legal rights. This is an unusual stance for undocumented immigrants to take, and in this chapter I describe how its development as an identity can be found in their narratives and *counternarratives,* or the contested discourse of illegality.

Why (Counter)Narrative?

I approached the study of illegality as an identity from the Vygotskian cultural-historical tradition in which human development is explained along multiple historical lines (Scribner, 1985). As such, I was interested in studying the development of undocumented immigrants from both personal-psychological and societal-institutional histories that are mediated by cultural tools. An initial theoretical premise was that illegality is an available identity afforded by social, historical, and political means and social structures such as the mass media, immigration policies, and popular opinion that position undocumented immigrants as "illegal" subjects unworthy of rights, targets of disparagement in popular discourse, and victims of exploitation in labor, housing, and other sites (Edstrom, 1993; Espenshade & Belanger, 1998).

In this sense, an "illegal identity" is made available by certain material conditions and narratives in the United States that presuppose both legal and illegal subjects. The history of militarization of the U.S.-Mexico border includes its exclusionary immigration policies that enable the existence of both documented and undocumented immigrants. On entering the United States, immigrants are identified and must identify themselves according to the legal terms that are already available to them (Solis, 2001). Consequently, "illegal immigrants" are normally unaware that, despite their irregular immigration status, they do have rights while residing in the United States, and they fail to stand up for their rights as a result of their illegal status and fear of deportation. However, such individuals know their own histories and reasons for becoming "illegal," which are ordinarily economic. Thus it is possible for them to confront societal and personal discourses in conflict that define their identities in legal terms.

Societal and personal discourses each tell a story that informs our thinking about undocumented immigrants, who they are, why they are in the United States, and what they do or do not deserve. These opposing, value-laden explanatory frameworks are defined here as narratives in conflict. Within the special context of a grassroots organization, Mexican immigrant families develop their identities through narratives and counternarratives of illegality that contest predominant notions and redefine illegality from new and different criteria. My research site made this study particularly unique in that participants were confronted both with societal narratives of rejection of undocumented immigrants and with community counternarratives of acceptance and inclusion of undocumented immigrants in U.S. society. Rather than identify themselves as "illegal" immigrants undeserving of rights, many became "undocumented" immigrants advocating for changes not only in their immigration status but also in their political access, visibility, and public voice, as well as in the enforcement of their rights even while they are undocumented.

To make sense of such conflicting narratives, I used social constructionism (Gergen, 1990) and poststructuralist theory (Henriques, Hollway, Urwin, Venn, & Walkerdine, 1984) to critically scrutinize seemingly coherent narratives about self, deconstruct assumptions about developmental universality, and examine the cultural and political bases of identity that reveal multiple narratives of individuals' self-understanding and variable social positioning, or sociopolitical and epistemological orientation toward the world.

I extended cultural-historical theory, then, to conceptualize narratives as cultural tools that mediate between societal conditions and personal experiences in goal-directed actions. The notion that societal narratives can be countered also presupposes that personal narratives are a source for understanding human development and conscious action in variable and multiple social, cultural, historical, and political contexts.

This definition of narrative also drew its theoretical foundation from many disciplines, because my intent was to trace both coherency and diversity in the ways that illegality is narrated as individuals speak and perform their identities. Some developmental views have defined narrative as a universal modality of thought that is culturally formed (Bruner, 1986; Nelson, 1996). For Bruner (1986), narratives simultaneously reveal uniformity and variability as they are produced through cultures and institutions. Multiple cultural narratives reflect potential worlds of individual knowing. Sociolinguistic narrative theory has defined narrative as comprised of uniform, structural components of storytelling (i.e., introduction, problem, and resolution) (Labov & Waletsky, 1967) that require a sense of coherency. However, for the purposes of my research, narratives were also understood to be revealing of tensions that point to narrative multiplicity, implicating cultural and cognitive variability.

In addition, narrative analysis has been useful in studying the deployment of power in society. Using narratives as a lens into individuals' social surroundings, Dijk (1993) found that certain narratives reproduced racism and social control in stories he examined about participants' neighbors. He found that in these stories, descriptions of immigrants and minorities recreated power relations from the narrators' position of white dominance. One might say that these stories were reflections of the narrators' reality. However, Freeman (1997) theorizes that narratives do not reflect but, rather, *constitute* culture. I argue that narratives are a cultural medium for the development of consciousness. Narratives about undocumented immigrants are produced in oral, written, and graphic texts by individuals and institutions in both dominant *and* disempowered social positions, as well as in individuals' actions oriented toward some goal. In this sense, language-based narratives, on their own, are not sufficient in identifying the "stuff" that makes up culture, but they are useful means of creating and reproducing culture within the context of goal-directed activities (e.g., textual, corporeal, or mental). Therefore, narratives here are defined as texts in the broadest sense. Narratives are both *material* (in the sense of being spoken, heard, read) and *conceptual* cultural tools that generate explanatory coherency in real-world activities. I propose that the value of narrative analysis in this study came from its grounded emergence through ethnographic data.

In my research, I focused on the texts produced by individuals involved in Tepeyac, an institution that generates a counternarrative about undocumented immigrants in which they are understood to be members of U.S. society whose legitimacy or "legality" is seen in their daily economic and cultural contributions. I found that Tepeyac's overarching narrative functioned to challenge existing narratives of power, which identify undocumented immigrants in disparaging ways, and to reposition them according to grounds that diverge from those that dominate public discourse.

Through Tepeyac's activities, public rallies, protests, placards, information bulletins, cultural events, and contact with the media, Mexican immigrants produce a countersocietal narrative about who they are and who they are not. That is, they present themselves publicly not as criminals but as law-abiding citizens who contribute to the welfare of the city.

The narratives produced by social institutions such as the mass media convey messages with implicit moral tones formed by the guiding political ideologies they are designed to maintain. Some have called such narratives "speech genres" (Bakhtin, 1986) or society's "grand" or "master" narratives (Lyotard, 1984). While societal narratives produce what I refer to as an "illegal" identity for immigrants who lack proper documentation, Tepeyac's counternarrative produces an "undocumented" identity that functions to legitimate Mexican immigrants' sense of belonging and entitlement in the United States, as well as to redefine mainstream notions of illegality. Thus, understanding how narratives and counternarratives produce a sense of identity requires an examination of points of conflict between those narratives *available to* and those *produced by* undocumented immigrants themselves. I propose that discourse psychology (Parker, 1997) must critically identify and analyze narratives through qualitative means that examine closely their divergent content, point of view, purpose, audience, and functions within cultural contexts and personal activities. More research is needed to reveal how individuals' self-understanding emerges in and through conflicting cultural narratives that reveal developmental diversity and variability.

Putting Narrative Theory in Practice

With this conceptual basis, one can now understand how certain sources of data were useful in this analysis of illegality as an identity. Because most of the Mexican population in New York is undocumented at this time,[3] my research study focused on the ways in which living illegally in the United States was narrated and impinged on the directionality of Mexican families' identity development: how they view themselves in this particularly complex social context and how their identities, as a frame of mind, orient their actions (or inaction) in the world around them.

Before I begin to delineate the process by which this theoretical background became empirical, I should say that I used narrative analysis as a grounded method (Strauss & Corbin, 1997). As I approached the data, my theoretical premises became guiding questions to understand whether illegality impinged on the formation of identity. In the process, the preliminary answers to my questions produced hypotheses, hunches, or insights that generated more questions to be examined against the data. Although ethnographic and data triangulation methods could have allowed the major finding I have described in this chapter to rest on its own, they would not have been sufficient to put my preoccupation with developmental diversity and variability to rest. Because this theoretical proposition underpinned my research goals, the process of going back to test a finding and generate further analytic questions with which to scrutinize the data only ended once such diversity was discovered in the midst of certain commonality.

In this sense, I have begun my own narrative backwards; I started with one end result, a major research finding, and will now explain how I got there. The following guidelines outline the steps I undertook in this research, and they should provide a means for the novice narrative analyst to approach other empirically investigative problems:

- Select and record common discourse markers useful in addressing the research question (e.g., topics, themes, content, use of indexicals, and discourse strategies that will be illustrated later).
- Triangulate preliminary findings with ethnographic data.
- Identify a narrative where discourse markers and cultural activities cohere.
- Turn ongoing theoretical assumptions into analytic questions.
- Refine, reclassify, or extend preliminary findings and theoretical premises.
- Check for counternarratives that explain data.
- Determine what commonalities remain after variability is discovered.

Such guidelines are intended for analyses that seek to examine coherency and variability simultaneously, but they should be theoretically based and modified according to one's research goals. Below I illustrate how this procedure took form, beginning with my initial research questions.

What are my participants' life histories? What is their understanding of the world and their place in it? How do they make sense of or justify their immigration status? With such questions in mind, I set out to design my project. I supplemented my field notes as a participant observer with a collection of Tepeyac's monthly information bulletin over 24 months. This source of data included a body of 270 articles detailing experiences, advice, and information written and illustrated by Mexican immigrants and directed toward others living in similar conditions. In addition, the writing project I conducted over a 3-month period ,with a total of 16 children and teenagers between the ages of 5 and 14, led to the production of an illustrated booklet containing both fictional and expository texts about Mexican children's experiences in the city and addressed prospective immigrant children and families. On its completion, the mothers of 5 focal children were interviewed to obtain their own life histories and expectations for their families' future.

Both the conversations that took place during the writing project and the group interview were audio-recorded and transcribed.

Texts were derived in three modalities: oral, written, and graphic (illustrations). Eventually, I chose to analyze them similarly in what turned out to be a first phase of analysis—although I initially wondered whether the oral and written modes called for different analytic means. According to Bakhtin (1986), there is no dichotomy between orality and literacy, since writing is dynamic and can be thought of as a response to previous oral or written discourse. The written texts produced by Tepeyac often displayed an oral quality (e.g., they were written in a familiar tone, using colloquial vocabulary and expressions in Spanish) and were dynamic in the sense that they addressed and responded to others. I found that the writing derived over the course of this project functioned to build a community based on similarities (e.g., political views, religion, social class, language) between the authors and their primary audiences.

Nonetheless, I came to see the written artifacts of the institution as fairly stable products of the shared identity and culture of Tepeyac, while I saw speech as a dynamic, interpersonal process that could potentially lead to more pronounced variations within the organization and between participants. Thus, I conceived of the oral data taken from the interviews and conversations with the children and their mothers as a source of individual contention to what Tepeyac, as a whole, represented. The children's interactions, unlike one-on-one interviews, also provided a setting where their own ideas, cultural knowledge, and identities were enacted and negotiated interpersonally in meaningful activities, rather than reported in less authentic ways or in an artificial context.

The written texts produced by the Asociación Tepeyac children and youth were analyzed in relation to their audiences, as were the discussions and conversations I transcribed, which were analyzed in relation to their interlocutors as well. As my intent was to see whether and how personal and societal trajectories become intertwined through the mediation of cultural tools, I approached the first phase of analyzing an enormous amount of text using the following categories to help me detect common narratives of illegality. (Recall that the findings derived from this initial phase of analysis were preliminary in the sense that they generated other questions and means of analyzing the data.)

Thematic Analysis. The different streams of data were analyzed for recurring *topics and themes* regarding participants' social position and self-understanding, to be used in detecting the common ground that unified the participants of Asociación Tepeyac. For example, the association's bulletins frequently conveyed the theme of injustice. As an example, in one article, titled "How Much Our Employer Steals From Us," the community was positioned as a collective victim of injustices in the workplace. In the article, a table listed what workers' salaries should be according to hours worked and legal minimum wage pay. Along with the text, an illustration depicted characters explaining the table to other people. In the illustration, one character was an employer wearing dark glasses and a suit, who was standing over a worker and smiling as he covered the worker's mouth to keep him from speaking. Since undocumented immigrants often work for less than minimum wage—and fail to report this infringement of their rights—the goal of the article was to raise awareness and provoke action against being silenced and treated unfairly by employers because of one's undocumented status. Other themes I identified across such texts included the themes of resistance/subversion, solidarity, difference, safety, and accomplishment.

Content Analysis. All the texts and transcripts were analyzed for three types of content in order to obtain a general sense of both commonality and diversity across participants that could reveal variable developmental outcomes. They included (1) uniformity and variation in ideologies about illegality, (2) cultural knowledge about living illegally, and (3) ideas, values, or assumptions in conflict.

For example, both *uniformity* in and *variation* between individual participants, between participants and Tepeyac, and between mothers and children served as analytic content and methodological counterarguments. That is, a commonality could be tested further by seeking alternatives or claims to the contrary within texts produced by the same person, the group, or Asociación Tepeyac. Once Tepeyac's identity and political stance became clear to me from its public documents, then I proceeded to question personal texts (discussions and conversations) with the initial finding in mind: *Do all of the individuals involved in the organization express the same perspective? Always? If not, what could be the source of the difference?*

The data were then analyzed for references to the specific places where *cultural knowledge* about being Mexican and living illegally was produced, assumed, or shared. This analysis also helped to question whether there were commonalities across participants, and of what they consisted. Goodnow (1990) states that relations of power, certain kinds of knowledge, and cultural values are embedded in "modeled messages," or implicit messages people draw from the routine arrangements of time, space, and activity. My initial observations of Asociación Tepeyac included noting how knowledge about being undocumented was produced in nonverbal ways. For example, its central office contains a large common room where meetings are held, and it is decorated with different objects that highlight its history and accomplishments as an organized community and as a national group. Portraits of Mexican revolutionaries, religious icons, photographs of Tepeyac's major yearly events, and artwork produced by community members tell a story about the organization and its identity, history, and values. Such non-verbal cultural knowledge also corroborated themes—such as religious faith, struggle, oppression, as well as strength, accomplishment, and cultural beauty—that were found in the written texts. In this way, it was possible to detect the common "undocumented" identity of the organization as part of its cultural make-up, which could be read across several forms.

Because I initially assumed that I would find a tension between undocumented immigrants' alleged illegitimacy in society and their own personal sense of righteousness, seeking points of *conflict* became important. Thus, the third content for which data were analyzed consisted of expressions of conflict, contradiction, or counterarguments that pointed to the multiple social positions Mexican immigrants and children occupy.

In the process of conducting such content analyses, I identified subtopics, especially across written texts, that included religion, health, sports, politics, and other aspects of cultural life in both Mexico and the United States. This allowed me to analyze illegality in relation to other issues that impact development and to determine, in qualitative terms, whether my analysis was valid.

Graphic Illustrations. As the various examples above demonstrate, graphic illustrations added strength to the message of a text and stood as a cultural means of expression that served to corroborate or check initial findings derived mainly from written and oral texts.

Discourse Strategies. Along with a general sense of the culture of Tepeyac and its members, I was interested in capturing the microdetails of cultural activity through language. Therefore, the discourse strategies of Tepeyac and of individual research participants were important to analyze in terms of what identities (assuming that being undocumented was one of many possible identities) could do, enact, or accomplish through language. Discourse strategies were identified to learn how individuals and institutions were positioned by themselves and others in actual language use through *forms of address* and selection of *audience* (e.g., the general public, other immigrants, children, etc.). Also, in the case of the discussions among children and teenagers whose dominant language was English but who were conversant in Spanish, instances of *code-switching* (Zentella, 1997) were analyzed as indicators of shifts in social position, cultural knowledge, topic of conversation, addressee, and meaning. For example, many of the youngest children who were U.S.-born were English dominant yet used Spanish lexicon to describe their experiences in certain activities, such as accompanying parents to rallies where they would demand *amnistía* (amnesty). They also code-switched to retell chants in Spanish they had learned at demonstrations.

Indexicality. Texts were also analyzed for *indexicality*, or linguistic pragmatic markers of identity that produce the social positions of the speaker and interlocutor. Some have argued that personal pronouns indicate positions of power and solidarity between interlocutors (Blas-Arroyo, 1994; Brown & Gilman, 1960) and that these social positions of differential power delimit what the individual can say and know (Harré & Gillett, 1994). In my analysis, I searched for typical pragmatic features of participants' social positions as indexed by personal pronouns (e.g., I, you, he, she, they; *yo, tú, él, ella, ellos*) and other indexes of spatio-temporal location (e.g., now, then, before, here, there, later; *ahora, entonces, antes, aquí, allá, después*) (Levinson, 1983). I considered these to be the most direct means of detecting the speaker's or writer's social positioning in language, as well as the changes to their positioning through their use of temporal contrasts (e.g., before, now) that could mark development of their identities. Many expository articles in the information bulletins, for instance, began in the first person singular, *yo*, yet often turned into the first person plural, *nosotros*, positioning the author as an individual representative of the community's experiences as a whole. Also, the authors often addressed the audience (other members of Tepeyac and other Mexicans) in the familiar, second person singular, *tú*, as a potential marker of solidarity. Accordingly, the data were analyzed for indexes to individuals' social position in reference or in contrast to another person or society. The table below illustrates these initial findings.

- U.S. born/Mexican born
- legal/undocumented
- child/parent
- peer/nonpeer
- older/younger sibling
- sibling/nonsibling
- boy/girl

- Mexican/Other ethnicity
- Spanish speaking/English speaking
- cultural supporter/assimilationist
- bilingual/monolingual
- Tepeyac member/nonmember
- U.S. resident/Mexican resident
- authority/subordinate

Sample of Social Position Indicators Identified in Texts

Social Structures. Data were also analyzed to see whether and how traditional social structures of identity, such as race, class, language, gender, or religion, were introduced in oral and written texts and used by participants to capture the broader, societal history of Mexicans in New York. The purpose of the analysis was to also determine whether immigration status was important to immigrants' formation of identity, as well as how it operated in conjunction with, or as an alternative to, other social structures of identity.

By the time I had read and analyzed the texts of the information booklets (the first source of data I approached) according to the categories above, I had already been a participant of Tepeyac for about a year. The ethnographic backdrop to the texts provided sufficient support for the idea that Tepeyac was serving as a cultural tool in the development of immigrants' identities. Tepeyac's mission statement, press releases, and placards at immigrants' rights rallies (e.g., "No Human Being Is Illegal" and "Who's the Illegal Alien, Pilgrim?") all pointed to a narrative about undocumented immigrants and their life conditions, rights, and entitlement to fair treatment. My second phase of analysis consisted of triangulating these findings (Denzin & Lincoln, 1994) across the data to examine how Tepeyac's counterinstitutional narrative of illegality was produced or understood by individuals, as well as how my participants came to adopt an uncommon political-epistemological stance wherein they identified themselves as "undocumented" rather than "illegal" immigrants. As noted below, this second analytic phase was useful in helping me to clarify my preliminary findings and refine my theoretical presuppositions.

Discovering (Counter)Narratives of Illegality

To illustrate this second phase, I begin with examples taken from the monthly information bulletins, in which individual authors extended the notion of belonging, entitlement, justice, and self-righteousness proposed by Tepeyac. Consider the following excerpt from an expository piece that illustrates a typical Mexican immigrant story, as well as the intervening role of Asociación Tepeyac.[4] It was written by an undocumented male member of the association and is titled "In the Struggle for Our Dignity":

> Poverty obligates us to emigrate to this country with the hope of earning good money and taking our family out of crisis in our beloved Mexico. And we risk our life when we cross the border. From there, on the border, our suffering begins as it is not so easy to cross. . . . Our hope is to soon pay off the money we brought that is often loaned at a high credit rate. That is what obligates us to work at the first job we find, without caring about the hours, nor the low salary, nor how one will be treated. . . . On some occasions, all of this [i.e., labor abuses and physical mistreatment] has to be reported to the police or to

Asociación Tepeyac so that help will come from our office. Do not be afraid of denouncing all of these violations. Because even as undocumented immigrants we have rights, because we are human, not animals to be treated in such an unfair manner by those children of arrogance and money. . . . If you are one of those workers, denounce those atrocities. Asociación Tepeyac is there to help us. It teaches us how to defend ourselves from those abuses. Remember that we are not alone. Asociación Tepeyac is there to help us.

In this text, the topic is immigration related and conveys the themes of economic survival, struggle, solidarity, and resistance to exploitation. This author assumes that poor economic conditions are what propel Mexicans to emigrate and find work, however arduous it may be. An analysis of indexicals demonstrates that many of his sentences (including but not limited to those quoted above) use the Spanish first person plural verb form ("we risk," "we work," "we are," "we have"), plural possessive pronouns ("our"), and plural self-reflexive verbs ("obligates us," "teaches us"). He uses inclusive grammar, as well as assumptions about shared affective stances ("beloved Mexico") to address other undocumented Mexican workers and position himself as one of them. The author also uses the second person formal imperative ("denounce," "remember") to persuade other Mexican immigrant workers like him to report human and labor rights' violations. He also builds solidarity by invoking trust in Tepeyac when he repeatedly assures the reader (positioned as a nonmember) that it "is there to help us."

The example illustrates how personal development is constructed through cultural means where members of Tepeyac address other members and other Mexican immigrants in the city. Indirectly, they also address the powers that be. Comparing this personal stance to the individual women's experiences orally narrated in their interview, I was able to detect more of the affective qualities that led to this development. For instance, in their group interview, all of the women I met, who had become community leaders through their involvement in Tepeyac, reported having been initially hesitant to participate in meetings and other activities that seemed political or public. For example, Mercedes and Lucía,[5] who are sisters, were invited by their niece and brother-in-law, already members of Tepeyac, to attend a meeting. Generally, members of the organization become involved initially as a result of various cultural and personal needs or interests. Some arrive independently after hearing of the organization in the media and desiring to somehow participate; some become members after seeking services, and others after being invited by co-workers, neighbors, relatives, or priests, as my participants illustrate. In the following excerpt, Mercedes and Lucía described their initial hesitance and consequent participation in Tepeyac, as well as the personal transformations they underwent and attributed to their community involvement:

Lucia: My brother-in-law used to tell me, "Why don't you go? My niece used to go there." But, no, no, no. "You're very boring. And what are we going to say? Mexicans don't even help each other." . . . And I would call him to say hello and he would invite us. I don't remember how we decided one day to check it out.

Mercedes: Yeah, but we didn't like it. I didn't. . . . When I would come [I would say], "That man [the executive director], I don't like the way he speaks," I tell her. "I don't like him."

Lucia: She didn't like him.

Mercedes: Later I told him that [laughter].

Lucia: And he helped us a lot in his meetings to, for example, to be able to communicate with you. For example, you're a professional, that is, now we talk to you [in the familiar] even though our English or our Spanish may be bad, right? Because we don't have as much education as you. Or for example, with the priests . . . all respect went to them. Not anymore. Because we place ourselves as equals

Mercedes: Not now. Now we speak. Now they tell me that I'm rude. And I tell him, "Oh Father, you're a saint" [sarcastically]. I didn't dare say that [before]. And me too, thanks to [the executive director]. . . . in his meetings he asks us [to speak].

Lucia: He makes us speak, he makes us read. . . . We had already forgotten about reading. . . .

Mercedes: Yeah, so then I started to like all that.

Clearly, an important characteristic of Tepeyac has been to invite participation from the ground up, and this participation is found, among other means, within its speaking activities. As these women state, the executive director was a central figure in implementing this working style, in which members could participate actively by voicing their ideas and learning to communicate with others as equally valid interlocutors—in spite of differences in their level of education or subordinate position in hierarchical relationships. The women later claimed to have extended this new skill to other areas of their lives, an ability that was linked to their sense of self, including their self-esteem. They went from being incapable or uninterested in speaking, to finding their voice without feeling embarrassed or degraded over potential flaws in their speech. They also came to believe that some people were genuinely interested in helping their community, and they were drawn to organized collective community work. In the following dialogue, we see how all three women's discourse strategies served to coconstruct a common narrative about how they gained self-confidence in the process of learning to speak as members of Tepeyac:

Mercedes: Before I used to think that if I spoke a word, they would laugh at me because I would say "Maybe I didn't say it correctly. Maybe I won't say it, I shouldn't say it. Maybe if I say this, they'll laugh at me. Maybe if I say this to the priest, he'll say no." Always things that . . .

Lucia: Negative things.

Mercedes: Really we weren't sure of ourselves. Well now, little by little, with all this . . .

Rosa: We learned to lose our fear.

By using the discourse strategy of completing each other's sentences, the women assumed a common explanation for their personal transformation from nonspeakers and nonmembers to speakers and active participants of Tepeyac. The transformation entailed learning to put their fears and doubts aside in favor of feelings of self-worth and self-confidence. Although Mercedes began by describing her own doubts, she concluded her thoughts by extending her self-evaluation to the other women ("we weren't sure of ourselves"). Rosa then acknowledged this collective positioning in her assessment, "We learned to lose our fear." In addition to building a common narrative through one key discourse strategy (sentence completion), they also used certain indexicals: first person plural verb forms (e.g., "we were," "we learned") and spatio-temporal markers (before, now). This collective process of learning to speak was described as a first step in their coming to learn to defend themselves and their community and becoming vocal and visible in spite of their undocumented status. The quote with which I began this chapter sums up this finding nicely.

The Extent and Function of Counternarrating Illegality

In order to determine whether children and youth involved in Tepeyac produced similar narratives of illegality, and whether their development of an undocumented identity was similar to that of their mothers, I examined transcripts of our meetings. Here, I illustrate my analysis using one session during which I asked my core group of participants to interview each other about other people's beliefs about immigrants, and about what they, themselves, believed about immigrants. Of the five focal children who participated in the writing of the booklet, only the two eldest children were able to respond to the question. David, a 14 year-old boy, and Karina, his 12 year-old sister, were both undocumented, but had arrived in the United States at a very young age. Their mother later informed me that only David recollected their traumatic border-crossing experience, although he was 4 years old at the time. Throughout our meetings, both children positioned themselves as advocates of their community and demonstrated a deep awareness of the difficult life conditions of undocumented Mexican immigrants in the city. On this occasion, their responses were no different. However, their responses also revealed that their identification of immigrants was expressed in terms not only of illegality but of other structures of power as well.

In their responses to my questions during this session, these children also defined immigrants in terms of class and language inequalities. When questioned about what other people thought about immigrants, Karina identified the "other" in "other people" as Americans. Specifically, she referred to employers and other adults and children who arrived in the United States prior to Mexican immigrants, describing them as people who think they are better than immigrants because they mistakenly think of them as "different" or unequal. Consequently, immigrants were identified as those who are treated unfairly by "Americans" according to a social order based on power and time of arrival in the United States. She stated, "Some people think that they're different. . . . They're disrespectful, like, people feel better than them but they're not. . . . Some Americans, like, when immigrants are working for them . . . they treat them bad." When questioned specifically about children who are immigrants, she responded, "Um kids? They treat them bad because since they're immigrants, they come here after them [Americans] so they don't know English and they make fun of them." Karina repeatedly made a distinction between adult immigrants, who are oppressed as a result of their social class and undocumented status, and children who are mistreated because of their minority language status.

While the youngest children in the focal group had not yet developed an explicit understanding of immigrants to be able to respond to my questions, Karina and David did demonstrate an important commonality with the larger community counternarrative, which was that they were capable of articulating their own and others' immigrant identities in terms of power and social injustice in ways that diverged from predominant societal narratives.

On the other hand, they also added other criteria for the identification of immigrants that went beyond the inclusion of legal and human rights as advocated by Tepeyac and its members, including their parents. In our interactions, the children included such social structures as socioeconomic class and language status as the structures of power on which immigrants and citizens are identified in U.S. society. Eventually, Karina and David's opinions about immigrants, which they expressed in this interaction, took the form of a text that was included in the booklet under the heading "Immigrants: The People Who Come From Mexico to Live in the United States." Such distinctions in their means of identification of immigrants, however, led me to raise questions of the remaining data produced by Tepeyac, the children's mothers, and the youngest children: *Do members of the community identify with people of other nationalities, languages, religions, and social classes? Do such social structures of identity intersect in any way with their undocumented status? Do the youngest children have an understanding of illegality? What other means do they use to identify themselves and others?*

My attempts to answer such questions led me to analyses that revealed important points of variability within the community. One such point was that although an "undocumented" identity was adopted by individual members of Tepeyac, including adults and children, being undocumented was not as central to the formation of children's identities *at this time* because this identity was not functional with respect to their immediate goals. I discovered that the formation of an undocumented identity is contingent on everyday life activities that would require illegal immigration status to be masked, surpassed, or offset (e.g., getting paid "under the table" or seeking services that require official identification). While David and Karina were the only focal children to discuss illegality explicitly over the course of our meetings, the younger children also demonstrated a developing awareness of the subject, such as knowledge that people move from one place to another and that the actual crossing is difficult. As mentioned earlier, the children were being socialized into the community's political life by accompanying their parents to rallies, demonstrations, and community meetings. On some occasions, Karina and David shared their cultural knowledge in the presence of the younger children, discussing how migrants are persecuted and die on the border and what families can do to retain their U.S.-born children if an undocumented parent is deported. In advice columns they authored, separately addressing children, teenagers, and adults, they alluded to illegality only in their advice to adults, who were warned about abuses on the part of employers and encouraged to demand minimum wages. David and Karina even considered naming the children's booklet "Illegal in New York," but they decided that illegality was not the only issue covered in their texts about the lives of Mexicans in the city. The booklet the children produced, with its collection of texts and illustrations describing the conditions of their own lives and communities, was itself a narrative about Mexican immigrants. Although rich on its own, it also served as a sharp contrast to the narratives of identity produced by the children's parents and other adults, as well as by Asociación Tepeyac.

The identities of undocumented persons, and of the U.S.-born children of undocumented immigrants, may produce different and variable developmental outcomes, which emerge from the cultural resources available to these individuals. These resources include narratives and counternarratives produced in society and institutionally that individuals can use to make sense of themselves and others. Narrative theorists need to understand how counternarratives also become available and function in individuals' identity development. The beliefs about illegality that define undocumented immigrants and their children as they reject, embrace, or produce such beliefs are outcomes of their participation in multiple activities and institutions. The notion that powerful narratives and counternarratives are simultaneously available to individuals—in making sense of self—makes identity a particularly complex, continuous developmental process. It presumes that if the quality of an individual's activities and narrativity change, so will the directionality of that individual's development.

In this chapter, I have attempted to illustrate how the formation of identity based on an institutionally produced counternarrative is one possible ontogenetic achievement enabled by the quality of an individual's participation in activities generated by a community-based organization. The sort of narrative analysis described in this chapter was useful in operationalizing cultural-historical theory, where the tensions between societal and personal development, as well as variations within wholes (e.g., institutions, individuals), were intended to be discovered rather than ignored or compressed. The background "noise" of traditional social science research may actually be a (counter)story waiting to be told. In this sense, the critical study of narratives provides a source for the retention of complexity and multiplicity in cultural analyses of human development.

Notes

1. This chapter is based on a dissertation project (Solis, 2002) that was completed thanks to the generous support of the Ford Foundation.

2. For a more detailed description of Asociación Tepeyac and its history in New York City since 1997, and through the course of this project, see Solis (2002).

3. As a result of two severe economic crises in Mexico in the mid-1980s and early 1990s, the Mexican immigrant population grew tremendously, turning into the third largest Latino group in New York City.

4. Tepeyac's information bulletin, *El Popocatepetl*, contains articles in Spanish authored by undocumented members of the community whose identities will remain anonymous in this chapter for purposes of confidentiality. All translations of original Spanish texts are my own.

5. All research participants' proper names have been changed to protect confidentiality.

References

Bakhtin, M. M. (1986). *Speech genres and other late essays* (V.W. McGee, Trans.). Austin: University of Texas Press.

Blas-Arroyo, J. L. (1994). De nuevo sobre el poder y la solidaridad: Apuntes para un análisis interaccional de la alternativa *tú/usted. Nueva Revista de Filología Hispanica, 42*(2), 385–414.

Brown, R., & Gilman, A. (1960). The pronouns of power and solidarity. In T. A. Seboek (Ed.), *Style in language* (pp. 253–276). New York: John Wiley.

Bruner, J. S. (1986). *Actual minds, possible worlds.* Cambridge, MA: Harvard University Press.

Denzin, N. K., & Lincoln, Y. S. (Eds.). (1994). *Handbook of qualitative research.* Thousand Oaks, CA: Sage.

Dijk, T. A. van (1993). Stories and racism. In D. K. Mumby (Ed.), *Narrative and social control: Critical perspectives* (pp. 121–142). Newbury Park, CA: Sage.,

Edstrom, M. (1993). La imagen de México en Estados Unidos: La inmigración mexicana en los medios impresos estadounidenses, 1980–1988. *Revista Mexicana de Sociología, 54*(4), 21–65.

Espenshade, T. J., & Belanger, M. (1998). Immigration and public opinion. In M. M. Suárez-Orozco (Ed.), *Crossings: Mexican immigration in interdisciplinary perspective* (pp. 363–403). Cambridge, MA: Harvard University Press.

Freeman, M. (1997). Why narrative? Hermeneutics, historical understanding, and the significance of stories. *Journal of Narrative and Life History, 7*(1), 169–176.

Gergen, K. J. (1990). Social understanding and the inscription of self. In J. W. Stigler, R. A. Shweder, & G. Herdt (Eds.), *Cultural psychology: Essays on comparative human development* (pp. 569–606). Cambridge, UK: Cambridge University Press.

Goodnow, J. J. (1990). The socialization of cognition: What's involved? In J. W. Stigler, R. A. Shweder, & G. Herdt (Eds.), *Cultural psychology: Essays on comparative human development* (pp. 259–286). New York: Cambridge University Press.

Harré, R., & Gillet, G. (1994). *The discursive mind*. Thousand Oaks, CA: Sage.

Henriques, J., Hollway, W., Urwin, C., Venn, C., & Walkerdine, V. (Eds.). (1984). *Changing the subject: Psychology, social regulation, and subjectivity*. London: Metheun.

Labov, W., & Waletsky, J. (1967). Narrative analysis: Oral versions of personal experience. In J. Helm (Ed.), *Essays on the verbal and visual arts* (pp. 12–44). Seattle: University of Washington Press.

Levinson, S. C. (1983). *Pragmatics*. Cambridge, UK: Cambridge University Press.

Lyotard, J.-F. (1984). *The postmodern condition: A report on knowledge*. Minneapolis: University of Minnesota Press.

Nelson, K. (1996). *Language in cognitive development: The emergence of the mediated mind*. Cambridge, UK: Cambridge University Press.

Parker, I. (1997). Discursive psychology. In D. Fox & I. Frillektensky (Eds.), *Critical psychology: An introduction* (pp. 284–298). London: Sage.

Scribner, S. (1985). Vygotsky's uses of history. In J. Wertsch (Ed.), *Culture, communication, and cognition* (pp. 119–145). New York: Cambridge University Press.

Solis, J. (2001). Immigration status and identity: Undocumented Mexicans in New York. In A. Lao-Montes & A. Davila (Eds.), *Mambo montage: The latinization of New York* (pp. 337–361). New York: Columbia University Press.

Solis, J. (2002). *The trans(formation) of illegality as an identity: A study of the organization of undocumented Mexican immigrants and their children in New York City*. Unpublished doctoral dissertation, City University of New York.

Strauss, A. L., & Corbin, J. M. (1997). *Grounded theory in practice*. London: Sage.

Zentella, A. C. (1997). *Growing up bilingual: Puerto Rican children in New York*. London: Blackwell.

3.2

Transcendent Stories and Counternarratives in Holocaust Survivor Life Histories

Searching for Meaning in Video-Testimony Archives

Sarah K. Carney

The issues that surround recovery from physical and psychological trauma have received tremendous attention within Western psychological literature (Foa, Molnar, & Cashman, 1995; Frazier & Burnett, 1994; Frazier & Schauben, 1994; Hanson, 1990; Herman, 1992; Koss, 1989; Lebowitz, 1993; Resnick, 1993; Roth, 1993). United States popular culture has, in turn, become fascinated with survival and recovery; the prevalence of self-help literatures, television talk shows, movies, magazine articles, and the like featuring "true-life survival" stories attests to the power of this cultural infatuation. A rapt social gaze follows "survivors" of all types—from victims of assault to cancer patients in remission. We thrill to stories of adversity met with strength or defiance. We are moved by the ways in which victims of horror overcome pain and betrayal. Survivors are idealized for and/or by the rest of us, as models of good citizenship or as examples of the power of religious faith, and there can be perhaps no better example of this process of almost deification than the ways in which U.S. culture and other Western cultures have written about and talked about survivors of the Holocaust (Des Pres, 1976; Langer, 1991).

In what have come to be seen as the ultimate survival narratives (Des Pres, 1976), stories about living through and despite the Holocaust—whether documented by historians, fictional, or autobiographical—reveal the powerful impact Western psychological theory has had on such literary constructions of trauma and recovery. Survival narratives of today (narratives of the Holocaust included) contain within them common clinical understandings and definitions of survival; in particular, that the victim of survival, though battered, will "overcome" or "move on" or, best yet, "triumph" over the trauma (Dye & Roth, 1991; Herman, 1992). These clinical assumptions are so strong, and so deeply entrenched in current Western understandings about trauma and healthy recovery, that they often go unscrutinized. They have become the dominant "survivor-discourse" (Romero & Stewart, 1999), and as such, they frame—and limit—the ways in which both survivors and witnesses can speak about atrocity. In order to be considered "healthy" or "good" survivors, victims are compelled to speak in this clinical language. Speaking otherwise, narrating stories that don't conform to the parameters of dominant "survivor-speak," is most often seen as indicative of pathology or illness (Dye & Roth, 1991), and narratives that suggest that triumph or transformation is not possible in the face of unimaginable horror are, for the most part, ignored. They may be cited as examples of "incurable" traumatic stress reactions, or even as the stories of malingering ex-victims wanting attention or sympathy, but mostly stories such as these are met with silence—by the clinician, by the bystander, and by the media at large.

Langer (1991) suggests that victims of the Holocaust have multiple voices, and that their narratives reflect their conflicting feelings about and ambiguity toward their own survival. Survivors, he argues, may write (or speak) from seemingly incompatible points of view—at one moment from a triumphant perspective, then at another moment as though lost. In some areas of psychology, indeed, in some parts of our culture, these competing voices are suspect, and researchers have occupied themselves in searching diligently for the "real" or "authentic" voice of the survivor (Gordon, 1993; Koss, 1989; Lefkowitz, 1997). Langer (1991) states that the goal of finding an absolute voice is doomed to failure, particularly in the face of what he calls "the moral quicksand of atrocity" (p. 138). Langer's theory may explain how survivors can be both triumphant and bitter at the same time, how they can express a gratitude to be alive as well as a nagging belief that they are dead, how Joseph Mengele can be framed both as a man who loved children and as a monster (Lagnando & Dekel, 1991), how Millu (1991) can recall walking through a field of flowers beneath a smoking chimney stack, and how Wiesel (1960) can write simultaneously about a beautiful April day and his march into Auschwitz for the first time. Multiply situated and unresolved voices create stories that seem odd when viewed from a traditional press for integration. They are, however, typical of Holocaust survivor narratives and of autobiographical narratives in general.

This chapter describes a portion of a larger project designed to shed some light on survivor-discourse in general and, specifically, on one that looked under the covers and scrutinized Western psychology's taken-for-granted assumptions regarding healthy trauma survival. I studied the narratives of Holocaust survivors, looking for the ways in which these storytellers both incorporated and resisted commonsense understandings about ways to live through atrocity. This project begins with the notion that mainstream, dominant narratives—such as those of trauma survival—may not reflect the real-life experiences of victims, and I suggest that the field of psychology might better understand (and perhaps help) victims if it were to open up its own definitions of health to include voices of those that have so far been overwritten, silenced, or disregarded. It is a call for discourse analysis to enter the ring of scientific legitimacy, for surely we have much to offer here. This chapter attempts to lift up nondominant versions of survival—here called counterstories (Romero & Stewart, 1999)—marking them as legitimate and understandable narratives of the effects of oppression that can stand alongside traditional, mainstream clinical narratives of health and recovery.

Video Project Background

I have analyzed videotaped narratives of Jewish Holocaust survivors collected by two major archival organizations: The Galiepter Foundation of Brooklyn, New York, and the Fortunoff Archives located at Yale University in New Haven, Connecticut. These particular foundations, and others like them, have the common goal of preserving the stories and memories of those who were victimized during the Holocaust by recording the life histories and experiences of people who managed to live through the war. They are the archives of autobiographies of survival, and as such they are an especially fruitful area for understanding the discourses that make up and frame narratives of atrocity. This adaptation of archival methods allowed for an analysis of the content of produced survival narratives as well as an examination of narrator and interviewer interactions; it enabled a glimpse at the actual production of a narrative of survival. The press for certain stories, the erasure of others—what Apfelbaum (2001) calls "the dread"—and the urgency to tell a "truth" became visible through this particular choice of method.

Both foundations recruit Jewish survivors to tell their stories while being interviewed and filmed by foundation trained staff. Typically, interviews begin with questions regarding the narrator's life prior to World War II— these would include questions about family, school, and holiday memories. Interviewers then usually shift into wartime memories. Survivors are invited to describe both their experiences at home and, if applicable, their deportation to and life within concentration camps. Questions next focus on the narrator's memories of liberation or the end of the war. As the interview winds down, interviewers tend to ask questions about the survivor's present-day life. These rebuilding questions spotlight current occupation, family, and personal issues. Fortunoff interviews end with these rebuilding questions. Interviewers from the Galiepter Foundation end the taped session with an invitation to the survivors to include a message to their grandchildren or to future generations based on their experiences during the Holocaust.

The data for this project were collected by watching and summarizing selected videotaped interviews and then searching interviews intensively for codes lifted from mainstream, clinical literature—specifically, the defining characteristics of healthy trauma recovery that have become so popularized that they are almost invisible. Survivor narratives were coded as traditional "survivor-speak" when narratives were *spoken, linear, emotionally resolved,* containing *heroic* themes, and followed current U.S. *psychological guidelines for healthy recovery.* Counterstories, in contrast, would be marked by *silences, fractured* and fragmented structures, *unresolved emotion,* the presence of *nonheroic* messages, and survivors' *rejection of standard psychological procedures.*[2]

The Transcendent Survivor

A traumatic event, according to Janoff-Bulman (1979), impacts some victims' most closely held beliefs about the world. It may shatter victims' sense of personal invulnerability, their sense that the world is meaningful and ordered, and their view of themselves as positive or good. The destruction of these beliefs, clinicians suggest, leads to a series of symptoms, such as depression, hopelessness, anxiety, aggression, and withdrawal—symptoms now held together under the label "survivor syndrome" (Burt & Katz, 1988). These symptoms, left untreated, may be long-lasting (Engdahl, Harkness, Eberly, Page, & Bielinski, 1993; Garbanno, 1996; Hanson, 1990; Resnick, 1993). As a result, treatment becomes centered around activities intended to help each victim reestablish her or his fractured beliefs and, more important, to integrate the traumatic experience into her or his personality and life history.

More recently, some clinicians and researchers have examined the act of surviving from an alternative, and yet complimentary, perspective—that of resilience. They ask: How is it possible that so many people who have suffered immense trauma manage to cope, adjust, and even thrive (Aldwin, Levenson, & Spiro, 1994; Draucker, 1992; Lyons, 1991; O'Leary & Ickovics, 1995; Robinson, Rapaport-Bar-Sever, & Rapaport, 1994; Spaccarelli, 1995; Whiteman, 1993)? Resiliency, as Valentine and Feinauer (1993) write, is "defined as the power or ability to return to original form or position after being bent . . . as well as the ability to overcome adversity . . . and rise above disadvantage" (p. 222). Resiliency implies transcendence. Work on resilience has gained momentum in recent years, and the researchers who adopt this perspective stress the possibility of finding good or positive outcomes of trauma. This idea holds a great deal of attraction for the field of psychology—indeed, one might argue that it is a collective fantasy that we all be saved—and its assumptions now form many of the traditional clinical theorems for surviving trauma.

Traditional psychological definitions of healthy survival suggest, then, that successful recovery from trauma involves recreating a life story that is, if not transcendent, at least resolved and integrated. The mandates of clinically approved survival represented by the literature of the survival movement, as well as by current psychological research—with its focus on resilience, state that, almost regardless of type of trauma, successful survival seems to involve two important steps for the survivor: the event must be seen as "in the past" and, in addition, the event must be integrated into the survivor's life history (Cohler, 1991). The challenge for therapists and survivors alike is to manage the initial and immediate turmoil generated by trauma, and then gradually to move toward the integration of the trauma into the survivor's sense of self—to reintegrate his or her life story as an assimilated whole.

Given the state of the literature and its focus on recovery from traumatic stress and resilience, what can we say are the criteria for traditional, mainstream, psychological discourse? First and foremost, there is a tremendous press for survivor narratives to have transcendent overtones. From there, transcendent stories have qualities that are particular and predictable. First, transcendent stories are stories that are spoken; silence represents pathology in the view of psychology (Alcoff & Gray, 1993; Lang, 1995). The goal for survivors is speech—private speech with the therapist (Foucault's notion of confessional speech) and then, optimally, public speech, political speech, and legal speech. Next, transcendent stories are stories structured by a linear progression of events. They, like all good stories (Gergen & Gergen, 1995), have a clear beginning, middle, and end. In addition, the emotional content in the stories is either resolved or controlled in the telling (Herman, 1992). Transcendent stories are stories with heroic themes and developed characters (Gergen & Gergen, 1995). The narrator describes events in a way that creates solid heroes or villains. Similarly, transcendent stories do not threaten cultural beliefs or fundamental ways of looking at the world (Janoff-Bulman, 1979). They have "happy endings" and use language that describes the hero's ability to surmount obstacles and overcome difficulty. In transcendent narratives generated within the field of psychology, health is often attributed to those survivors who correctly use the dominant clinical language (posttraumatic stress disorder, depression, anxiety disorder, etc.) and agentic language to describe their experiences. Similarly, healthy survival is attributed to those who use traditional coping language and/or dictates—the marshaling of social support, the use of professional therapists, the pressing of legal action (Fine, 1992). Vast amounts of data were obtained by using each of these codes and applying them to the selected autobiographical accounts of the Holocaust. It is not possible, given the volume of the work, to include them all here; I have selected one to look at more specifically—the urgent press for heroism. Let us turn, then, and look more closely at this criterion for the development of transcendent stories and to the Holocaust narratives themselves that embody it in interesting and intriguing forms.

The Heroic Narrative

One way for a narrative to be considered transcendent or "healthy" is that survivors allow themselves as well as their stories to become texts for purity and wisdom gained through the transcendence of inhuman events. The survivor of trauma is viewed by our culture as the possessor of certain knowledge, insight, and understanding that the rest of the nontraumatized world does not, and cannot, possess (Des Pres, 1976; Epstein, 1979; Greenspan, 1996; Ringelheim, 1995; Whiteman, 1993). He or she is positioned as a "hero/ine" (Des Pres, 1976; Wiesel, 1962). Survivors, says Des Pres (1976), are proof that "human heroism is possible" (p. 54). Heroism is made up of both an acceptance of this implied unique wisdom and a willingness to cast the self and the other "characters" in his or her story as determined, steady fighters—as courageous battlers of injustice and as brave "surmounters" of atrocity. Survivors come back to tell the "rest of us" how they saved themselves and others, about the enrichment of their lives due to their experiences, about their appreciation for each day, and about their higher realization of life's fundamental goodness (Frankl, 1977).

Anderson and Gold (1994) suggest that the cultural preoccupation in the United States with attributing heroics to survivors of trauma reflects a well-meaning attempt by professionals to help victims by assuring them of their inner strengths; they indicate respect as well as sense of conviction that recovery is possible. Attempts to create "strengths" from struggles stem, they argue, from a real desire to help or to try to ease the pain of those who are suffering.

The tendency to glorify and deify victims of atrocity is not, however, one that is purely therapeutic. In addition, cultural tendencies to romanticize survivors, to turn them into heroic soldiers of injustice, may be attempts to alleviate the cultural fears that spring up when worldviews are threatened (Janoff-Bulman, 1979). Capitalist societies have much invested in notions of personal freedom and individual power. The notion that at any moment our lives might be disrupted, that we may be powerless in the face of evil, or that we might engage in atrocity ourselves is profoundly discomforting. In the face of that discomfort then, it seems only natural for the culture to attempt to shore up chaotic images and messages of powerlessness with smooth, seamless discourses of heroism and transcendence (Greenspan, 1996).

Attributions of heroism, of saintliness, or of martyrdom to survivors of trauma frequently come from outside the narrator's personal story of survival. Readers, editors, listeners, therapists, family, and/or friends frequently interpret for or attribute to the survivor a heroic quality.[3] Similarly, editors and reviewers have taken cultural and psychological notions of heroic survival and then used these discourses to construct descriptions of traditional transcendent survivors.[4]

These types of narratives contain a combination of the two survival imperatives or heroic mandates: the individual or collective triumph over horror and atrocity (by skill, by intelligence, or by force) and the attribution to the survivor of a privileged view of human existence. They indicate that it is only by living through atrocity—the worst the world can provide—that an individual can truly achieve such an understanding of the fragile beauty of life (Frankl, 1977; Ringelheim, 1995). Des Pres (1976), in his account of life in the death camps, writes, "It seems clear that the ordeal of survival becomes, at least for some, an experience of growth and purification" (p. 21).

How did these cultural expectations about the presence of heroics within survival stories play out in the data I collected? As tellers of survival narratives, these particular survivors were certainly cognizant of the fact that heroic stories were anticipated by their listeners. However, it was also clear that few narrators were willing to represent themselves as heroes; the role of hero/ine was often only reluctantly accepted by these narrators and frequently then with suggestions that what had occurred was "no big deal" or what "anybody else would have done." Survivors downplayed incredible stories of bravery; their few words and frequently emotionless discourse belie the danger they were in and the risks they took.

Survivors' stories of their own generosity, of kindness to other people, and of personal acts of courage are notably detached and often conclude with an apology; survivors suggested that they were not, in fact, courageous, but stupid or not thinking. M.A., for instance, describes finding a wallet full of enough money to feed her family for a month. Rather than keeping the money, she returns it, but she brushes off the idea that her gesture was a particularly noble one: "I was an idiot, but this is upbringing." Similarly, in her interview, C.R. describes assisting a girl who needed to buy a ticket to Budapest to escape the Nazis' advance. C.R. says that she went with the girl to the train station, gave her her own birth certificate, and bought the ticket for her. She does not feel that she did anything particularly heroic, however, for she concludes her story:[1]

> Today when I'm thinking back . . . I could have killed my whole family with this. If I would buy the ticket and just give it to her and go . . . not to give mine birth certificate . . . this wouldn't be nothing. Just for this . . . you can see how . . . s s stupid I was [smiling and nodding slowly]. And that's it. [Silence] And I hope that she lives. [Silence] And maybe . . . if I would have to do it again . . . I would again not think twice. Just today I would know why I am doing it. That time I was . . . I think very naive.

Few narrators in this sample represent themselves as having lived heroic lives during atrocity, and they, in combination and agreement with the many autobiographical accounts I have read, almost never suggest that they, as survivors of the Holocaust, possess a unique understanding simply because of their experience of suffering. In fact, many suggest the opposite—that their suffering made them more callous. Attributions of heroics seem to be a criterion for transcendence that is accepted or allowed to be tacked on from outside rather than being self-acclaimed. Survivors may allow such descriptions; however, it seems that they rarely assert them themselves.

Heroic stories are present within these narratives, however, and they come in dramatic form. Parents, siblings, friends, strangers, and even Germans may be cast in the role of hero/martyr/savior, and, when this occurs, all of the transcendent language and culturally wished-for heroic themes emerge. Frequently, the heroes of these narratives are dead, and often they died while saving others or in sacrificing themselves for others.

Heroes were "cast" in interesting ways by the narrators of my sample: most heroes, according to these narrators, died during the war, becoming the "drowned" that Levi (1986) spoke of so eloquently.[5] For example, A.S. recalls how his mother saved another mother and her child who were stranded as the Germans invaded their Polish town:

> And they . . . they didn't have . . . they didn't know where to go. So my mother says to her . . . her name was Flussberg. . . . "What are you sitting here . . . you gonna get killed! Come! Don't wait!" So we . . . we rent a . . . horse and buggy . . . and this family went with us. Today this boy is alive in Israel. He always . . . when I go there he always tells me without my mother he wouldn't be alive . . . today.

Similarly, S.F. describes the heroic sacrifice by his mother, who went without food so that her sons could have more to eat:

> I have a very good mother. I go home . . . and she get me supper and she's not eating. And I ask her: "For what you don't eat?" So I . . . I don't have nothing more. And she don't eat and she get me to eat. "You have to have . . . you're young . . . and that's it."

Family members were not the only heroes of the war, however, as these narrators demonstrate. S.F. describes General Eisenhower as a hero, as his efforts got S.F. and his family relocated to the United States. F.I. recalls the murder of Rosa Rubotto (a Jewish prisoner of Auschwitz who helped smuggle the explosives that blew up one of the crematoriums near the end of the war): "She was the most wonderful human being—if she could do anything she really risked her life to be able to help somebody." Rubotto was hanged for her actions.

Nor were Jews and allies the only heroes, as M.A., L.H., and A.S. make clear. Some of the Germans (the SS and other camp workers) were also singled out for their exceptional heroics. For instance, L.H. recalls Hungarian camp workers who tried to keep prisoners' spirits up by telling them "Eat everything, food is life," as well as by passing messages for them. And A.S. states,

> And we had a . . . instructor . . . an SS in Auschwitz. His name was Mueller. He . . . he was in civilian clothes . . . he didn't wear a uniform but he told us he was an SS . . . but he was a master bricklayer. One night . . . afternoon he took us all together and he told us, he says "You. . . better learn this trade," he says, "That's the only way you gonna survive. And I'm gonna help you . . . to survive," he says. This . . . was . . . was one SS in Auschwitz. In fact

we looked for him after the war . . . we tried to find him. He organized soup for us . . . bread . . . [sigh] . . . he was very nice. [Voice cracks] He was a human being.

Thus we as readers or viewers (or, perhaps, interviewers) expect to find heroic themes of survival, and we are not disappointed, though the characters are perhaps not who we had anticipated. Heroic themes are tricky, slippery concepts when applied to the narratives of Holocaust survivors, as these data bear out. The role of hero/ine, it seems, is reluctantly and only momentarily tolerated, and survivors' discomfort with this attribution is fairly visible. Instead, these narrators choose to celebrate and memorialize family members, strangers who offered seconds of kindness, and even some Nazis themselves, who may have (knowingly or unknowingly, intentionally or unintentionally) offered help or saved a life. The mantle of hero, as these narratives demonstrate, is, perhaps, a heavy one, which is troubling to the survivors themselves. Their narratives read, more often, as the stories of ordinary people caught up in extraordinary circumstances, who have the luck, good fortune, or fate to have met up with the "true heroes" of the Holocaust.

The Counterstory—The Life History That Does Not Integrate

If traditional clinical and popular conceptions of survival and recovery are best signified through the construction of transcendent narratives, what do we do with those stories and parts of stories that do not so conform? If we as qualitative interviewers and researchers wish to think more expansively about the data we collect, at some point we have to begin to account for the ways in which our data fail to support our hypotheses—the ways our data fail to comply with our stated or unstated assumptions. In survivor narratives, in particular, stories do not always neatly splice into our U. S. cultural assumptions about healthy recovery. Close reading of these stories leads us to the idea that, in many ways, survivors of trauma tell tales that often disconfirm, even defy, the now nearly standardized recommendations for and explanations of trauma. Survivors may tell oppositional narratives—stories that call into question the theories and suppositions of traditional psychology. These new perspectives are disturbing—they threaten to topple the fragile framework for knowledge a culture so painstakingly builds. Accepting them, let alone embracing them, feels difficult. But if our goal as psychologists is to build a more inclusive psychology, a more encompassing psychology, even just a smarter psychology, we have to learn how to examine critically what we take for granted. The criteria for transcendence may be turned completely around when they are confronted with the data of actual survival narratives. If spoken narratives are healthy, how can we account for the fact that many survivors do not speak? If transcendence means the linear structuring of a narrative, how do we evaluate the fragmented, jumpy, scattered nature of many life story interviews? If, in order to be considered healthy, survivors must allow their stories to become moral models, fables for heroism, or myths of transcendence, how do we account for those who refuse to narrate such heroics? How do we hear stories that question our fundamental beliefs about the world? Finally, if transcendence means a certain fluency with the medical model and social discourses of health, how do we hear the voices of those who resist and refuse such support and assistance? How do we allow alternate conceptions of survival—diverse versions of health—to sit at the same table as the accepted, even trumpeted, traditional vision?

The first step toward legitimizing counterstories is to hear them. If we can recognize without judgment (or diagnosis) the existence of alternate views and positions, we will have come a long way toward broadening our conceptions of recovery from victimization. In the next section of this chapter, I will reconsider the earlier analyzed criterion for transcendence—the presence of heroic themes—this time analyzing the data for the opposite of transcendence—counterstories.

Survival Without the Phoenix

I have just stated that one of the most culturally potent mandates (in the United States) is that survivors describe their experiences in transcendent language and position themselves (or at least allow themselves to be cast) as hero/ines in their narratives. Stories of survivor-heroes flood our lives daily; our popular media have become incessant producers of phoenix-like transcendence.

I began this research with a suspicion that survivors themselves are living in a stew of discourses, some of which are more dominant or persuasive than others, and that there is no one authentic, real or raw story of survival. I wondered, do Holocaust survivors rest uncomfortably with notions of heroism and martyrdom and with assumptions about the spiritual transcendence gained through suffering? I assumed that this would be a difficult question to answer, given the overwhelming cultural pressures for hero stories. In fact, many, if not most, survival autobiographies and interviews include anti-heroic narratives and messages. Many survivors describe the non-heroic acts and behaviors they engaged in to survive (Epstein, 1979; Langer, 1991; Levi, 1960; Millu, 1991; Wiesel, 1960, 1962), and many suggest that suffering did not enhance their spiritual or philosophical existence (Greenspan, 1996; Levi, 1986; Ringelheim, 1995; Wiesel, 1962). Extensive reading of Holocaust narratives, in fact, leaves one with the sense that there lies a huge gulf between the actual life stories produced by survivors and the translations they receive in film, television, books, and other mass productions.

Frankl's (1977) book *Man's Search for Meaning*[6] aside, much of the witness literature calls into question this notion of the hero-survivor. In reality, spiritual growth was a luxury—and a virtually impossible one. In fact, many Holocaust narrators state that survival in a concentration camp entailed a violence, ruthlessness, and hardness that was antithetical to any kind of spiritual or philosophical transcendence. Prisoners stole from one another, beat each other, turned their backs to cruelty, and watched mutely as their families and friends died off. The message of the stories many survivors tell is not of the blessing of suffering but of the brutalizing, degrading force that turned them into brutalizers themselves.

Survivors were far from invulnerable to Nazi assaults, as Hollywood and other cultural producers of survival might have us believe; in many of these narratives, the "invincible" human spirit turns out to be completely susceptible and porous with respect to learning to act with stunning cruelty in order to survive. The experience of the Holocaust, Langer (1991) writes, and particularly the experience of the concentration camps, "crushes the spirit and frustrates the incentive to renewal" (p. 99). Despite pressures to tell stories to the contrary, survivors maintain that their actions were far from noble and were by necessity primarily selfish, hard, and brutal. Levi (1986) argues that we should not be surprised to hear that prisoners victimized other prisoners. The Nazi concentration camp, he states, was designed to bring out the worst in its inmates. Oppression, he stated, produces more oppression—not justice, kindness, or sympathy, and especially not heroes.

In the stories I watched, many of the narrators noted the cruelty of fellow prisoners in their narratives. A.R., for instance, recalls Slovakian prisoners pointing to the chimneys of Auschwitz and saying, "You see? Your father and mother is dead already—those flames are your parents burning." Narrators also recalled being the victims of theft by other prisoners. A.R. recalls fellow prisoners stealing the cabbage her brother had smuggled so carefully to her: "So they took from me . . . that was . . . so big . . . the hunger." M.A. remembers her entrance into Auschwitz-Birkenau. When she woke up the first morning, she found that her shoes and comb had been taken. She says that she was pushed, beaten, and scapegoated by other prisoners; even the Jews, she states, were cruel to one another. Similarly, L.H.

recalls how the Polish and Czechoslovakian prisoners used to beat up and scream at the Hungarians. Later, when she reflects on the fact that Jews hurt other Jews, she says that they tried to keep that information secret:

> Don't admit this in front of the Goyim . . . let's be quiet about this, it is our shame . . . we felt bad about that . . . but it was the truth . . . why should the whole world know about that . . . that Jews did that to other Jews? But it happened . . . the Germans had a special meaness . . . the dirty jobs they gave to the other Jews.

In their narratives, these survivors note their own brutal behavior as well as that of others. They do not apologize for such actions, however. They understand and explain them by stating that the violence of the camp—the hunger, the beatings, the cold, and the terror—produced the violence among themselves. The brilliant oppression of National Socialism managed to create the context in which the oppressed would victimize their own, a circumstance that is perhaps the most destructive legacy of the Holocaust. Few narrators fail to mention their participation in atrocity, their existence in Levi's (1986) "gray zone"; their implication defies cultural notions of heroics under adversity. Certainly, they provide us with a version of survival that calls into question the moral vision put forth by Frankl (1977). Trauma, as Erikson (1995) has suggested, seems to have as many centrifugal as centripetal forces.

Survivors of the Holocaust have also had much to say about the second mandate for heroic stories: that survivors allow for the suggestion that their experiences ennoble them. Wiesel (1960) questions just such an assumption when he asks, "Where is God to be found? In suffering or in rebellion? When is a man truly a man? When he submits or when he refuses? Where does suffering lead him? To purification or to beastiality?" (p. 12).

The interviews I studied have particular moments where it seems an advocation of a privileged viewpoint might be expected or anticipated. Both protocols include a question about what survivors would like to tell future generations, after all their experiences. This question, I believe, flags an assumption that survivors must possess, by virtue of their experience, a special insight, perhaps a unique vision of what it will take to make sure a Holocaust never reoccurs. Notably, not one of the narrators in my sample answered from a position of privileged knowledge. Their answers were vague; one (C.R.) suggested that future generations should be kind. L.H. said that she wanted future generations to be nice and educated in the Jewish faith. A.A. wished future generations, "All the best. That includes everything. Health, parnassah [income], mood." Clearly, these narrators are not suggesting that they possess any more awareness or moral stature than any non-survivor. Their wishes for the future are ordinary, somewhat conventional, and unceremonious hopes. Thus the antihero and non-privileged perspectives discussed in this section provide dramatic examples of counterstories; they stand in opposition, or at least, as alternatives, to traditional portrayals of survival.

Some Concluding Thoughts

In this chapter, I described only a small portion of a much larger study on survivor-discourse (Carney, 1998). In it, I examined the ways Western society now privileges certain versions—certain discourses—of survival and recovery and pathologizes others. In particular, I explored the ways U.S. culture embraces and legitimizes survival narratives that follow specific psychological and cultural formulations about healthy survival. In this project, I suggested that "good" or healthy survivors must tell their stories, they must structure their narratives linearly, they must express and then resolve emotions associated with the traumatic event, they must allow their narratives to become examples of heroism and must avow a privileged moral and intellectual awareness as a result of their experiences, and they must utilize the support systems and treatments recommended by the culture. Though not individually responsible for their oppression, healthy survivors take individual responsibility for their healing, and it is worth underscoring that cultural recommendations for recovery ignore a cultural critique in favor of an individualized medical model.

This project takes seriously the concepts of master and counternarratives (Romero & Stewart, 1999) and examines these ideas in a particular collection of autobiographical narratives. Some survivors refuse to let the culture, as represented by listeners, off the hook. They tell what can be called "counter-dominant stories." Some survivors suggest that these individual-ized prescriptions serve to reinforce societal belief systems that maintain oppression. Their narratives remind us that focusing on whether or not a survivor has visited a therapist takes our gaze away from the perpetrator of the crime, and it takes our attention away from the culpability of the culture in which the crime occurred.

When survivors refuse to switch their gaze and take on personal responsibility for recovery, interviewers, therapists, listeners, and/or cultures react in one of two ways: they pathologize and thus dis-empower the counter-story by labeling the survivor as depressed or mentally ill or they rewrite the counternarrative in socially acceptable ways. Both are effective strategies for reinstituting and reaffirming the values and beliefs of the dominant social system. With the first, we learn to feel sorry for (or despise) the survivor; with the second, we learn to admire her or him. Much of the clinical work done in the 1970s and 1980s attempted to do the first, while much of the resilience work being done in psychology at this time attempts to do the second. This project, instead, attempts to uncover the multiple discourses floating in actual narratives of survival; it allows counterstories and master discourses of resilience to stand next to each other, recognizing that each plays an important part in the story of survival.

I would like to end this chapter with two overriding conclusions that I think spring from this work. One has to do with critical discursive research in general, and the other with the implications of this study in particular. The first is a note about the materiality of discourse. Those of us who engage in discourse analysis are so often asked: Is discourse material? Is it alive? Can we touch it? Can it touch us? These are questions that plague us—they keep those of us who do work on narratives up at night. Is talking about the ways we talk an intellectual exercise, interesting but of little practical use? Of what value is knowing that knowledge is constructed from particular viewpoints and frameworks? Who cares about the work we do? There exist ongoing and sticky debates over whether narratives and discourse can be considered "material" or whether material conditions and contexts stand both within and outside of discourse (Ussher, 1997). It is the quintessential postmodern argument. One side suggests that narratives, in the end, are just stories, symbols, and signs. Narratives, these theorists state, may organize or galvanize social change; however, they in and of themselves do not create change—they do not put food on the table, they do not put warm coats on children. On the other side of this debate are discourse theorists who suggest that narratives are, in fact, the final and essential materials of any social system. In the study I am presenting here, I acknowledge the importance of ongoing discussion—and I realize that stories are not food, are not heat, and are not safe places to live. But at the same time I draw primarily on and frame my theoretical argument from those who suggest that discourse—and narrative—are what constitute, define, and construct the material world. With this task, I see narratives as much more than "just stories." Material conditions have roots in discourse. While hunger may not be discursive, poverty—its reasons, justifications, explanations, legitimations—is. Narratives of responsibility or of deservingness construct material conditions; it is through these cultural narratives that material resources are allotted and distributed. Thus, this work begins with the assumption that stories are more than "only discourse." It begins, quite straightforwardly, with the idea that altering social discourse has the potential to alter existing social conditions.

In addition, and more specifically, this work demonstrates in a concrete manner that the ways in which we talk about a "thing" (surviving, health, recovery) can impact material effects. It stands, I hope, as an example of how our discourse work can clarify real-life social arrangements. Framing Holocaust narratives as counter-dominant and master narratives, and allowing for traditionally ignored, discredited, or pathologized versions of a story to emerge, exposes some unsettling implications—and these implications are surely material in nature. If, as clinicians have argued, survivors are heroes, if survivors are transcendent, if survivors are privileged through their experience of suffering, we are then led to the natural next question: What, then, can be wrong with such oppression? For if victimization functions to create a better form of person, where is the impetus to stop events like the Holocaust from happening? Psychology's focus on resilience and transcendence—and indeed our entire culture's fascination with survivors of any sort—reveals our discomfort with thinking about the real cost of oppression and the ways in which our own practices and assumptions reinforce unequal power relations. In glorifying transcendence, we risk saluting oppression, since it seems, the one produces or makes the other possible. A sober thought, and one that reminds all of us who take discourse analysis seriously that our findings may have powerful implications.

In this chapter, I have argued not for the impossibility of transcendence but for embracing a variety of possible stories. If counterstories are legitimate, our assumptions about oppression, about surviving, about cultural and individual health, and about the fragility of our philosophical beliefs have to become more complicated. Listening to those voices that question mainstream, dominant conceptions of the ways the world works does not cause the social system to fall apart—it causes it to grow. Current, socially acceptable narratives of survival are shrunken; they are smaller than they should be. Including and legitimizing different realities, viewpoints, and a greater variety of narratives influences—and alters—social discourse. Discourse analysis has, then, a large role to play in further broadening future conversations about survival, health, and recovery.

Notes

1. Ellipses mark pauses or hesitations in quoted interview material.
2. The following is a brief description of the narrators:

All were English-speaking, Jewish survivors of the Holocaust, and all were deported to concentration camps. Six of the interviews described here are of women, and four are of men. Five of those interviewed were Polish, three were

Czechoslovakian, one was Hungarian, and one was Rumanian. Almost all of the narrators were sent first to Auschwitz/Birkenau; however, from there most were sent to other locations. They were either sent to work camps or marched to other concentration camps as the Allies advanced toward Poland. Their long and, for most of them, nearly fatal journeys make a particularly grim atlas: from Auschwitz this small sample of survivors marched to and through camps such as Bergen-Belson, Magdelberg, Mathausen, Lenzing, Peterswaldaw, Langenbielau, Langwy-Thil, Heilbronn, Dachau, Passau, Christianstadt, Ravensbruck, and Mulhov before they were finally liberated.

Only two of these interviewees had finished their formal schooling before the war began. For the rest, growing wartime tensions and the needs of their families forced the end of their schooling. Based on their stories and the ways they described their lives, social standing, and economic privilege prewar, one of the narrators appears to have come from a wealthy family, five could be described as coming from middle class backgrounds, and four either stated or implied that their families had been poor. Only one of the women had worked outside of the home before the war began, while the men had worked various jobs.

All of the narrators experienced profound and devastating family losses. As is common for Holocaust survivors, very few of their family members survived. Only one of the interviewees was reunited with his parents—such reunions were highly unusual. The rest found what family they could through painstaking and rigorous searching. Some sisters or brothers survived, some aunts or uncles, some cousins, but far too few, and these narrators, like so many others, found that their large families had been devastated by the Nazis.

The interviews analyzed were conducted in English with American, English-speaking interviewers; however, a variety of languages (words or phrases) peppered the stories of the survivors. They used a collection of languages—Yiddish, German, Polish, Russian, Czechoslovakian, Hebrew, and interesting versions of what both Levi (1986) and Langer (1991) mention as a sort of "language of the camps," or prisoner jargon, to communicate their experiences. All the interviews were composed of a mixture of languages and, because of this, some portions of the video summaries have been translated. In general, survival stories took a while to tell—the average length of this sample of interviews was 1½ hours, with the shortest interview lasting for 1 hour and the longest running for 4½ hours.

All interviewees describe the painful processes of rebuilding their lives after the war and reestablishing normalcy post-chaos. All but one of these narrators married fellow survivors. None of the interviewees remained unmarried. All the survivors, in addition, had children either postwar or, in the case of the oldest interviewee, prewar. Five of the narrators stated that they have grandchildren, and two mention their great-grandchildren. Two of the women worked outside of the home postwar, while the rest of the women married and became wives and mothers, supporting their husbands and reestablishing their homes and families. The men began to look for work in a new country, finding jobs in a variety of primarily manufacturing areas.

3. For example, Epstein (1979) quotes a child of Holocaust survivors:

> I thought that my parents were good, generous people who were ethical in their business dealings and respected by their community. I thought that the war had made them that way, that being good was their way of conquering the evil of their experience, and that this was true of all survivors. (p. 314)

4. For example, the inside flap jacket of *When They Came to Take My Father: Voices of the Holocaust* describes the book in the following manner:

> Never in history has there been an event more horrifying than the Holocaust—the human loss inconceivable, the after-shocks felt for generations. But in the midst of the misery was forged a strength of spirit and humanity that shows in the faces and stories of its survivors. Captured here with clarity and truth are fifty images of survival, portraits of the men and women who lived through the brutality to triumph over oppression; survivors truly. (Kahn & Hager, 1996)

5. Levi (1986) said that the true heroes of the concentration camps did not survive—that survival necessitated being willing to exploit family, friends, and strangers for a piece of bread.

6. Frankl's (1977) work has become a Holocaust classic and is perhaps emblematic of the heroic narrative. Frankl maintains that survival of the Holocaust necessitated finding a transcendent meaning in the suffering. He stresses the moments of beauty within Auschwitz—a lovely blue day, the music playing as prisoners go off to work in the morning, the singing, the art produced—and it is because of these moments, he argues, that he and others like him have more appreciation for life. Frankl's work contains within it two themes: first, that the common prisoner of the camps was ennobled by his or her experiences and, second, that the human spirit is transcendent.

References

Alcoff, L., & Gray, L. (1993). Survivor discourse: Transgression or recuperation? *Signs, 18,* 260–290.

Aldwin, C., Levenson, M., & Spiro, A. (1994). Vulnerability and resilience to combat exposure: Can stress have life-long effects? *Psychology and Aging, 9,* 34–44.

Anderson, L., & Gold, K. (1994). I know what it means but it's not how I feel: The construction of survivor identity in feminist counseling practice. *Women and Therapy, 15,* 5–17.

Apfelbaum, E. (2001). The dread: an essay on communication across cultural boundaries. *Critical Psychology: The International Journal of Critical Psychology, 4,* 19–34.

Burt, M., & Katz, B. (1988). Coping strategies and recovery from rape. *Annals of the New York Academy of Sciences, 528,* 345–358.

Carney, S. (1998). *Transcendence and counter-story: The construction of narratives of survival.* Unpublished manuscript.

Cohler, B. (1991). The life story and the study of resilience and response to adversity. *Journal of Narrative and Life History, 1,* 169–200.

Des Pres, T. (1976). *The survivor: An anatomy of life in the death camps.* New York: Oxford University Press.

Draucker, C. (1992). Construing benefit from a negative experience of incest. *Western Journal of Nursing Research, 14,* 343–353.

Dye, E., & Roth, S. (1991). Psychotherapy with Vietnam veterans and rape and incest survivors. *Psychotherapy, 28,* 103–120.

Engdahl, B., Harkness, A., Eberly, R., Page, N., & Bielinski, J. (1993). Structural models of captivity trauma, resilience, and trauma response among former prisoners of war 20-40 years after release. *Social Psychology and Psychiatric Epidemiology, 28,* 109–115.

Epstein, H. (1979). *Children of the Holocaust.* New York: Penguin.

Erikson, K. (1995). Notes on trauma and community. In C. Caruth (Ed.), *Trauma: explorations in memory* (pp. 183–199). Baltimore, MD: Johns Hopkins University Press.

Fine, M. (1992). Coping with rape: Critical perspectives on consciousness. In *Disruptive voices: The possibilities of feminist research.* Ann Arbor: University of Michigan Press.

Foa, E., Molnar, C., & Cashman, L. (1995). Change in rape narratives during exposure therapy for posttraumatic stress disorder. *Journal of Traumatic Stress, 8,* 675–690.

Frankl, V. (1977). *Man's search for meaning: An introduction to logotherapy.* Boston: Beacon.

Frazier, P., & Burnett, J. (1994). Immediate coping strategies among rape victims. *Journal of Counseling and Development, 72,* 633–639.

Frazier, P., & Schauben, L. (1994). Causal attributions and recovery from rape and other stressful life events. *Journal of Social and Clinical Psychology, 13,* 1–14.

Garbanno, J. (1996). The spiritual challenge of violent trauma. *American Journal of Orthopsychiatry, 66,* 162–163.

Gergen, M., & Gergen, K. (1995). What is this thing called love? Emotional scenarios in historical perspective. *Journal of Narratives and Life History, 5,* 221–237.

Gordon, L. (1993). Women's agency, social control, and the construction of "rights" by battered women. In S. Fisher & K. Davis (Eds.), *Negotiating at the margins: The gendered discourses of power and resistance.* New Brunswick, NJ: Rutgers University Press.

Greenspan, H. (1996). On being a "real survivor." *Sh'ma: A Journal of Jewish Responsibility, 25,* 1–3.

Hanson, R. (1990). The psychological impact of sexual assault on women and children: A review. *Annals of Sex Research, 3,* 187–232.

Herman, J. L. (1992). *Trauma and recovery: The aftermath of violence—from domestic abuse to political terror.* New York: Basic Books.

Janoff-Bulman, R. (1979). Characterological versus behavioral self-blame: Inquiries into depression and rape. *Journal of Personality and Social Psychology, 37*(10), 1798–1809.

Kahn, L., & Hager, R. (Eds.). (1996). *When they came to take my father: Voices of the Holocaust.* New York: Arcade.

Koss, M. (1989). A conceptual analysis of rape victimization: Long term effects and implications for treatment. *Psychology of Women Quarterly, 13,* 27–40.

Lagnando, L., & Dekel, S. (1991). *Children of the flames: Dr. Joseph Mengele and the untold story of the twins of Auschwitz.* New York: William Morrow.

Lang, M. (1995). Silence therapy with holocaust survivors and their families. *Australian and New Zealand Journal of Family Therapy, 16,* 1–10.

Langer, L. (1991). *Holocaust testimonies: The ruins of memory.* New Haven, CT: Yale University Press.

Lebowitz, L. (1993). Treatment of rape trauma: Integrating trauma-focused therapy with feminism. *Journal of Training and Practice in Professional Psychology, 7,* 81–99.

Lefkowitz, B. (1997). *Our guys: The Glen Ridge rape and the secret life of the perfect suburb.* Berkeley: University of California Press.

Levi, P. (1960). *Survival in Auschwitz—The Nazi assault on humanity.* New York: Macmillan.

Levi, P. (1986). *The drowned and the saved* (R. Rosenthal, Trans.). New York: Summit.

Lyons, J. (1991). Strategies for assessing the potential for positive adjustment following trauma. *Journal of Traumatic Stress, 4,* 93–111.

Millu, L. (1991). *Smoke over Birkenau* (L. S. Schwartz, Trans.). Philadelphia: Jewish Publication Society.

O'Leary, V., & Ickovics, J. (1995). Resilience and thriving in response to challenge: An opportunity for a paradigm shift in women's health. *Women's Health Research on Gender, Behavior, and Policy, 1,* 121–142.

Resnick, P. (1993). The psychological impact of rape. *Journal of Interpersonal Violence, 8,* 223–255.

Ringelheim, J. (1995). Women and the Holocaust—A reconstruction of research. *Signs, 10,* 741–761.

Robinson, S., Rapaport-Bar-Sever, M., & Rapaport, J. (1994). The present state of people who survived the Holocaust as children. *Acta Psychiatrica Scandinavica, 89,* 242–245.

Romero, M., & Stewart, A. (Eds.). (1999). *Women's untold stories: Breaking silence, talking back, voicing complexity.* New York: Routledge.

Roth, S. (1993). The process of coping with incest for adult survivors: Measurement and implications for treatment and research. *Journal of Interpersonal Violence, 8,* 363–377.

Spaccarelli, S. (1995). Resilience criteria and factors associated with resilience in sexually abused girls. *Child Abuse and Neglect, 19,* 1171–1182.

Ussher, J. M. (1997). Towards a material-discursive analysis of madness, sexuality and reproduction. In J. Ussher (Ed.), *Body talk: The material and discursive regulation of sexuality, madness and reproduction* (pp. 1–9). New York: Routledge.

Valentine, L., & Feinauer, L. (1993). Resilience factors associated with female survivors of childhood sexual abuse. *American Journal of Family Therapy, 21,* 216–224.

Whiteman, D. (1993). Holocaust survivors and escapees: Their strengths. *Psychotherapy, 30,* 443–451.

Wiesel, E. (1960). *Night.* New York: Bantam.

Wiesel, E. (1962). *The Accident.* New York: Bantam.

3.3

Women of "The Greatest Generation"

Feeling on the Margin of Social History

Abigail J. Stewart and Janet E. Malley

Americans have a powerful cultural narrative about "the greatest generation," expressed in its most romantic form by Tom Brokaw (1998):

> 1940 was the fulcrum of America in the twentieth century, when the nation was balanced precariously between the darkness of the Great Depression on one side and the storms of war in Europe and the Pacific on the other. It was a critical time in the shaping of this nation and the world, equal to the revolution of 1776 and the perils of the Civil War. . . . The nation turned to its young to carry the heaviest burden, to fight in enemy territory and to keep the home front secure and productive. These young men and women were eager for the assignment. They understood what was required of them, and they willingly volunteered for their duty. (p. 3)

Authors' Note: We are grateful to the nine "Round Robins" and their several family members who generously cooperated with the needs of this study. We are also grateful to Elizabeth Coe, Kristin Coon, Julie Konik, Tracy Landskroener, Marie Miller, and Deb Serafin for assistance with transcription. Special thanks go to Edith Parker for starting it all, and to Colette Daiute, Cynthia Lightfoot, David G. Winter, and Timothy Stewart-Winter, for helpful comments on earlier drafts.

In this chapter, we will develop a less romantic, more modest, and more complex narrative about the experience of one group of women from this generation. Their experience is quite particular, and it certainly cannot be read back into that of the entire generation. But by examining the women's own perspective on their place in history, we can see some of what the familiar cultural narrative obscures. For this analysis, we draw on a study of nine women who graduated from an elite women's college in 1943, married men who participated in World War II, and remained part of an enduring friendship network over the next 60 years. These women have narrated their lives through "Round Robin" letters to each other from 1943 into the present[1] and in interviews with us over the past few years. Here we rely only on the interviews to examine how key social events affected the women's lives (both in their own view and in ours) and how gendered discourses often shaped their understanding of their place in those social events. We are struck by how much these women's life stories include references, as Brokaw's vision would suggest, to the larger social events, patterns, and movements of the second half of the 20th century in the United States (World War II, the postwar baby boom, the civil rights movement and school desegregation, the Vietnam War, and the women's movement, to name a few). In many instances, these women's lives involved direct participation in these events. In others, the women were peripheral to them. Interestingly, this complex relationship to social history may have offered the women a certain zone of freedom or autonomy from which to critique events and formulate independent perspectives on them.

Our analysis will show that these women felt themselves to be part of a very particular generation in history, one shaped by World War II and the Depression that preceded it. In some instances, particularly World War II, they saw their husbands, and men like their husbands, as the central social actors. In those cases, they saw themselves not so much as participants in important historical events but, rather, as supportive bystanders. This partial marginality to the course of social history—perhaps because it was coupled with long periods of necessarily independent coping—seems to have offered them a measure of autonomy from their husbands' perspectives, despite their commitment to playing supportive roles in their husbands' public lives. The women used this autonomy to create quite independent ideas about social events, even as they sometimes denied their own place in them. In narrating their own experiences, these women often referred to culturally available narratives for representing women's lives (perhaps most notably, "Rosie the Riveter"), but they often simultaneously expressed the ways in which the narrative did and did not fit their own experience. While these cultural narratives offered useful common reference points, they were seldom simply adopted or rejected by this group. (See Romero and Stewart, 1999, for a discussion of how "some women directly challenge particular master narratives they find confining, distorting, or oppressive," while at the same time "the master narrative is often partially reproduced in the new narratives women construct" [p. xvi].)

The narrative analysis technique we employ in this study was developed and taught by McClelland and others, under the broad rubric of "thematic analysis" (see McClelland, 1964; Smith, 1992; Winter & McClelland, 1978). According to this method, any text—produced for personal, literary, cultural, political, or research purposes—can be examined for thematic content that might reveal the ideological, motivational, and idiosyncratic meanings individuals and groups attach to words, relationships, symbols, and institutions. Analysis of thematic content generally involves noticing recurring themes, as well as patterns of association of content (themes that co-occur, or combine images in distinctive ways), in a single text and comparing different texts (or sections of texts) to detect particularized meanings by contrast. These two procedures (interpretive analyses of association and of contrast) sometimes yield a codified set of categories that enables systematic content analysis of many texts (e.g., to assess the achievement, power, and affiliation motives and other psychological constructs). In other cases, though, the thematic analysis of single documents or a pair or set of documents is itself the goal. In all cases, within this approach to content analysis, systematic coding of texts is always secondary to an initial thematic analysis in which patterns of association and contrast are uncovered (for the most complete account of this procedure, see Winter, 1973, Chapter 3). This method of thematic analysis is quite similar to other content analysis techniques or techniques of qualitative data analysis. Specifically, it shares many features of methods of interpretation (Geertz, 1973; Ochberg, 2003), constant comparison (George, 1979), logical combination and induction (Becker, 1998), and grounded theory (Charmaz, 2000; Denzin & Lincoln, 1994; Glaser & Strauss, 1967). All of these techniques involve the inductive generation of themes through interpretation and the identification of patterns of association and contrast.

In this chapter, we use thematic analysis to explore how our particular sample of nine women describe their relationships to social history. We approach this question both directly and indirectly, through the women's responses to explicit questions about their experience of World War II and through their descriptions of their own lives in terms that reflect their participation in some social and cultural events (such as civilian support for the war effort and the postwar baby boom). They narrated for us their experiences of these years in retrospect—with full knowledge of all that came after. We then examined those narratives to identify the common and idiosyncratic features of their experiences, with the hope that thematic analysis of these first-person narratives would yield new understanding of the psychological significance of this generation of women's encounters with social history. Following the techniques described in Romero and Stewart (1999), we explicitly compared the resulting thematic accounts to published historical analyses of this period, as well as to widely shared cultural accounts of these same experiences. Through this process, we identified the features of the women's narratives that have been largely ignored or submerged in the "official story" of this generation of women.

Who Are the Women?[2]

Nearly half of the Round Robins[3] came to an elite eastern women's college from East Coast communities; one came from the South, a couple were from the Midwest, and two came from the West. Only a few of these women came to college with much familiarity with either the nearby city or the school itself; three had family friends or relatives who had previously attended this college, but for most this area was uncharted territory.

While some of the women came from families that were financially well-off, most of the women were middle-class and a few benefited from scholarships to attend college. Some arrived at college in 1939 having already decided what they wanted to study and persisted with those initial intentions. Others explored several disciplines before selecting a major or shifted from their initial expectations. Their majors ranged from psychology, sociology, and political science to zoology, English literature, and art history.

As the parents of the baby boom generation, it is not surprising that all but one of the women were married within a few years of their graduation in 1943, with the one exception pursuing a career for several years before she married. These new families dispersed geographically, usually in response to the husband's employment and often to places far from where the women had grown up. As a result, when we met them, the women lived literally all over the country—nine women in nine different states and in four different regions. All of the women had at least two children and almost all began their families within 2 years of their marriages. While their children were young, none of the women had paid employment; however, they were involved with their communities and engaged in a variety of volunteer activities. In their later adulthood, when their children were older, two pursued education and related careers, one assumed a high-level administrative position, and a fourth started her own business. The remaining women continued to be seriously engaged in volunteer activities and at least two contributed significantly to their communities through their work in civil rights.

The patterns historians and social scientists have identified as influencing women generally in the second half of the 20th century can be seen in the Robins' accounts (Chafe, 1972, 1991; Hartmann, 1982; May, 1988). Their lives were shaped by their early experiences of growing up in reasonably financially secure families free from want but during the Depression (Elder, 1974). Even more, World War II defined the period of their young adulthood (Stewart & Healy, 1989). They entered adulthood having achieved more education than their mothers' generation. They met and married men who served in World War II, and they endured long separations from them at the beginning of their relationships (Malley, 1999). An appreciative government rewarded these returning war veterans—whose educations, early careers, and family lives were disrupted by the war—with financial and educational assistance (Cohen, 2003; Coontz, 1992).

The war was, in fact, critical in setting the tone for the Robins' early family lives, as well as their postcollege work lives. Over the course of the war, men were increasingly called to serve in the armed forces, seriously depleting the available labor pool at home (Polenberg, 1968). As concern for the country's ability to maintain war production in the face of diminishing laborers grew, women were encouraged to enter the paid workforce, including in jobs thought to be inappropriate and even dangerous for women to hold (Winkler, 1986). This was an important shift in social expectations concerning gender roles for college-educated married women and mothers (roles that had previously required women to tend to the needs of their families and stay out of the labor force). Women responded to the national need and entered the labor force in unprecedented numbers (Anderson, 1981; Chafe, 1990; Hartmann, 1982). This significant growth in paid labor force participation by women was, however, short-lived. While career opportunities expanded for some women as a result of their employment during the war, most women left the paid workforce at the end of the war (Anderson, 1981; Chafe, 1990; Hartmann, 1982). Concern about jobs for returning servicemen resulted in almost immediate job terminations for women workers. Women were encouraged to resume their homemaker role, to attend to the needs of the returning husbands and nurture those who were viewed as the country's future hope—their children (Anderson, 1981; Hartmann, 1982; Michel, 1987).

During the postwar baby boom period, the young women of this generation (usually represented as white and middle class without comment) were subject to a range of cultural representations. They were heralded as committed homemakers, wives, and mothers (Meyerowitz, 1994), vilified as overbearing "moms" (Wylie, 1942/1955), and eventually defined as victims of the feminine mystique and the suburbanization of America (Friedan, 1963; Meyerowitz, 1994). During the late 1960s and 1970s, feminist scholars—often the daughters of this generation of women—argued that the Robins' generation had been confined in a gender role that left them isolated, socially devalued, and unfulfilled (see, e.g., Breines, 1992; Coontz, 1992; Skolnick, 1991). Some women of the Robins' generation—and some Robins—took advantage of the new opportunities for women associated with both social change and their own children's adulthood (Stewart & Healy, 1989). But we have heard little from women of this generation themselves about how they viewed these experiences at the time and how they view them now, in hindsight.

A few years ago, a colleague of ours who knew about our previous research studying college-educated women encouraged us to contact the Robins and interview them. With only a general notion that it would be valuable to document this group's experience, we followed her advice, and began to interview the women, who were then in their early eighties.[4] It took us 3 years to make arrangements to interview all nine of the women in their homes; in the course of those interviews, we also met the three husbands who are still living. The interviews were lengthy and open-ended; they generally took the form of a life narrative, with a special focus on the period of the Robins' acquaintance, from college to the present. In the course of the interviews, the women were invited to reflect on the different periods and eras in their family lives, and on different social historical events and movements. All of the interviews were tape-recorded and transcribed verbatim. We read the interviews over several times and constructed, across the nine interviews, the typical accounts the women offered of different periods of their lives. For the purposes of this chapter, we have focused on four narrow periods: college (1939–1943); the postcollege war period (1943–1945); the immediate postwar period (1945–1950); the early 1950s (1950–1955). We identified for each period a dominant or typical narrative; we also noted important deviations from the dominant narratives.

College During the War Years: A Narrative of Distant Thunder

World War II had just broken out when the Robins began college in 1939. For some, the war was a distant event, irrelevant to their lives, at least in the beginning. Liz Wiley remembers, "I was sort of unconscious of what was going on. I didn't have anybody in the military and I don't remember thinking about it." For others, the war was an immediate presence in their lives. Margaret Fowler, who traveled across most of the country to attend college, recalls, "I got on the train for my freshman year in college on the day that the war started in Europe, September 1 or September 3, 1939. It was on the radio that the war was started in Europe."

At school, Ellen Maxwell remembers gathering in a student's dorm room after dinner to listen to radio updates. For many, the war was a constant backdrop to everyday activities—especially after Pearl Harbor. Many of the Robins described blackouts at night and air raid drills. The war touched the lives of some directly as brothers, friends, and boyfriends enlisted. Hannah Singer remembered that, "we were much more aware of uniforms. My brothers went, one by one, into the service. Different friends had boyfriends who went off, certainly by the time of senior year."

As the war progressed and the United States joined the conflict, it intruded more and more into their daily lives. Some told stories of refugee professors distraught over what was happening in their homelands. Hannah remembered her French teacher, who "was so fragile, and she was so, so sad about what was happening in Europe. You could almost feel her mourning for what was happening to the world she knew." Many also mentioned with great pride the role of the college's female president, who took a significant war job in Washington while they were in school.

The Robins were active participants in the war effort while in school, testing soils for victory gardens, knitting hats and scarves, sewing bandages, and attending USO-sponsored events. Liz remembered, "A lot in the class were engaged. We were making bandages and going in and dancing with the USO boys and really in the effort of saving the Reynolds Wrap from our chewing gum, and all those things."

The constant undercurrent of the war as the Robins entered early adult-hood—concern about what was happening to friends, relatives, and acquaintances, as well as about how to help—impinged on their lives in ways that made planning for their own futures difficult, if not irrelevant. Although the women's college experiences included expanding horizons and exploring future options, the reality of the war and the demands it made on them and their peers eclipsed those activities in important ways. Beth became engaged when she was in her junior year. She and her fiancé planned to delay marriage until they had some financial stability; however, his enlistment, and concern about his departure for the war, hurried the decision along and they were married just before she graduated. Others deferred plans for graduate school, and instead attended specialized train-ing to provide needed military-related services (e.g., decoding). During these years, then, the Robins saw themselves as on the sidelines of important events but not as irrelevant to them. They made contributions to the war effort during college, and they felt they had a responsibility—and eagerness—to continue to do so after college.

After College: Supporting the War by Being or Helping Rosie the Riveter

Graduating in 1943, when the country was fully involved in the war, the Robins felt an obligation to set aside early aspirations for further education and careers in such fields as medicine, library science, and archeology; the war—and marriage—sidelined those hopes. Sally Kennedy mentioned to us that her one regret was not having pursued law school: "I thought for a while during my junior and senior years of going to law school and I think that probably World War II is the biggest reason I didn't do that. I would have liked to do that. . . . We all thought we had to get out and do something for the war effort."

What Sally did instead of law school was work for the government as a Washington intern. While still in college, she and two other Robins were selected for specialized military-related training for the government, and they were immediately placed in positions in Washington D.C. upon graduation—Liz Wiley worked on decoding and Dorothy Williams catalogued maps for the Navy. While it was distracting and preoccupying, the war also opened up other kinds of opportunities and provided a level of excitement and adventure. Though disappointed not to be in law school, Sally was pleased to be working in Washington. "I wanted to work for the government. This was an extension of political science [her major in college], and Washington was an exciting place to be at that time."

Others pursued paid employment that helped the war effort in different ways. Two of the Robins (Donna Peters and Hannah Singer) were involved directly in war production—like Rosie the Riveter. Several worked in daycare facilities and saw themselves as helping Rosie. Margaret Fowler recalled,

> We all knew what we were going to do when we graduated was take a job having to help some way with the war effort. . . . I thought, well maybe what I could do when I left college was to help take care of children of war workers. And I took a course my senior year so that I had some background on the care of children left at daycare centers by "Rosie the Riveter."

A few of the Robins pursued clerical positions, some more and others less directly tied to the war effort. None of these jobs lasted very long and most of the women stopped working as soon as, or shortly after, they got married. But these experiences were critical to their development. As Dorothy Williams said,

> I think we did feel in those early war days that we were in the center of things. I think we each—those of us who were married or about to get married—felt as if we were a team. And we [women] were doing what was expected of us as well as they [the men].

The short-term nature of these "war" jobs, and the uncertainties stemming from the war, made postgraduate planning difficult. Hannah Singer recounted, "I didn't really make a very good plan for myself after college. I wasn't sure what I wanted to do." She ended up following her roommate home and found employment in a factory. Donna Peters was also unsure about what to do after graduation. While she admired women who did do so, she herself did not want to join the WAVES. After a year doing factory work, she got a job with the Red Cross and then took a job in an army hospital, providing social services to wounded veterans. Eventually she went to Washington, D.C., and, after a few short-term jobs, worked for the government in the Marshall Plan Division. Her work brought her to Europe, and she spent a year writing to the Robins from Vienna and another year writing from the Netherlands.

Donna was the only one of the Robins who continued to work for several years after graduation. For her, it was certainly a life of independence and adventure, but it was also a somewhat lonely experience living in a foreign land separate from all family and friends and in some ways "out of synch" with her peers. She did eventually marry (in 1951, a man she had met in Europe in 1950). Her new husband was being transferred to the United States, so Donna left her government job in Europe and moved back to the States right after the wedding. Her marriage marked the end of her paid work for a significant period. She didn't want to "start all over again job hunting and try-ing to figure out what I was going to do." It was only after her two children were older that she pursued graduate training and a career as a librarian.

As the country waited for an end to the war, the lives of the Robins—as well as those of their peers—were put on hold. Though married, or at least engaged, they couldn't settle down and begin families while their husbands were in the service. Many of them went home and lived with their parents while their husbands were away, and they worked at war-related jobs. Beth Thornton, who was married just before graduation, went to live on the East Coast to take advantage of the occasions when her husband's ship would be in port and they could spend a few days together. Even though she was other-wise alone, she passed the time pleasantly. "I lived alone but I knew [the city].

I felt comfortable there. . . . I was used to being alone. . . . At college, after all, I'd lived without my family and I had some college friends around." Beth took secretarial courses—she and her husband thought that she would need to work in the beginning of the marriage to help support the family—and did some clerical work. She didn't remain long, however, because her husband's ship was sent to the Pacific and she followed him to the West Coast. In response to our question about how her experiences of World War II affected her, Beth pointed to her need to take care of herself, despite the fact that she was married. "I guess I just learned to get along on my own; I had to."

For those whose husbands were still in the United States, it was not unusual for these young brides to criss-cross the country, following the men from one military post to another. The logistical and emotional difficulties of such an existence were highlighted by Beth Thornton, who had just spent some time rereading her wartime correspondence with her husband when we talked with her:

> It's interesting seeing how one couple survived the war. I mean it was these let-ters. . . . Everything depended on the mail—this was the only communica-tion. . . . At the time I thought it's even worse if he did come home for a while, because he comes in for three days and they then go out again, and then he comes in for four days and we hope the ship has to go into dry dock. . . . It wasn't always possible [to see him, even] if I was on the right coast. I moved out to [the West Coast] at the beginning. . . . But sometimes, when it was out in the Pacific, it would be three months between when we'd see each other and then it would be very briefly. I mean a couple of days.

Another example was provided by Dorothy Williams who recalled an arduous plane trip of several hours from Maryland to her family in Wisconsin, where there were medical and social resources available to her when she had her first baby. While life's uncertainties were normative for the times, and perhaps for that reason easier to handle, they were never-theless stressful. Sally Kennedy also remembered about this time,

> You know, it was so much a part of what everyone else was doing that I don't know that we thought it was all that unusual. It was difficult, but not as diffi-cult as it would have been if you were the only person doing it, or if you were a very small segment of society that was doing it. It wasn't easy doing that; it's something that was just accepted.

Others described the difficulties more directly—especially the emotional toll exacted by the war. Rita Stanton remarked, "It was a stressful time because . . . all the women you knew had somebody overseas."

This immediate postgraduation period was a complicated time for the Robins. We got a real sense from them of the excitement, adventure, and general optimism they recalled about this time. They explored opportunities for employment, as well as a lively social life with servicemen. They experienced a national community coming together to support the war effort and the centrality of their families of origin as places of refuge in periods of uncertainty or the absence of their husbands. They traveled and managed on their own and thrived in their independence and competence. Despite their mostly positive accounts of these times, there was also a subtler, but real, intimation of the difficulties the war years brought to their lives.

The Robins' experience of the war after college also nearly always included their connection to their husbands' experience (except in the case of Donna Peters, who met her husband after the war). During the war, and certainly during the subsequent years, their husbands' experiences of the war often were critical features of their marital and family landscape. Those experiences in many ways took center stage once the men came home, retrospectively transforming some of the women's own wartime experience to marginality, in their own estimation. At the same time, the differences between the men's and the women's experiences during this period, and the fact that the experiences were intense and formative for both, set the stage for their lifelong habit of respecting each other's separate spheres.

Husbands in the Military: Actors on the World Stage

All of the women's husbands were in the military during the war, but they did not all view their military experience in the same way. One was a career military man, who rose through the ranks to quite a high level and "never thought of leaving the Navy" according to his wife, Liz Wiley. In contrast, Beth Thornton's husband "wasn't dying to fight. He was not pro military or anything like that. . . . He didn't like military life, but he enjoyed what he did on the ship." Beth Thornton said of her husband, "He had tremendous admiration for the Marines and what they did, but . . . he just boggled against the kind of autocratic and silly routines—that's what he found boring too."

For all of the men except Liz Wiley's husband, the war disrupted an education or a career, in addition to the establishment of a family. Beth Thornton's husband's law school education was interrupted, and Rita Stanton's husband didn't have a chance to start law school. Margaret Fowler's husband, who was a little older, had to halt the building of his law practice to serve in the war. Similarly, Ellen Maxwell's husband, who had finished medical school, missed a key date for starting a residency, so he continued to lose time in getting his career started. Many of the men were able to take advantage of the G.I. Bill to complete their educations, but all of them felt they were "behind" in their adult lives (Elder, 1986).

Nevertheless, for many the military offered a very positive experience of an all-male world, in which they were exposed to men who were very different from them and at the same time likable, even admirable. For example, Rita Stanton said that her husband

> was a company captain and he had fifty men under him from, as he said, the coal mines of Pennsylvania. So he got to know a lot of different backgrounds and people, and I think he was very popular with his men. I think he thought they were the salt of the earth.

The war, then, broadened their husbands' experiences of American men—to include men who were less educated, came from different regions and ethnic groups, and had vastly different skills and life experiences. The war also took them to Europe, to the Pacific, and all over the United States; most of them traveled long distances and saw places very different from their places of origin—both within the United States and around the globe. For example, Beth Thornton's husband

> went everywhere. He went to India, he went to Rio, he went to Aden. . . . He went to Italy; he went to England. Back and forth to England. Back and forth to France. He went to Naples; he went to Egypt. And first starting with the Atlantic—going out taking troops to England and for North Africa. You know, now, looking back at it, I see that it was the course of the war. And then it shifted to the Pacific, and there were longer trips, there were longer between times.

Finally, although only a few of the men had serious encounters with danger in battle, those who did had experiences with deep and long-lasting effects—effects that shaped their marriages and family lives. Beth Thornton contrasted her husband's experience of the war with that of another man she got to know after her husband died:

> [My friend] fought a real war. I mean, this is in the trenches, and he had night-mares for years, things he couldn't talk about, you know. He—it was the bad war, the whole, all that business fighting through towns and seeing his mates lying in the trenches, and it was just really awful. But [my husband] wasn't in that.

In contrast, Margaret Fowler said of her husband that

one of the defining moments of his life was his service in the navy, and he went through some dangerous things, and survived, and saw a lot, and was always so proud of it.

He was in the Battle for Leyte Gulf, which was a major battle in the Pacific, that really turned the war around. . . . And he was a great student of how all that took place . . . it was a major thing in his life, and I tell you, he had a major turning on the light—epiphany—while he was on board ship. During the Battle . . . they really thought their carrier was going to be sunk, and that the Japanese fleet was going toward them. And the captain said that anyone who wanted to could go to the chapel for Holy Communion and so [my husband] did that, and he took Holy Communion next to a colored steward, and it changed him. Or it advanced him. He always considered himself a decent person. But it just gave him something that led to his working on the open schools movement.

At the same time, Margaret noted that her husband "never believed in talking about feelings." He felt that "men didn't talk about feelings—they had to be strong men." One of their children "was very angry with him" about this, but Margaret "dealt with that by finding other people to talk to about my feelings."

Rita Stanton's husband was certainly affected by his war experience. He

went overseas in February of '44 and just before the D-day—you know, they were grouping, and he was with the army division, so they didn't go [on] D-day. They were stationed in England. Then in July they moved and well, actually, in July they landed in Brest. He was wounded in October of '44. He was sent to England to recuperate. He'd been shot in the knee, or below the knee, so he had a cast and surgeries and so on. Then he was shipped back to the States.

I know when he first came back I was quite concerned about him because he seemed—and I didn't know him that well—but he seemed terribly nervous . . . and had particular little tics, that eventually went away. But he was very close to one of the friends that he'd known all through the service, and who actually lasted, and didn't come home until '45.

She found that she "learned more when [the two men] were together," because her husband did not talk directly to her about his experiences. She said that both after the war and later on, after her husband and his friend had retired, they "would talk about the war, and I know it made him probably more appreciative of life. He was very serious; he was a workaholic, very dedicated to his profession and to the community."

It is impossible to know whether these men were changed by their war experience or would have had the emotionally reserved personalities and intense postwar community commitment and career drive that they had under all circumstances. In any case, the Robins understood the sacrifices their husbands had made to serve their country, and they were eager to begin lives with the men they'd married. They were happy to center their postwar households on the demands of their husbands' careers, partly out of respect for the importance of their husbands' roles in the war.

After the War: Setting Up Separate Domains

All of the women viewed their war work as temporary, and they were eager to be united with their husbands and to set up permanent households. Even so, their expulsion from the workforce was sometimes dramatic and painful. For example, Ellen Maxwell was living at home with her parents, and working in a child-care center, tending children of women who were working in ammunition plants.

> The day that the war ended in Japan, that was the end of that. They closed it overnight. . . . The head teacher called me and said, the war is over and so is your job. . . . I didn't dispute it because the whole thing was, I'm sure the women who worked in the munitions factories got the same . . . because otherwise they would've needed the child care. It shut down, but in just one day.

Ellen had enjoyed the work, and her own husband was not home yet, so she found another job in a nursery not tied to the war effort. After her husband came home, she moved with him to his residency location, started looking for a job,

> and then discovered I was pregnant. I was feeling lousy, lousy, so I did nothing but sit around home feeling lousy. And then I took a couple of courses . . . in interior decorating and in sewing and really getting ready to be a housewife.

Like Ellen, all of the Robins quickly became mothers, and they had more children than is common today for educated white women in the United States. Two of the women adopted two children each. The remaining women had three, four, and five each. Dorothy Williams also helped raise several "foster" children as part of her work for the American Field Service. Though all of the women described wanting to be mothers, and enjoying many aspects of motherhood, it is also clear that they also felt considerable pressure in this area. For example, Beth Thornton recalls the difficulty she and her husband had conceiving before they adopted.

> It bothered me when everybody kept saying, "Why don't you [two] have children, or when are you [two] going to have children?" You know, it's hard. . . . It wasn't that easy and you have to pay attention to when you ovulate and all that kind of stuff. . . . And the last thing the [doctors] said to me was, "Well, now, I think we'll just have to think about more drastic measures." And I remember going home . . . and saying . . . "Why don't we just adopt?" It was harder for him to think about it. . . . I think he felt he didn't need this, and I felt all my friends were having babies. . . . I don't think I thought of alternatives. I just thought, well, this is what—yeah, I wanted children. And I loved having them.

Another Robin who felt the pronatal pressure of the time was Donna Peters. Unlike the other Robins, after the war she continued to work, eventually ending up in Europe helping with reconstruction activities. But Donna was aware that her path was different from most. She said, "At that time, there wasn't such a strong feeling that everybody had to do this [work on reconstructing Europe]. A lot of my friends had married and were having children and moving around the country with their husbands."

The Robins, having quit their jobs or had them disappear, having traveled long distances to set up new households, having finally united with their husbands who were earnestly trying to make up time lost in their careers, and having populated their homes with offspring, found themselves creating and running their households (Coontz, 1992; Skolnick, 1991). Men were doing important work in a public sphere, work that kept them away from home and domestic intimacy much of the time. Ellen Maxwell described this pattern vividly:

> He would leave the house at six in the morning or even earlier. I would not get up. He would get up at five a lot of mornings and be off, and he wouldn't be home until 7, 7:30. And I would feed the children and get them to bed, and then we'd have dinner late . . . I felt it was necessary. I would've liked to have it otherwise, but I sort of felt I was necessary, and helpful in helping him do what he was trained to do. So in that way I wasn't malcontent with my situation at all.

The Robins were more than willing to raise children, give up their work in the labor force, and manage their husbands' personalities and needs. To some degree, they lived out the postwar dream of large families thriving in suburbia (see Cohen, 2003). For example, Ellen Maxwell described this period:

We lived in an area—the man developed it with the idea that he wanted all young people who had at least two children. It was a very unique neighborhood, where the children roamed freely. We didn't have to lock doors at that time. Kids were always coming in and out of the house. And there were lots of playmates for the children. In the early stages, all of us were at home. I was just doing what I'd expected to be doing, and it was a great neighborhood to be in.

This period was not idyllic or uniformly satisfying for all of the Robins. Part of the problem, of course, was that many of the women had enjoyed their wartime jobs and had experienced the stimulation of work. For example, Dorothy Williams was interested in world geography and worked in Washington during the war making maps and as a map librarian. She recognizes in retrospect that she would have liked to have gone to school to become a librarian. Instead, she worked as a volunteer for many years for the American Field Service Student Exchange Program and hosted many students from other countries. Similarly, in retrospect, Beth Thornton wished she had gone to graduate school. She commented,

It never occurred to me that I—I mean, I'd gone to graduate school for two semesters, and I'd gotten A's, and you know. It was years later that I then went back to graduate school. . . . Why didn't I ever think of continuing when I went back years later . . . ? Why didn't I think of continuing to commute? Never occurred to me. I don't think it was the expense. I think it never occurred to me. After all, this is the way the war marked me. We had been separated. And every single letter he wrote or I wrote is we couldn't wait till we got back together again. And so it just never crossed my mind that I would do this. I mean, if he was ready to leave, we left.

We heard from some of the women that one important reason they didn't seek paid employment was their husbands' attitudes. Sally Kennedy said,

I never really worked after [the war] until I was 58 years old. My husband had the feeling that—like many men in that day and age—that they had to be able to take care of their family. That was the bottom line. So after our children were all grown . . . I went back to work full-time.

Before that time, she had been very active in volunteer work, including serving on national boards and as president of an organization involving 11,000 adult volunteers. During the years that she did not have paid employment, she felt that she "had some really tough years." She said, "You felt that you were over-trained for what you were doing. Even though, intellectually, you know that raising the next generation is important, you still feel a lack of fulfillment." Beth Thornton found these years difficult too.

> After the children I was at home with them, and I didn't have sitters cause we couldn't afford it. [My husband] was extremely busy . . . and I resented that because some weeks he'd be gone every night. He'd be gone to a meeting. And I really did resent that a lot. And he started talking about being chairman . . . and I said, "No, I don't want that." I said, "I just never see you." And I was home with children all day alone. Yes, that got to me. . . . That was hard. I really resented it.

One way the Robins reconciled their eagerness to make a public contribution with the pressures of their domestic roles was to get involved with volunteer activities. For example, Hannah Singer helped to found and run a kindergarten. Later on, she got involved in housing issues through a neighborhood association, and through that she worked on race relations. Similarly, Donna Peters said that she "volunteered in the school library where [my kids] were in elementary school, and . . . got interested in school libraries. . . . Eventually I started going to library school . . . and got a job." When the women did pursue these interests, they felt absolutely responsible for taking care of their domestic responsibilities fully, too. For example, Donna Peters said, "I remember talking with another friend who was going [to school] at the time. We weren't going to do anything to upset our families. Keep everything just the way it was and do everything else yourself."

Many of the Robins made extensive community contributions through volunteer work—sometimes supporting their husbands' two-person careers—for many years (see Seidenberg, 1974). Liz Wiley saw it as very much a part of her role to be a "service wife."

> You didn't get a job. You didn't do anything except take care of kids, and as a service wife you were expected to entertain. They made formal calls—the commanding officers. You called on them and left your calling cards. And then they returned your call and you hoped that you looked sort of presentable when they drove up with their driver and came in. I remember one of [my husband's] commanding officers called on us . . . and we were in a Quonset hut, and we'd had some ridiculous argument . . . and I'd hung my bra on the light switch in the kitchen, and I said "It'll stay there till you"—and he looked out the front window of the Quonset and I said, "Oh, my Lord, Captain and Mrs. Something are coming to call with their white duds." And he said, "Get the bra out."

Later Liz had to meet more formal social demands:

> In Washington it was a more formal kind of life. . . . You had to entertain and you had to go to lunch and you had to go to balls and you had to do a lot of sort of formal stuff because the more senior you get, the more kind of Navy wife-ish duties you have to take on.

Margaret Fowler played a similarly supportive role during the years when her children were young and her husband was pursuing a political career. Even then, though, Margaret began to get involved with school desegregation activities, as soon as the Supreme Court handed down the *Brown v. Board of Education* decision in 1954. She pointed out that

> the children understood. They knew mama was busy and going to meetings, that sort of thing. But always, when the children were little, I almost always was home at 3:00. Cause I had to cook dinner and [the housekeeper] went off at 5:00. I just thought it was important to be here.

Even though Margaret and her husband "would say to each other in the middle of the night, segregation is wrong," her husband "kept himself independent" of the organizations she created and joined. "He didn't want his name associated because he wished to be a free agent and not tied down by policy decisions that somebody's sitting around deciding what we're going to say and do."

Later Margaret had her own significant volunteer career, working on civil rights and programs to support poor people's claims to welfare rights, for over 20 years. Although many of the Robins could point with genuine pride to many accomplishments in their volunteer careers, they also knew that theirs did not come with the same recognition that their husbands' careers did. Margaret Fowler said,

> My husband got lots of awards for his excellence, and his professionalism. . . . And one of the awards came with a $500 prize, for [him] to do what he wanted to. And to my complete surprise he gave it to my work. . . . See, so he really respected it.

Thus, throughout the 1950s the women lived out their commitment to supporting their husbands' careers and their children's development, and many of them drew deep satisfaction from those efforts. They also quietly sustained intellectual interests and political, religious, and community involvements that offered them some autonomy and satisfaction. Cultivating that autonomous zone made it easy for several of them to transition into active careers and to express independent political convictions after their children were grown. Ellen Maxwell said, "I was very much for what the young people were doing in the '60s. I could identify with that, and I thought that . . . their goals were good. They wanted to participate in government, and in their education."

She felt more strongly about this than her husband did, but their differences about politics did not pose serious conflict. "It wasn't an issue at all. It was just discussions." During the Vietnam War, many of the women were more sympathetic to their children's objections to it than were their husbands. And they were not reluctant to show it. Perhaps the habit of independence and respect for each other's very different experiences in the course of wartime separation enabled both the men and the women in these couples to concede each other some freedom and autonomy, and not to expect too much deference.

Learning About Women's Wartime and Postwar Experiences From Narratives

The narratives the Robins shared with us offered us real insight into some of the complex meanings of war work for women, of men's war experiences for their families, of the postwar baby boom, and of women's volunteer activities in the 1950s. They enabled us to see how women viewed themselves as marked by the history they shared with their husbands but experienced so differently. Their narratives revealed the real sacrifice and loss these women experienced, along with their genuine willingness to accept the constraints they faced at various times in their lives. Finally, the narratives allowed us to understand the autonomy that was offered the women by their relative freedom from centrality in the public sphere (partly because of the official public rhetoric that valued, even glorified, home and domesticity, or private space, during this period) (Hartmann, 1994; Michel, 1987). These women fully recognized that, in contrast to their husbands, they were free from the demand for military service and control by work institutions. They were also freed from their husbands' control by their husbands' busy career lives, by their own personal confidence and independence (derived in part from their education and wartime experience), and by a public ideology of separate spheres. Collectively, these narratives offered us a less romantic but richer, more complex, and more psychological understanding of the experience of this group of women from "the greatest generation." It is, moreover, an account that helps us understand how and why women like the Robins— white, well-educated, attentive to national and world events, and confident of their own opinions—supported the next generation's active questioning of a very different war, of contemporary race relations, and of the domestic gender arrangements they observed while growing up.

Notes

1. Round Robin letters involve the circulation of letters to all members of a group, in sequence, with each member who receives the packet adding a letter and

removing her last letter. Thus, every packet each woman receives contains nine letters (one from each person) and is sent on its way with a new letter from the recipient and the old one removed.

2. In describing the women and in quoting them, we have obscured identifying details, including names, and the name of the college, as part of our confidentiality agreement with the women. Thus all the names used here are pseudonyms.

3. In many letters, the women in this group addressed themselves collectively as "Robins" (as in, "Dear Robins"). We have adopted their nomenclature.

4. We should note that complete sets of the letters written by four of the women from 1943 to 1993 are archived at the college library. We have read these letters, as well as those of two others—Dorothy Williams (which are in her possession) and Margaret Fowler (her later letters). We are focused in these analyses only on the retrospective narratives in the interviews, and we hope in future writing to explore the similarities and differences in the women's constructions of their experience at the time and in retrospect.

References

Anderson, K. (1981). *Wartime women: Sex roles, family relations, and the status of women during World War II*. Westport, CT: Greenwood.

Becker, H. S. (1998). *Tricks of the trade: Or how to think about your research while you're doing it*. Chicago: University of Chicago Press.

Breines, W. (1992). *Young, white and miserable: Growing up female in the fifties*. Boston: Beacon.

Brokaw, T. (1998). *The greatest generation*. New York: Random House.

Chafe, W. H. (1972). *The American woman: Her changing social, economic, and social roles, 1920–1970*. New York: Oxford University Press.

Chafe, W. H. (1990). World War II as a pivotal experience for American women. In M. Dietrich & D. Fischer-Hornung (Eds.), *Women and war: The changing status of American women from the 1930s to the 1950s* (pp. 21–34). New York: St. Martin's.

Chafe, W. H. (1991). *The paradox of change: American women in the 20th century*. New York: Oxford University Press.

Charmaz, K. (2000). Grounded theory: Objectivist and constructivist methods. In N. K. Denzin & Y. S. Lincoln (Eds.), *Handbook of qualitative research* (2nd ed., pp. 509–536). Thousand Oaks, CA: Sage.

Cohen, C. (2003). *A consumers' republic: The politics of mass consumption in postwar America*. New York: Knopf.

Coontz, S. (1992). *The way we never were: American families and the nostalgia trap*. New York: Basic Books.

Denzin, N. K., & Lincoln, Y. S. (1994). *Handbook of qualitative research*. Thousand Oaks, CA: Sage.

Elder, G. H. (1974). *Children of the Great Depression: Social change in life experiences*. Chicago: University of Chicago Press.

Elder, G. H. (1986). Military times and turning points in men's lives. *Developmental Psychology, 22*, 233–245.

Friedan, B. (1963). *The feminine mystique*. New York: Dell.

Geertz, C. (1973). *The interpretation of cultures*. New York: Basic Books.

George, A. L. (1979). Case studies and theory development: The method of structured, focused comparison. In P. G. Lauren (Ed.), *Diplomacy: New approaches in history, theory and policy* (pp. 43–68). New York: Free Press.

Glaser, B. G., & Strauss, A. L. (1967). *The discovery of grounded theory: Strategies for qualitative research*. Chicago: Aldine.

Hartmann, S. (1982). *The home front and beyond: American women in the 1940s*. Boston: Twayne.

Hartmann, S. (1994). Women's employment and the domestic ideal in the early Cold War years. In J. Meyerowitz (Ed.), *Not June Cleaver: Women and gender in postwar America, 1945–1960* (pp. 84–100). Philadelphia: Temple University Press.

Malley, J. E. (1999). Life on the home front: Housewives' experiences of World War II. In M. Romero & A. J. Stewart (Eds.), *Women's untold stories: Breaking silence, talking back, voicing complexity* (pp. 53–70). New York: Routledge

May, E. T. (1988). *Homeward bound: American families in the cold war era*. New York: Basic Books.

McClelland, D. C. (1964). *Roots of consciousness*. Princeton, NJ: Van Nostrand.

Meyerowitz, J. (Ed.). (1994). *Not June Cleaver: Women and gender in postwar America, 1945–1960*. Philadelphia: Temple University Press.

Meyerowitz, J. (1994). Beyond the feminine mystique: A reassessment of mass culture: 1946–1958. In J. Meyerowitz (Ed.), *Not June Cleaver: Women and gender in postwar America, 1945–1960* (pp. 229–262). Philadelphia: Temple University Press.

Michel, S. (1987). American women and the discourse of the democratic family in World War II. In M. R. Higonnet, J. Jenson, S. Michel, & M. C. Weitz (Eds.), *Behind the lines: Gender and the two world wars*. New Haven, CT: Yale University Press.

Ochberg, R. (2003). Teaching interpretation. In R. Josselson, A. Lieblich, & D. P. McAdams (Eds.), *Up close and personal: The teaching and learning of narrative research* (pp. 113–134). Washington, DC: American Psychological Association.

Polenberg, R. (1968). *America at war: The home front, 1941–1945*. Englewood Cliffs, NJ: Prentice Hall.

Romero, M., & Stewart, A. J. (Eds.). (1999). *Women's untold stories: Breaking silence, talking back, voicing complexity*. New York: Routledge.

Seidenberg, R. (1974). *Corporate wives—Corporate casualties*. New York: AMACOM.

Skolnick, A. (1991). *Embattled paradise: The American family in an age of uncertainty*. New York: Basic Books.

Smith, C. P. (Ed.). (1992). *Motivation and personality: Handbook of thematic analysis*. New York: Cambridge University Press.

Stewart, A. J., & Healy, J. M. (1989). Linking individual development and social changes. *American Psychologist, 44*, 30–42.

Winkler, A. M. (1986). *Home front U.S.A.: American during World War II*. Arlington Heights, IL: Harlan Davidson.

Winter, D. G. (1973). *The power motive*. New York: Free Press.

Winter, D. G., & McClelland, D. C. (1978). Thematic analysis: An empirically-derived measure of the effects of liberal education. *Journal of Educational Psychology, 70*, 8–16.

Wylie, P. (1942). *Generation of vipers*. New York: Holt, Rinehart & Winston. (Revised in 1955)

3.4

Culture, Continuity, and the Limits of Narrativity

A Comparison of the Self-Narratives of Native and Non-Native Youth

Michael J. Chandler,
Christopher E. Lalonde, and Ulrich Teucher

This chapter is all about how it is that Aboriginal[1] and culturally mainstream adolescents differently undertake to story their own and others' lives. It details a developmental and cross-cultural program of research that (1) begins by obliging young participants to argumentatively redeem their beliefs about their own personal persistence in time, and related matters of sameness and change in the lives of various familiar story characters, and (2) ends by undertaking to submit participants' responses to several different forms of narrative analysis. Although this work is carpeted wall-to-wall in narrativity (i.e., the work is all about life narratives, it employs published narratives as stimulus prompts, it collects respondents' spontaneous narratives as primary data, and it employs various forms of narrative analyses), a main conclusion to be drawn from all of these efforts is that only about half of what of our respondents actually have to say seems best characterized as narrative-like in structure. Of course, by some especially forgiving lights, just about everything (e.g., Leonardo Da Vinci's painting *The Last Supper*, as well as the question "Could you pass the salt?") qualifies as a narrative. The work reported here is not like that; it has instead the different aim of working out what might qualify as an appropriate contrast class—a class made up of things said about self and others to which the rhetoric of narrativity scarcely applies. To anticipate the conclusion to which this chapter leads, our research prompts us to conclude (1) that there are two contrasting ways of understanding the topic of personal persistence—one Narrativist,[2] one not and (2) that Native and non-Native young persons subscribe to such views in ways that are "culturally appropriate." Well before coming to these conclusions, however, it is important for us to begin by clarifying how we intend to use and restrict the notions of "narrative" and "narrative analysis" in ways that are meant to ensure that some things, at least, are left to the side.

A Show of Colors

In certain colorful but typically still ghettoized quarters, talk of narrativity has, of late, become very much the talk of the town. Many reading this book likely frequent, if not inhabit, just such places, and in the process such readers have picked up enough of the local patois that words like "narratological" and "narratory" no longer seem outlandish. Elsewhere, however, including most of the usual haunts of psychology's more polite society, things are quite otherwise. Homebound critics of this more mainstream variety are often impatient with, if not intolerant of, all talk of narrative matters—an imagined affectation of speech that is routinely discounted as simply the next in a long line of dubious French fads. In such methodologically more circumspect quarters, narrative analysis tends to be bracketed and dismissed along with other so-called qualitative (by which is meant suspect) methods, all of which are judged to be favored only by the quantitatively challenged. In such company, merely being suspected of consorting with known narratologists is often seen to be enough to tarnish one's scientific reputation.

Given such "uptown" attitudes—this "them" versus "us" drawing up of sides—a chapter such as this would do well, you might imagine, to begin by clearly displaying its true colors, declaring plainly for or against narrativity. We mean to give no such satisfaction. Instead, the more Janus-faced position to be developed here will be spoken out of both sides of our mouths at once, sometimes for and sometimes against the prospects of adopting a narrative approach. We mean to do this illustratively, by way of example, pointing off in two different directions at once. One of these lines of sight shows that large parts of a data set we are currently assembling demand being analyzed and understood using tools of narrative analysis. The other identifies whole stretches of data in which narrative or relational forms are either entirely missing or in especially short supply. In brief, we regularly find occasions for narrative analysis—but *not* whenever and wherever we look.

Before going on to provide backing for these oppositional claims, two things, at least, need to be taken up by way of introduction. First, and in order to set the context for our own ambivalent account, we need to begin with at least a rough sketch of the broad program of research from which our examples will be drawn. Second, and because our claim is that the language of narrativity applies to some but not all of our data, we need to get especially clear about what we are and are not prepared to call narrative-like. The first of these tasks is, far and away, the simpler of the two.

Folk Conceptions of Selves and Identities

Broadly speaking, our research focuses on the question of how young people think about and respond to questions concerning the persistence of their own and others' identities. More particularly, we are interested in possible variations (age-related variations, cultural variations) in those forms of self-understanding that promote and preserve the conviction—we suggest the necessary or "constitutive" conviction—that we each deserve to be seen as "numerically identical" (i.e., as persistently ourselves despite the inevitable changes that time holds in store). Although our reasons for saying so are still to come, the thrust of our findings is that what young people have to say about the paradox of their own personal persistence amounts to one or the other of two broad solution strategies. One of these—what we have called "Entity" or "Essentialist" solutions (Chandler, 2000, 2001; Chandler, Lalonde, Sokol, & Hallett, 2003)—involves an accounting system according to which persistent persons are understood as analogous to stobs in the stream of time, enduring "things" that, while subject to inevitable wear and tear, nevertheless possess certain more or less abstract but always enduring bits or pieces that are said to defy time by remaining relentlessly the same. Change, in this view, may well be inevitable, but it is not ubiquitous, and selfhood is owed to the parts of ourselves that stay the same. In short, Essentialist strategies discount or turn a blind eye to change and are imagined to work by defeating time.

Alternatively, other individuals undertake the identical job of vouchsafing their own and others' personal persistence not by pointing to some imagined (Essentialist) "something" that has putatively remained hidden from the ravages of time but, rather, by understanding all of the admittedly distinct time slices that make up their own or others' biography as related chapters in what is argued to be one and the same life. Solution strategies of this second "Relational" or "Narrativist" sort succeed by running a continuous thread of meaning through what are recognized to be substantively different incarnations of the self. Practitioners of this Narrativistic logic believe themselves to have succeeded in solving the paradox of sameness within change so long as some unbroken chain of linked circumstances can be forged that binds together life's various changing moments.

Of these two contrastive ways of attempting to make a case for personal persistence, Essentialist solutions, while still in need of some better explanation of their own, have the easy virtue of involving "things" or essential parts that can be straightforwardly named or indexed. That is, warranting one's own perpetuity by pointing to the enduring presence of, for example, one's strawberry birthmark, or arguing for one's numerical identity by repeatedly dragging out the same signature soul, may well be bad metaphysics, but, at least, doing so involves indexical gestures that point to something in particular to which personal persistence is supposedly owed.

By contrast, claiming, for example, as Dennett (1978) does, that selves are something like a "narrative center of gravity," or insisting, as do many of our own research participants, that one's own and others' continuing identity is vouchsafed by something like a gapless story we choose to tell about ourselves, is altogether less straightforwardly declarative and requires rather more explaining. A stab in the direction of just such an explanation follows. It follows in three parts.

Part one has nothing directly to do with selves per se, and is concerned instead with what is variously had in mind by calling something— anything—a narrative. Next, we consider some of what is meant by those who have imagined, in some metaphorical sense, that selves are analogous to personal narratives, that lives lived are like stories told, and that methods common to narrative analysis can serve as useful source models for analyzing the intricacies of selves or persons. Finally, and apart from the issue of whether selves actually *are* somehow narrative-like in character, we take up the still more focused question of whether people of any or all stripes actually *think* of themselves and others in narrative terms. We take up these three separate matters in turn in the three subsections that immediately follow.

How to Recognize a Narrative When You Meet One

Scholarly talk about narratives—like where they begin and end and how they might best be analyzed—did not, of course, get its start with attempts, such as our own, to characterize à la mode matters of personal persistence, nor, for that matter, with any other issue of contemporary psychological concern. Narrative analysis is much too old for that. Rather, long before being belatedly pressed into service by latter day social scientists, narratives and their analysis were the familiar stock and trade of literary scholars and semiologists whose thoughts strayed only occasionally, if at all, toward systematic examinations of the process of identity development. Consequently, anyone bent upon turning some part of this venerable academic tradition to their own different and more work-a-day purposes is naturally obliged to begin by attempting to sort out how the term "narrative" was traditionally played on its own home court.

Although any serious plan to attempt a full exegesis of the notion of narrativity, and the myriad forms of analysis to which narratives are commonly subjected, is beyond the necessarily limited scope of this summary account, it does not require a full account for the reader (even if he or she is not an insider) to quickly come to the realization that, outside of the social sciences, as well as in, the general enterprise of narrative analysis continues to be in what Mishler (1995) charitably calls a "state of near-anarchy" (p. 88). One large part of this confusion is owed to persistent disagreements over what a narrative is and what, if anything, it is not. Another concerns the possible aims, methods, and procedures of narrative analysis. Some potential gain in understanding is to be had by separately taking up these broad questions before turning to the more localized issues of if and when something narrative-like might serve as a metaphor or source model for better understanding matters of the self.

Although demanding too much in the way of up-front definitional precision is an uncharitable first move in any interdisciplinary venture, it probably goes without saying that social scientists are unlikely to make much headway in figuring out whether people can be usefully understood as somehow narrative-like unless or until some progress is made in learning to recognize when one is or is not in the presence of anything that deserves to be called a narrative. As it is, even this much in the way of precision is extremely hard to come by. Still, on the assumption that any concept term that applies everywhere and without remainder automatically falls short of meeting the minimal standard of being discriminating, what we are looking for is a contrast class—something that being a narrative is not.

Awkwardly, not everyone who seems eager to promote the potential utility of narrative analysis seems equally ready to play by these familiar rules. Jameson, for example, argues that narratives are simply "the central function or instance of the human mind" (Hardt & Weeks, 2000). Similarly, Turner (1996) counts narratives as "the fundamental instrument of thought . . . our chief means of looking into the future, or predicting, or planning, and of explaining" (pp. 4–5), and Barthes (1966/1987), going Turner at least one better, works to defend the claim that "narrative is universal, international, trans-historical, and trans-cultural: it is simply there, like life itself" (p. 7). All of this seems strangely reminiscent of Monsieur Jordan in Molière's (1670/1992) *Le Bourgeois Gentilhomme*, who, in his 40th year, came to the insight that all of his life he had been "speaking prose without knowing it." However potentially clarifying looking at the world through narrative lenses might initially appear, if narratives prove to be all that there is to see—if narratives really are "like life itself"—then, in the absence of any real contrast class, we would all appear to be better off dropping the constant prefix "narrative" and simply going on with life itself, much as before. Alternatively, one could work to set some sort of limits on runaway narrativity by trying to work out some criteria by means of which certain things could be fairly designated as narratives and others not. Unfortunately, few if any of these attempts at even minimal precision are uncontroversial.

Working to satisfy at least this minimal standard, some (e.g., Polkinghorne, 1988, p. 13) have proposed that in written reports, at least, the term "narrative" is standardly used to distinguish prose from, for example, graphics. The germ of the idea at work here is obviously that things without words fail to qualify as narratives. Others are quick to disagree. Wildgen (1994), for example, makes a persuasive case that Leonardo Da Vinci's painting *The Last Supper* is a perfectly acceptable narrative rendered in oil and egg tempera. Others, going for length, suggest that narratives necessarily consist of triptychs or sentences or paragraphs and cannot be rendered as single pictures or words or phrases. Even this much can hardly be taken for granted, however. For some (e.g., McQuillan, 2000, p. 10), even "Pass the salt" and "Help!" easily qualify as narratives. Worried that all this gives too much away, some hold out for a group of words expressing a complete thought (e.g., "The cat sat on the mat"), while still others raise the ante, requiring at least two such thoughts (e.g., "The cat sat on the mat, then the dog sat on the mat") that do not logically entail or presuppose each other (McQuillan, 2000, p. 323). More commonly, many (e.g., Harmon & Holman, 2000, p. 36) hold out for some patterning of events, or insist on "plots" or other "schemes" that recognize the contributions that certain events make to the development and outcome of others (Polkinghorne, 1988, p. 18). Each of these increasingly demanding claims has its own critics. Frank (1995), for example, will have none of the necessity of plots or patterns, claiming that they rule out of court "chaos narratives" and other disjointed and fragmentary accounts that seem all but obligatory in the narration of traumatic events. Near the limit, there are those who insist that simple stories only become narratives when they can boast having beginnings, middles, and ends (e.g., Abbott, 2002, p. 194). As Rorty (1987) points out, however, even "squirrels, a particular patch of pachysandra, and the Mediterranean basin all conform to the condition: they have life stories with beginnings, middles, and ends" (p. 66).

Faced with this much in the way of "elasticity"(McQuillan, 2000, p. 323) and what Bell (1994, p. 172) calls the "rich charge of suggestiveness" that circulates around the term "narrative," many have come to the conclusion that the word qualifies as an instance of what Danziger (1997, p. 148) calls "essentially contested concepts," such as love or freedom, that possess an inescapable and seemingly inexhaustible supply of ambiguity born of the different interpretive interests that have prompted their use.

All of this persistent confusion about where narratives end and things that are not narratives begin is obviously cold comfort to social scientists, such as ourselves, who continue to hold out hope that something is to be gained by seeing otherwise intractable psychological problems in their most narrative-like countenance.

Whatever Narratives Are, Are Selves, Lives, or Life Stories Somehow Narrative-like?

A rather long list of reasons can and has been offered up in support of the intuition that narrativity is, if not the "essential genre" (Flanagan, 1996, p. 67), or "natural" (MacIntyre, 1984), or "native tongue" (Weintraub, 1975) of the self, then it is at least "natural to think of the self in narrative mode" (MacIntyre, 1984, p. 192), and to assume that it represents our "best" and most "privileged" way of giving voice to it (Kerby, 1991). However true this may be of selves caught in some frozen moment, it seems truer still of selves seen or understood in their fully diachronic aspect. This is widely seen to follow because narrativity is "the language structure having temporality as its ultimate referent" (Freeman, 1984, p. 9). As Dilthey (1962, pp. 201–202) put it, "the connectedness of life can only be understood through meaning"—meaning that works to build bridges between the disparate time slices that together form the archipelago of our lives (McAdams, Diamond, de St. Aubin, & Mansfield, 1997). On such accounts, "selves are understood to be the narrative embodiment of lives told (Spence, 1982), and "it is in telling our stories that we give ourselves an identity" (Ricoeur, 1985, p. 214)—what, as indicated earlier, Dennett (1978) has termed a "narrative center of gravity."

Although we are, no doubt "story-telling animals" (MacIntyre, 1984, p. 201) who "find it natural to think of the self in narrative mode" (p. 192), there are good reasons to be slow to equate selves with personal narratives and to be cautious about dissolving the process of identity formation into a species of literature. Support for such caution comes from many quarters. Ong (1982), for example, warns against eliding the difference between thought (and its oral expression) and written texts. Thought, he argues, "is nested in speech, not in texts" (p. 75). Moreover, a life lived is always in "the midst," its beginnings, middles, and endings ascertainable only in posthumous biographies conjured up by other people. Being always in "the midst," lives, according to Bell (1994), lack the organization and intrinsic meaningfulness that characterizes narratives, in which everything is put there by some real or implied author. In short, lives may sometimes be lived like a story, but they are not stories, they are lives. On these and related arguments, it would seem unwise to attempt to indiscriminately raise narrative to a universal principle.

On How to Do Narrative Analysis

Even if it were clear, as it obviously is not, what does and does not qualify as a narrative, it would still be necessary to work out what constitutes narrative analysis, as opposed to some other form of analysis. As previously mentioned, Mishler (1995, p. 88) points out that this unsettled matter, like the definition of narrative itself, is also in a state of "near-anarchy" that works to obscure often incompatible differences in the numerous distinctive uses to which the term is often put. Imposing some sort of order on this tangle of meanings consequently seems a necessary first step in any effort to get clear about one's own and others' work. Some part of this housecleaning operation can be accomplished by simply throwing things out. As Bell (1994, p. 172) points out, in at least some instances, the idea of narrative analysis is used primarily as an "illustrative analogy," (that is "the reference to narrative could in fact be removed without damage to the substantive case"). Such instances, he suggests, and we agree, should probably be left to the side. Doing just this much helps to clear the decks, but it hardly solves the problem. The number of radically different things all reasonably called by the same name still continue to be awkwardly thick on the ground. In response, there have been numerous efforts to somehow classify the diverse ways in which serious talk of narrative analyses might be ordered up (e.g., Cortazzi, 1993; Langellier, 1989; Riessman, 1993; Young, 1989). Especially helpful among these, we find, is a "typology" recently proposed by Mishler (1995), as a way of sorting out what he regards as three distinctive "models of narrative analysis."

According to Mishler (1995, p. 90), the full panoply of contrastive approaches to narrative analysis lends itself to being rough-sorted into the following not altogether mutually exclusive bins, having to do, in turn, with the study of (1) narrative *"reference"* (i.e., the relations between events and their representation), (2) narrative *"structure"* or "textual coherence," and (3) narrative *"function"* (i.e., the work done by, or problem-solving function of, narrative strategies). On this account, most psychologists, along with other "life-scientists," most commonly employ brands of narrative analyses that qualify as instances of Mishler's last and most *functional* model, by spelling out the kinds of work that narratives are thought to do, the settings in which they are produced, and the effects they are assumed to have. The analyses of narrative *structures,* by contrast, are more often the work of literary scholars, who commonly focus their attention on matters of textualization, including explorations of the poetics of narratives. Finally, what Mishler characterizes as *reference* models of narrative analysis all share a common interest in temporality, and they take as their common task the job of explicating the nature of whatever "tying relations" are assumed to hold between the "telling" and the "told," that is, between scholars' interpretations and the actual texts that they mean to interpret.

Such type-three referencing relations, according to Mishler (1995), tend to come in one or the other of two basic types. The first and most familiar of these involves efforts to recapitulate or reconstruct the "told" from the "telling," or to fashion some veridical temporal ordering of events from their often scattered representations. Historians are commonly numbered among those most committed to such reference models and often (though, of course, not always) view their task as making sure their own particular telling is somehow "true" to (i.e., that it stands in a veridical referencing relation with) the "actual" events being told about. Something similar is also frequently taken to be the common business of interviewers or therapists or other students of life histories, whose job, by these lights, is seen to be that of correctly mining the resources of some patch of discourse, or some stretch of text, situated in the "tale world," in an effort to accurately reconstruct what really and truly transpired.

Alternatively, one can undertake to run the relation between the told and the telling in the opposite direction by attempting to make what Mishler (1995) calls "a telling from the told" (p. 100). The clearest instance of this strategy can be seen in the efforts of certain comparative historians, political scientists, and sociologists who work to "narrativize" often large-scale social processes or events, and for whom narrative is a mode of *theorizing* or *interpretation*. World War I was, for example, almost certainly different from World War II, and both differed from the innumerable wars that preceded and followed them, but they can all be imagined to find their place in some overarching narrative that is argued to make them all of a piece.

Our own research efforts, and our own focal uses of the term "narrative," find their best place in Mishler's last "reference" model of narrative analysis, or at least they do so with an important difference. Mishler's working example of moving from the told to the telling is a shifting train of large-scale social events seen to be in need of being narrativized or interpreted by historians or political scientists. The resulting "theories" offered up by practitioners as a way of imposing some common meaning on distinctive slices of historical time are then tallied up by Mishler as instances of his third key forms of narrative analysis. In our own research, by contrast, we confront individual young people (not historians or political scientists) with "evidence" of dramatic changes (not sweeping historical changes, but personal changes) in their own and other people's unfolding lives. We then invited them (our research participants) to "theorize" about, or interpretively redeem, their own commonly held conviction that they and others somehow go on being one and the same continuous or "numerically identical" person despite agreed upon evidence of personal change. The scale of events and the theoretical maturity of our respondents is obviously different from those Mishler had in mind, but the formal task of creating a "telling from the told," of providing some interpretation or "folk" theory to account for personal persistence in the face of change is not.

Despite other similarities, one key point of difference importantly distinguishes our own analyses from those of Mishler. Perhaps because the temporal dimension running through the large-scale social events featured in his examples was never in doubt, Mishler seems prepared to take more or less any form of associated theorizing as inherently narrative-like in character. Although the self-continuity warrants offered up by the young participants in our own research did, naturally enough, always consist of large or small stretches of discourse about personal sameness and change (and so perhaps qualify as "narrative" accounts under some especially loose definition of the term), they were not, as we will go on to argue, always offered as "Narrativist" or "Relational" accounts that were intended to "make a telling from the told." Rather, as we go on to show in detail, only some, but not others, of our interviewees share in the premise that their identities are altered in any fundamental way as a consequence of the passage of time—and so experience some need to search out what Mishler calls prospective "tying relations" intended to connect up the successive time slices that form the archipelago of their lives. Others, as we will go on to demonstrate, imagine instead that whatever it is that they judge to be the kernel of their own or someone else's identity somehow manages to hide out from the ravages of time and, consistent with this view, they work to vouchsafe their personal persistence by repeatedly pointing out those features of theirs that they imagine to have persisted unchanged in all of the episodes that taken together form their personal biography. Such Entity or Essentialist (as opposed to what we earlier characterized as Relational or Narrativist) accounts are meant, then, to discursively redeem their claims for self-continuity or personal persistence, but, as we insist here, they are not, in any strong sense, narrative-like accounts meant to "make a telling from the told," however many words might get used up in the telling.

In brief, then, these are the assumptions and claims that have guided the program of research that we now mean to briefly summarize as our own working example or case in point. First, contemporary talk of narrativity and narrative analysis is so richly Byzantine and so apt to go flying off in all directions at once that it would be a serious disservice to our readers to simply launch into yet another such profligate account without first trying to find a plainer way of speaking—a way that leaves room for some remainder (some one or more contrast terms) and that ends up characterizing some things as narrative-like and others not. Second, because we are interested in not only sorting out what is narrative-like and what is not but also determining where so-called narrative analysis is and is not appropriate, we attempt to trade on and further extend Mishler's recent stab at developing a typology of alternative forms of narrative analysis and find our own place in his descriptive framework. Doing this allows us to mark some of what various participants in our ongoing program of research actually do in response to our interview protocol as being of a Relational or Narrativist form—a way of moving "theoretically" from the told of one's life to a possible interpretive telling. On this account, other response forms (Essentialist or Entity forms) common to other of our research participants, although naturally made up out of words, are hardly the sort of stuff that can serve as the proper grist—at least for the sort of narrative analysis that we have in mind. In short, we proceed in an effort to convince you that sometimes we are in possession of data that has a meaningful narrative structure and that profits from narrative analysis and that on other occasions we are not. What follows is an effort to line out these two distinctive classes of responses that cross-cut our data, and to make the point that what is narrative-like and what is "remainder" interestingly divides itself along cultural lines.

A Distinction in Search of a Method

Our research question, you will recall—the interpretive problem that we have so far posed to more than 400 adolescents—is how young persons understand themselves or others to be "one and the same" continuous or temporally persistent individuals despite the inevitability of personal change. What we claim and mean to show is that what respondents say in response to this line of inquiry sometimes does, and for others does not, deserve to be understood as having a narrative structure. Here, in detail, is how the question was put and how the answers offered up appear to rough-sort themselves into what we have termed Essentialist and Narrativist responses.

The Personal Persistence Interview

When asked directly, young persons, it will not surprise you to learn, are typically neither eager nor especially quick to share their best thoughts about how it is that selves in general, or they themselves in particular, can be understood to "embody both change and permanence simultaneously" (Fraisse, 1963, p. 10). That is, directly confronting adolescents with the question of interest—"How is it that you are still the same person despite the fact that you have changed?"—typically draws little more than a bewildered stare. Our own more roundabout way to seriously engage young people in discussions about self-continuity or personal persistence regularly begins by asking them to describe themselves, first in the present, and then at a point (depending on the age of the participant) either 5 or 10 years in the past. Our purpose in drawing out such self-descriptions has been to confront our young interviewees with evidence of obvious changes in their own lives. How, we routinely press them to explain, can you justify or warrant the claim that you are still the same person when you have changed in all of the important ways that you have listed out? Several hundred such structured interviews later, it has become clear that even preteens can be counted on (1) to acknowledge the paradox of persistence and change as it applies to the details of their own lives and (2) to work to offer up a set of reasons that they believe is sufficient to reconcile their own apparently competing claims about the permanence and malleability of their own identity.

Still, as effective as this technique has proven to be, launching immediately into a long series of personal questions is hardly the best way to begin an interview of almost any kind. This frontal approach, with its clear emphasis on the continuity of the self, also fails to adequately assess the participants' thoughts about persistence in the lives of others. To avoid awkwardly beginning with "tell me all about yourself," and to gauge the thoughts of our participants on the general issue of change and continuity, our interview protocol opens by first focusing attention on persistence in the lives of others.

We could, of course, have elected to minimally shift the spotlight off of our participants and onto some friend or acquaintance—someone about whom they are well positioned to comment. But such a strategy would have been problematic. Obviously, different participants know different people, some of whom will have changed a lot and others only a little. Without some ready means of equating or controlling for these differences, there would never be a way of being sure that our participants were addressing a common question. The solution to this procedural problem that we eventually settled on involves persistence and change in the lives of fictional story characters drawn from classic works of literature (e.g., Victor Hugo's *Les Misérables* and Charles Dickens's *A Christmas Carol*). Such stories of character development—or *bildungsroman* (Kontje, 1993)—are stories that set out to document lives that are transformed in some profound and followable way over time. Such stories typically succeed or endure, at least in part, because the persistence of the character across these transformations is somehow followable and believable.

What such heroes and heroines may lack, when set against the flesh and blood relevance of friends and acquaintances in the everyday lives of our research participants, they more than recoup in common coinage and in allowing us more control over how their biographical details are presented. The first target of that control is the length of the story. If beginning an interview with personal questions is bad, asking a taciturn teen to wade through original works by Dickens or Hugo might seem worse. Overcoming these obstacles proved relatively simple. We used "Classic Comic" versions of these familiar narratives—comic books that, as the series title implies, are pint-sized, graphic retellings of classic works of literature in which the story is reduced to a handful of densely illustrated pages. In the case of *A Christmas Carol*, we also used an extensively edited version of the 1951 Alistair Sims film. Also, because our research eventually came to involve young people from aboriginal cultures—adolescents for whom works drawn from the Western European literary tradition might prove especially "foreign"—we also made use of counterpart First Nations stories that were similarly edited and presented in either comic book or video format.

In creating these heavily abbreviated and easily digestible story materials, we worked to retain all of the crucial plot elements such that, after reading or viewing the story, our adolescent participants could easily report what the main character was like at the beginning and end of the story, as well as recount the radical changes in the life and person of the character that had occurred over the course of the narrative. In ways meant to directly mirror the procedures employed in asking our participants about continuity in their own lives, we worked to first obtain their "before and after" descriptions, and then pressed them to provide an account of the continuities in the lives of, for example, Scrooge or Jean Valjean.

There, in a nutshell, is our personal persistence interview protocol. We begin by focusing on changes in the lives of others as depicted in either comic book or video format, and then broach the topic of persistence of the self by asking about the details of change with the participants' own lives. The data of interest concern the various ways in which young people of different ages and cultural backgrounds undertake to resolve the paradox of personal persistence. Because the full details of how such data are derived and coded from the typed transcripts of these interviews have been reported elsewhere (Chandler et al., 2003), they will not be repeated here.

Even a cursory glance at these transcripts reveals, much as you might expect, that some young people have much to say about these issues, others relatively little. Some are quite sophisticated in their treatment of the topic, while the arguments offered by others are rather simplistic. Although there is no inevitable relation between the length of the transcripts and various measures of the sophistication of their contents, it generally proved to be the case that sophistication increases with age. Older adolescents, on average, exhibit more complex forms of thought and language than do their younger peers. That much is hardly surprising. While there is more to say about differences in complexity, of more immediate interest are differences in the *form* of the arguments that young persons employ when reasoning about personal persistence.

As noted above, our work has led us to identify two default solution strategies (Essentialist and Narrativist) that are employed by young persons asked to justify their commitment to the persistence of identity. Essentialist strategies aim to defeat time by making a villain of change and by seeking sameness in those features or aspects of the self that have managed to endure despite change in other quarters. Such strategies range from claims about concrete aspects of the self remaining constant across time (e.g., a person's name or favorite activity) to increasingly abstract notions of personality traits and enduring souls. Though such claims differ in the level of abstraction at which they are pitched, they all trade on the heartfelt conviction that perdurability is maintained, at some more or less subterranean level, through structures or features that remain unaffected by what are judged to be more trivial changes to surface layers of the self. Narrativist strategies, by contrast, begin from the opposite shore and proceed by granting the point that change is neither always nor only apparent and by concentrating instead on sets of functional or narrative connections between what are admitted to be different instantiations of a person's identity. Here, sameness is found in change when a person's life is rendered in some followable storied form. Not all of the young persons who employ this strategy are, of course, equally skilled at constructing narratives. The youngest often conflate "chronology" with "plot" and point to the simple sequence of life events—like beads on a string—as the thread of a narrative. Like early "picaresque" novels, or medieval romances, the least sophisticated of these accounts fail to count as transformational stories of character development and often lack any real plot or coherent change in the characters. Still, the types of narratives employed range upward in sophistication from maturational, cause-and-effect plots through convictions that the only real "plot" to a person's life is the story created in each of an endless series of attempts to interpretively reread the past in light of the present.

Within these two broad approaches to the problem of personal persistence, we have thus far identified and empirically distinguished five different "levels" or sets of ordered and increasingly adequate ways of framing either Essentialist or Narrativist arguments. The sequencing principle that we employed as a means of sorting responses into higher as opposed to lower levels concerns the extent to which the argument makes room for evidence of both sameness and change. At the lower end of the Essentialist sequence, for example, change is effectively ignored and the argument consists of a listing of features (name, or hair color, or street address) that remain the same. Similarly, the least sophisticated of the Narrativists simply list off changes in serial order, and life is understood as simply "one damned thing after another." Farther along in this ascending sequence, the contest between change and sameness is more apparent. In the middle, at Level 3 for example, Essentialists adopt "preformist" or "epigenetic" accounts that see change or novelty as the coming to fruition of some always present but previously hidden aspect of the self: "Monsieur Madeline was inside Valjean all along. It's just when he helped those people in that burning fire, he changed. Madeline came out and stayed out." Level 3 Narrativists, on the other hand, find continuity across change by rendering the present as the inevitable consequence of the antecedent causal events of their own individual pasts. At the highest levels, Essentialists begin to wrestle with the possibility that the theorylike self-understanding they have labored over may require constant or perpetual revision and that their efforts may amount to nothing more than the creation of an endless succession of working hypotheses. Endstate Narrativists face the similarly disquieting realization that each and every plot that they wrap around the events of their life is just one among any number of plausible readings and that their only real hope of finding continuity lies in their own continuing efforts to interpretively reread the past in the light of the present.

Knowing that young persons can, under the right circumstances, be urged to produce arguments that we can reliably classify as being either Essentialist or Narrativist in form, and at one or another of five levels of complexity, is just the beginning. Before rushing into cross-cultural comparisons, we first wanted to know whether individual young persons wield these arguments with any degree of regularity or selectivity. That is, do they use one solution strategy with regard to the circumstances of their own lives and another when asked about Scrooge or Valjean? Or are they consistent in using the same form of argument regardless of whether the target character is the self or another and irrespective of the cultural source or medium (comic or film) in which the story appears? Similar questions can be posed regarding development. Does the chosen strategy endure over time, or are all bets off when trying to predict reasoning from one testing session to the next? Finally, and regardless of the general form of the chosen strategy, does the complexity of reasoning increase over the course of adolescence and into adulthood? To anticipate some of the answers to these questions, our work has shown that young persons typically employ the same strategy for self and others, and that they do so in ways that are largely unaffected by the medium through which we present the topic or the cultural source of the stories we employ.

Although scarcely "inductive" in the full bottom-up sense, it was not the case that our Essentialist and Narrativist scoring categories were born into the world fully formed. Rather, we found ourselves several years into this still ongoing program of research before becoming convinced that the various flavors of Essentialist thought initially identified were not exhaustive of the things that young persons (even culturally mainstream youth) had to say on the topic of their own and others' personal persistence. In our early studies, which featured young persons living in the comfortable shadow of our own ivory tower, it was almost universally the case that these culturally mainstream participants answered in ways that we have since come to label as some variant Essentialist thinking. When we did occasionally find, within the transcripts of these participants, responses that we would now confidently classify as examples of Narrativist thought, such commentaries, typically provided only by the oldest and seemingly most sophisticated of our urban sample, were read (i.e., miscoded) as an advanced (Level 5) form of Essentialist thinking. Where some see all things as narrative, we once saw none.

We have come to see in hindsight that this single-mindedness resulted from the fact that both we and our research participants are equally steeped in a cultural tradition heavily committed to seeing almost everything by Essentialist lights—a view according to which genotypic truths (including supposed truths about the self) are always imagined to be hidden away in the depths and distinct from mere surface appearances. In such a view, the changes that inevitably mark individual lives can be discounted as trivial phenotypic variations on some bedrock of Essential sameness.

What we came to suspect, however, and subsequently went on to explore, was the prospect that Essentialist solution strategies do not represent the full range of possible responses to the problem of personal persistence. That is, although we are all arguably obliged to come to some working understanding of our own and others' personal persistence in time, it increasingly struck us as problematic that the only workable solution to the problem of sameness within change had, once again, emerged as the product of Euro-American, Enlightenment thought. What struck us as required, in order to plumb the depths of our own ethnocentric bias, was some contrast group of young persons whom we had good reason to suspect might not automatically share in our own reflexive "metaphysics of substance" (Polkinghorne, 1988). One such coincidentally ready-to-hand group, located just beyond the shadow cast by our own university community, is the Aboriginal peoples of Canada. The intuition that we set out to test was that Narrativist conceptions of self-continuity would be consistent not only with the interpretive and oral traditions of such Aboriginal groups but also with their more thoroughgoing "metaphysics of potentiality and actuality" (Polkinghorne, 1988). Whereas Euro-American cultures are commonly said to promote structural or Essentialist strategies, First Nations communities, we reasoned, might support more narratively based or functional approaches to the problem of personal persistence. In the section to follow, we mean to demonstrate that what the majority of adolescents drawn from these two groups actually have to say about such matters reflects these same contrasting cultural traditions.

The Distribution of Essentialist and Narrativist Strategies Across Cultural Groups

The Aboriginal peoples of Canada comprise a remarkably diverse set of cultural traditions. In British Columbia, where our research has been conducted, there are 196 separate First Nations communities (bands), 29 tribal councils, and 16 distinct language groups. The issue of deciding which of these cultural groups to invite into our research enterprise was made even more complicated by the fact that some members of the First Nations live on government sanctioned "reserves," others are scattered in cities and towns across the province, and still others regularly live both "on" and "off-reserve." Judging it important to at least attempt to represent this geographic and cultural diversity, we were fortunate to gain the cooperation of two First Nations communities, one situated on a reserve located within the boundaries of a major urban center and the other located on an island some 30 miles off the west coast of Vancouver Island.

Young persons from each of these communities, along with a comparison group of non-Native youth, were asked to complete our Personal Persistence Interview. A subset of these participants completed the interview again after a 2-year interval. Transcripts from these interviews were then coded and each participant was given a "Track" (Essentialist or Narrativist) assignment and a "Level" (1–5) score. Some of the manipulations that did not differentially affect performance included the use of different story presentation media (using comics versus video) and the cultural source of the stories themselves (Native versus non-Native stories). Similarly, no gender differences were anticipated or observed. As in our previous work, age differences were apparent in the Level scores—with older participants receiving higher level scores than their younger counterparts, indicating the expected increase in complexity of reasoning with age. No differences in reasoning complexity were observed between the cultural groups, nor between those who employed Essentialist and Narrativist strategies.

More important, however, are the results by cultural group and the results of our longitudinal follow-up. Our hypothesis that reasoning about matters of personal persistence is, like other conceptions of the self, "culturally contingent" (Holland, 1997, p. 163) was supported by a strong dissociation between the groups: Over 86% of our Native participants employed Narrativistic forms of reasoning, compared with less than one quarter of the non-Native youth. Within the Native group, Narrativist reasoning was employed in virtually identical proportions by the Native youth living in urban and remote settings. Among the Native youth tested across a 2-year interval, the proportion using Narrativist forms of reasoning actually increased from two thirds to nearly 90%. While the form of reasoning appeared consistent at follow-up, the Level or complexity showed a statistically significant increase.

It might have been the case that the First Nations youth who employ Essentialist practices—those who behaved in countercultural ways—were somehow more "Westernized." That is, they might represent failures of enculturation or accelerated acculturation, or otherwise indicate a loss of commitment to their culture of origin. If that were so, then one should expect Essentialist First Nations youth to be less intensely committed to their Aboriginal cultures than their First Nations peers who adopted Narrativist strategies. This was not the case. On multiple measures of cultural identification, both Essentialist and Narrativist First Nations youth show equal, and decidedly high, levels of commitment to Aboriginal culture. The distribution of these different solution strategies is neither entirely determined by cultural membership nor obviously yoked to a person's sense of belonging to one culture or another.

Summary

In the world of concept terms, scope is the enemy of precision. "Narrativity," which many have come to regard as borderless, and market as being of unlimited scope, is no exception. What we have attempted to argue and demonstrate in this chapter is that talk of narrativity without remainder (without some contrast class to which the term "narrative" scarcely applies) threatens to become too imprecise for words. In our own empirical efforts, we have worked to show that important individual and cultural differences can be usefully illuminated by drawing on insights owed to what is, for most social scientists, a newly emerging narrative tradition. At the same time, as our illustrative data show, not everything that some of our young participants had to say, and practically nothing said by others, especially lends itself to being seen in its most narrative countenance. Such contrasts, in our view, are the real stuff out of which the future of narrative analysis will be made.

Notes

1. The term "aboriginal" refers to indigenous people in general, while "Aboriginal" is meant to reference specific groups within Canada. The Aboriginal peoples of Canada consist of three distinct groups: First Nations, Inuit, and Métis. The First Nations were once termed "Indian." The Inuit were formerly referred to as "Eskimo." The Métis trace their origins to marriages between the First Nations and European settlers.

2. As will become apparent shortly, the terms "Narrativist" and "Essentialist" will be used throughout this chapter to refer to one or the other of two data scoring categories.

References

Abbott, H. P. (2002). *The Cambridge introduction to narrative*. Cambridge, UK: Cambridge University Press.

Barthes, R. (1987). *Criticism and truth* (K. P. Keuneman, Trans.). London: Athlone. (Original work published 1966)

Bell, M. (1994). How primordial is narrative? In C. Nash (Ed.), *Narrative in culture* (pp. 172–198). London: Routledge.

Chandler, M. J. (2000). Surviving time: The persistence of identity in this culture and that. *Culture and Psychology, 6*(2), 209–231.

Chandler, M. J. (2001). The time of our lives: Self-continuity in Native and non-Native youth. In H. W. Reese (Ed.), *Advances in child development and behavior* (Vol. 28; pp.175–221). San Diego, CA: Academic Press.

Chandler, M. J., Lalonde, C. E., Sokol, B., & Hallett, D. (2003). Personal persistence, identity development, and suicide: A study of Native and non-Native North American adolescents. *Monographs of the Society for Research in Child Development, Serial No. 273, Vol. 68, No. 2.*

Cortazzi, M. (1993). *Narrative analysis.* Washington, DC: Falmer.

Danziger, K. (1997). The historical formation of selves. In R. Ashmore & L. Jussin (Eds.), *Self and identity: Fundamental issues* (pp.137–159). New York: Oxford University Press.

Dennett, D. C. (1978). *Brainstorms: Philosophical essays on mind and psychology.* Cambridge: MIT Press.

Dilthey, W. (1962). *Pattern and meaning in history: Thoughts on history and society.* New York: Harper.

Flanagan, O. (1996). *Self expressions: Mind, morals and the meaning of life.* New York: Oxford University Press.

Fraisse, P. (1963). *The psychology of time.* New York: Harper & Row.

Frank, A. W. (1995). *The wounded storyteller: Body, illness, and ethics.* Chicago: University of Chicago Press.

Freeman, M. (1984). History, narrative, and life-span developmental knowledge. *Human Development, 27,* 1–19.

Hardt, M., & Weeks, K. (Eds.). (2000). *The Jameson reader.* Malden, MA: Blackwell.

Harmon, W., & Holman, C. (2000). *A handbook to literature* (8th ed.). Upper Saddle River, NJ: Prentice Hall.

Holland, D. (1997). Selves as cultured. In R. Ashmore & L. Jussin (Eds.), *Self and identity: Fundamental issues* (pp. 160–190). New York: Oxford University Press.

Kerby, A. P. (1991). *Narrative and the self.* Bloomington: Indiana University Press.

Kontje, T. C. (1993). *The German bildungsroman: History of a national genre.* Columbia, SC: Camden House.

Langellier, K. M. (1989). Personal narratives: Perspectives on theory and research. *Text and Performance Quarterly, 9,* 243–276.

MacIntyre, A. (1984). *After virtue: A study in moral theory.* Notre Dame: University of Notre Dame Press.

McAdams, D., Diamond, A., de St. Aubin, E., & Mansfield, E. (1997). Stories of commitment: the psychosocial construction of generative lives. *Journal of Personality and Social Psychology, 72(3),* 678–694.

McQuillan, M. (2000). *The narrative reader*. London: Routledge.

Mishler, E. G. (1995). Models of narrative analysis: A typology. *Journal of Narrative and Life History, 5*, 87–123.

Molière, J. B. (1992). *Le bourgeois gentilhomme* (N. Dear, Trans.). Bath, UK: Absolute Classics. (Original work published 1670)

Ong, W. (1982). *Orality and literacy: The technologizing of the word*. London: Methuen.

Polkinghorne, C. (1988). *Narrative knowing and the human sciences*. Albany: State University of New York Press.

Ricoeur, P. (1985). History as narrative and practice. *Philosophy Today, 29*, 213–222.

Riessman, C. K. (1993). *Narrative analysis*. Newbury Park, CA: Sage.

Rorty, A. O. (1987). Persons as rhetorical categories. *Social Research, 54(1)*, 55–72.

Spence, D. (1982). *Narrative truth and historical truth: Meaning and interpretation in psycho-analysis*. New York: W. W. Norton.

Turner, M. (1996). *The literary mind*. New York: Oxford University Press.

Weintraub, K. J. (1975, June). Autobiography and historical consciousness. *Critical Inquiry*, 821–848.

Wildgen, W. (1994). *Process, image, and meaning: A realistic model of the meaning of sentences and narrative texts*. Philadelphia: John Benjamins.

Young, K. (1989). Narrative embodiments: Enclaves of the self in the realm of medicine. In J. Shotter & K. J. Gergen (Eds.), *Texts of identity: Vol. 2. Inquiries in social construction series* (pp. 152–165). London: Sage.

3.5

Once Upon a Time

A Narratologist's Tale

Mary Gergen

Reflections in the Looking Glass: Critical Gazes

The title of this book seemed to invite a story about my development as a
student of narratives and some reflection on how the study of narratives, as
well as narratives themselves, have changed for me over time. The story
begins near the dawn of narrative studies in psychology and ends in the present. To begin, I express my critical views concerning traditional methods
within psychology, and I suggest the qualities of a more inclusive science,
one especially suited to narrative studies. Following this, I trace my encounters with narratives through the research projects with which I have been
involved; I also unveil some of my concerns about the social ramifications
of narratives' cultural potency. In the end, and it is a happy, if challenging,
ending, I speculate about what narrative analysis might be and become, and
in my ruminations I find myself far from where I began.

Exploring the Barren Plains of Experimental Psychology

About 15 years ago, I organized a conference at my university on
the theme of feminism and its impact on the academy. In relation to this

conference, I edited *Feminist Thought and the Structure of Knowledge;* in it, I expressed my dreams of how the field of psychology would be different if feminist ideas became more central to its research pursuits (M. Gergen, 1988b).

> Feminist-inspired research would endeavor to recognize that scientists, subjects, and 'facts' are all interconnected, involved in reciprocal influences, and subject to interpretation and linguistic constraints. In addition, scientific endeavors would be treated as value-laden and would be formed with specific value orientations in mind. This research approach would treat scientists as participants in the research project along with the subjects of research and not as superior beings who maintain a knowledge monopoly among themselves. (p. 94)

This vision, to advance a value-based, participatory, and contextually sensitive science, has been with me since that time, and serves as a background for my work in narrative psychology (see Denzin & Lincoln, 2000).[1]

Theorizing Narratives: Pilots and Pilgrimages

Writing Our Way Into the Narrative World

Critique is a compelling preoccupation that can fill one's life; envisioning new theories is exciting; creating new modes of research that fulfill all the demands of critique and the potentials of theory is difficult. In the mid 1980s, pioneers in psychology, including Ted Sarbin and his colleagues at the University of California at Berkeley and Santa Cruz, set out in this direction as promoters of narrative work (Sarbin, 1986; Sarbin & Kitsuse, 1993; Sarbin & Schiebe, 1983). Writing about our narrative explorations at Sarbin's invitation, Kenneth J. Gergen and I became convinced that there was much of value to share with others. During the 1980s, Ken and I worked on theoretical expansions of the idea of narrative to include notions of selves, relationships, and science itself. (K. Gergen & M. Gergen, 1988). We brought into our studies literary theory and philosophical ideas that treated narratives on a more conceptual level.[2] We wrote about their shapes, their forms, and, most importantly, how the cultural repertoires of narratives influenced human life (K. Gergen & M. Gergen, 1988). Adding to the earlier position taken by Ken (K. Gergen, 1973) that social psychology was history, we edited *Historical Social Psychology* to illustrate the diverse ways that social psychologists employ narrative studies (K. Gergen & M. Gergen, 1984).

Connecting Narrative Analysis to Social Construction

The study of narratives went hand in hand with our burgeoning interest in social constructionism (K. Gergen, 1985). Once we had been drawn to the idea that social groups were creating their conceptions of reality together, it was a reasonable extension to recognize the central importance of social groups in creating and sustaining the stories by which reality is formed and transformed. If story forms are produced within cultures to make sense of life, then central questions became "What are the stories available in a culture?" and "How do the stories we tell influence how we live?" Furthermore, taking feminist theory seriously concerning the patriarchal privileging of male voices, I was especially sensitive to the question of how silences and gaps in story forms can delimit who we are and can become.

Investigating Narrative Forms: Pilot Work

We began our empirical work by collecting narrative forms with Swarthmore College students. We asked them to write a brief story about some aspect of their life from childhood to the present. In order to analyze the various stories, we invented an analytical tool we called the "story line."[3] In one typical format, we gave each student a paper with a time line on the x axis and a scale of negative to positive on the y axis. The students were asked to draw a line that would express how positive or negative their lives were over that time period. For example, we asked them to tell the story of their lives as students. In general, these outstanding students wrote success stories, and from them they created highly positive and upward, progressive narratives from kindergarten to college. When we asked about social life, there was much more variety in the narrative forms, with many peaks and valleys for most students. Relationships with mother had one form of narrative for some students, while those with father often had another. Each question garnered a different story line.

This pilot work gave us three warning signals about narrative analysis. First, it cautioned us against assuming that any given "life story" was comprehensive; second, it signaled that no one story was accurate as a description of a life; and, third, it alerted us to the difficulty of finding generational stories—because cohorts of people did not necessarily have the same story to tell, despite the historical similarities of their lives.

What Is the "Truth" About Narratives?

These important realizations, in particular, that narratives are more than, less than, or other than "what really happened," set our work apart from that of some who regarded narratives as "truths" about individuals' lives. Many practitioners in forensics, therapy, social work, education, and psychology (particularly those in humanistic psychology and the psychology of women) had long held, often unwittingly, that stories can be true. What a person recalled from childhood or from some traumatic or difficult situation, if told under the right conditions, would thus be an accurate, if highly personalized, representation of the facts.[4]

As social constructionists, we did not require that narratives be true or false in any absolute sense, but rather we considered them renditions of events, cohering to certain cultural standards, which made sense of life to someone in a particular context. In addition, a narrative was almost always created to give meaning to events in the past. As many narrative theorists have emphasized, we make stories of the past and live into the future.[5] The importance of this realization has taken many forms, including research by others indicating that the nature of any narrative about one's past is also influenced by current stations in life and relations with others.[6] In taking this viewpoint, we diverge from the course of many others interested in narrative analysis.

Narrative Effects: Potentials and Deficits

The Relationship of Stories, Optimism, and Health

Regardless of how "truthful" life stories are, many research studies, including my own work with older people, indicate that the kind of story a person generally tells about some period in his or her life can have dramatic consequences for that person's well-being. In my dissertation research, I found that older people who were able to tell stories about how they had voluntarily chosen to give up activities were healthier and happier than those who said they gave up things because they were too old, too sick, or otherwise too restricted in their possibilities (M. Gergen, 1980).[7] I will never forget my uneasiness at asking Annabelle, who was 93, if she had thought about getting married again. She replied that she had no plans to remarry because she hadn't found anyone she particularly fancied. None of her stories highlighted her age, her physical limitations, or her narrowing social opportunities, all of which she could have described. (Annabelle lived for another 9 years, but she never did remarry.) Recent research on 200 older married couples also indicates that those who tell stories about how wonderful their marriage is have higher levels of life satisfaction and health than those who do not (O'Rourke, 2002).

Missing Stories, Missing Lives: A Quixotic Adventure

Defining the Monomyth: A Hero's Tale

While the right stories can create satisfying lives, so too the absence of good stories can have the opposite effect. Taking the notion seriously that without the right stories, certain lives cannot be lived, I have considered the fate of girls.[8] According to Joseph Campbell (1956), a noted theorist on storytelling, there is basically one story in Western culture, the monomyth, which is the framework for all stories. The story is of a hero who sets off on a quest. As the hero confronts various challenges—fearful, dangerous, powerful, and/or seductive—he is changed. He becomes wiser, more powerful, and more spiritual. I realized as I reflected on this plot that the hero is presumed to be male. Female characters serve supporting roles—mothers, sisters, maidens-in-distress, sirens, witches, crones, or princesses, who, with their sizeable dowries, are given in marriage to the heroes. I recognized, too, that the plot of heroine stories was a distorted version of the monomyth, with a passively expectant protagonist caught in a difficult situation.[9]

Missing the "Heroinic" Story

Consider the most common plots of popular fairytales: Cinderella scrubs the floor; Sleeping Beauty sleeps; Snow White makes supper for elves; Rapunzel spins as her hair grows. I began to wonder whether the missing stories in our culture had anything to do with the missing heroines. Is there something about our narrative traditions that has impeded women's progress in the public realm? Might this help to explain why so very few women reach the highest professional, corporate, and academic positions? Would missing stories contribute to the fact that single women often are poor and vulnerable to abuse? What stories are available for girls, and would it make a difference if the stories they told were different?[10]

In the beginning of this adventure, I had the intuition that girls need to have stories that approximate the monomyth, instead of fairy tales in which virtuous damsels wait for a prince to save them.[11] Where are the stories that emphasize the wonderful futures of girls who solve difficult problems, invent new products, or govern nations? Conversely, where are the stories about the girls who drop out of school to have babies? Such missing stories could have vital potential for changing the lives of girls.

Tapping a Narrative Source: The Popular Autobiography

These thoughts led me to an investigation of the popular autobiographies of contemporary heroes and heroines.[12] My method of studying these texts was at the beginning very systematic. I coded and sorted phrases that related to the variables of my study (e.g., those related to achievement, success, failure, mentoring, career aspirations, setbacks, resilience, diligence, high expectations, as well as to friendship, family, love, interpersonal concerns, and physical state).

Soon, however, I became disenchanted with this approach. Besides being a seemingly endless task, given the number of books I had been reading, I came to believe that the analytical method of deconstructing stories into coded piles actually was undermining the aims of the research. It was as though I had a house before me, and I had decided to dismantle it to make various piles of bricks. The narrative structure was of central importance to me, and I did not want to lose it in the process of analysis.[13] I wanted to incorporate bigger swatches of material into my project, which was to identify the major differences between the stories told by women and by men.

As quickly became apparent, the cultural conventions of telling a woman's or a man's story were so powerful that it was possible to pick up a book and ascertain the gender of the author within a page. The differences were so clearly stereotyped that even when the ghost writer of two autobiographies was the same, one could tell whether the coauthor was a woman or a man. For example, in *Iacocca: An Autobiography,* with William Novak, a noted second author of celebrity autobiographies, the first sentence is: "Wherever I go, people always ask me the same questions. How did you get to be so successful?" The first sentence of *Mayflower Madam: The Secret Life of Sydney Biddle Barrows,* also with William Novak, is: "On the evening of October 11, 1984, I had to endure one of the most dreaded rituals a single woman in our society can undergo: I went on a blind date."[14]

Gender Differences: The Monomyth and the Minimyth

To summarize this research (M. Gergen, 1992), I found dramatic differences between these stories. As I expected, men's stories invariably followed the monomyth framework. Each man was a hero on a quest: breaking the sound barrier, saving Chrysler, drilling oil wells, making touchdowns, or saving big corporations from ruin. In the end, they all won, usually against great odds and single-handedly! Any material that distracted from this story line, including family life and bodily conditions, was almost nonexistent. The women's narratives, in contrast, were less resolved. The women also described their personal achievements with great joy, but typically they didn't take all the credit for their successes. In their stories, they stressed the satisfactions and disappointments of others, as well as their own; they mingled their love lives with their professional achievements; they sacrificed professional success for family benefits, and they wrote extensively about those they loved. Martina Navratilova, for example, described winning her first Wimbledon tennis championship as fulfilling her father's ambitions and included in her tale of triumph a hug from Chris Evert, her defeated opponent (M. Gergen & K. Gergen, 1993).

Escaping the Rut of the Monomyth

I was not certain that borrowing boys' stories would create new possibilities for girls. It seemed to me that women's narratives, while messy and disordered, encompassed life more fully than did men's narratives, which were stuck in the groove of traditional monomyths. Men were characters in a story that centered on professional success, and they were as good as their last "touchdown." While I could see that women's stories did not encourage single-hearted sacrifice for the sake of professional merit, I thought they did succeed in combining two narratives: professional success and private relational fulfillment.

It seemed that the individual's position in society could be constrained by narrative forces beyond the potential of the individual to overcome them.[14] My curiosity led me to ponder how narratives might be recast so that they would be supple and multifaceted enough to encompass women's lives. Beyond that, I wondered how men might be encouraged to tell their stories and to live their lives in similar ways as well. Perhaps the first victims of the Procrustean cast of the monomyth were men themselves. From a Foucaultian position, narratives served as disciplinary discourses, shaping lives. Yet, with Foucault, I saw potentials for resistance.[15]

Craft Warnings on a Sea of Ambiguity

Troubling About Narratives

Regarding the impact of the gendered nature of narratives on life, it became clear to me that narratives themselves were expressions of hierarchical social arrangements. If, as one might argue, there were a number of strongly segregated narrative forms that were cast for various players on the stage of life, then social life would be very stable and potentially oppressive. Not only would there be narratives of gender but, also, of age, race, class, and nationality.[16] Clearly this is the case, if one considers the ways in which older people are cast in our culture's stories of life span development. Almost always aging is portrayed as a time of decline, DEPRESSION, withdrawal, and lassitude.[17]

There is a limitation, however, in simply regarding stable narratives as productive of stable social orders. Or perhaps one might say, an escape hatch from the egg crate of segregated cells is always a potentiality. In most Western societies, people do not just have one major role to play, nor one narrative to tell. From our earlier research with Swarthmore students, we could clearly see that people could tell many ministories. A person might be a poorly paid janitor during the workweek, a revered softball coach on Saturday, and an authoritative deacon of a church on Sunday. Which narrative would encompass all the social roles such a person might play?

An alternative theoretical possibility more suited to our postmodern times could be that stories are malleable and multifaceted, not rigid hollow shells shaping the lives of people, as had previously been theorized. Perhaps the popular autobiography only promoted the most prominent narrative forms, and people in ordinary life have more options than it first appeared to me. If the gender of the person telling the story could create such a shift in the subject matter and style of the monomyth, then perhaps temporal shifts in social role or in a particular relationship could also alter the narratives told. Perhaps people could become, if they were not already, designers of their own narratives, fashioning for each situation a story composed of the narrative forms at hand. If these various possibilities were possible, then many new research questions might be raised. Are all narratives equally rigid or fluid? If they are less than rigid, to what degree are they so, and under what conditions? Could people learn new narratives? How difficult might it be? These questions have occupied my attention in recent years.[18]

The Natures of a Narrative: Flexible and Firm

To address the issue of the flexibility or firmness of narratives as they are told, it is important to consider that there is no theoretical limit as to what narrative must go with what life circumstance. Consider the award-winning movie *Life is Beautiful*, in which the Italian father tells his son stories that cast being sent to a concentration camp as a game. One might consider this the extreme of narrative flexibility.

If there is no compelling case that narrative must align in a special way with life, then what factors do tend to regulate the choices made? There are practical, social, and psychological influences that must have an impact on the outcome. People are under the sway of many conditions. What do they do? It is not clear. Recall the joke about the twin boys who are presented with a room full of manure on their birthday. One boy is highly distressed, while the other plows through it enthusiastically, saying, "There must be a pony in here somewhere!"

Reflexivity and a New Narrative Adventure

I became especially interested not in the study of narratives as they relate to other facets of life, as I had once been, but in the question of how narrative analysis might be most productively done; my concern was related to my wondering how, if narratives are not stable entities, we can best study them. Surely there is a vibrant history of narrative research, with many scholars contributing fascinating accounts of people's lives and life stories. Clearly one could do something, but it became a bit murky to me what it all has meant. How is a narrative created? How is it constrained or liberated? What is the nature of a research-based narrative study? How can we study an "it" if the "it" is not there?

And beyond my own doubts, further questions emerged concerning the participants in our endeavors. Were the people we interviewed aware or not of the potential fragility of their narratives? If people became convinced that their narratives were constructions, open to change, what impact would this have on their sense of their own narratives and their sense of who they were? Would this notion of the instability of narratives have negative implications for their sense of integrity? Most likely. In American culture, people's stories about themselves are assumed to have a great deal of consistency. Only liars and "crooks" freely change their narratives from one moment to the next. If this is the assumption, might the notion that narratives are fragile social constructions be rejected by most people? Most likely.

My colleague Sara N. Davis and I set about discovering what people would say if we asked them about the stability of their narratives (M. Gergen & Davis, 2003). We wanted to know if people were aware of changing their narratives in various situations, if they were aware of why they changed them, and, in addition, whether they could change them in the interview situation if we asked them to. We began our research by each interviewing five people. We asked them to tell us a story about some "life transition" they'd experienced. We suggested that this event did not have to be especially significant, traumatic, or negative. As it turned out, the stories they told were some combination of these. After they had finished, we described in some detail our view concerning the potential malleability of stories. We then asked them about their views on this. Could they tell the story in different ways? When might they tell this story differently?

While we sought to encourage our storytellers to consider their different tellings, we realized that the fact that they had just told this particular story to us would make it more difficult to tell a radically different version and still seem to be a reasonably coherent, honest person. Unless the tellers were rather sophisticated about narrative construction, it might appear that they lacked moral fiber or had been deceitful in their narratives if they admitted to making up different versions in different situations.

Changing the Story: Factors Favoring Change

Yet, we did find that our participants could describe how they had changed their stories—if not in the present moment, at least in other situations. For example, one respondent, who had a stormy relationship with her father, reported frequently editing certain details about his death. If she does not say that her father died on her birthday, she is able to avoid "excessive" emotional reactions from others that require a response from her that she regards as hypocritical.

Another respondent, who described the death of her mother when she was a young child, reported that her story has changed considerably over the years. As a child, she seemed unable to talk about it at all. In adolescence, she became more able to tell a story of her great loss. As an adult, she could tell a story about the severity of the loss, as well as about how it led to a greater and earlier maturity on her part. In her case, time and maturity had greatly changed the nature of her story. In another interview, the discussion about reflexivity between Sara and a participant led to some revisions in her story within the interview setting. The story became more satisfying to the participant as a result of their conversation. She left the interview a happier person than she had been when she arrived.

In general, we observed that people changed their narratives, knowingly, when confronted with the possibility of an unwanted response from a listener or from a desire to preserve a particular form of identity. Their stories also changed with increasing maturity and verbal competency, and as they took on new meanings of their pasts through therapy or other interpersonal encounters. For some, an awareness of gaining some greater psychological benefits from change helped to shift the narrative in a different direction as well. The theoretical potential of social constructionism to allow people to change their stories was irrelevant for all but one of the storytellers, who will be described below. Changing narratives was not a theoretical decision!

Strongly Held Stories: Favoring Stability

We also found that stories can become so ingrained that it appears to the teller that there is no possibility of revision. In addition, the identity of the teller and the teller's subsequent relationships with others who are involved with this identity are so dependent on the "truth" of special stories that to significantly alter a story would mean that the life circumstances of the teller would be called into question. This proved to be the case for one young woman who told a harrowing story of her childhood. While she told a shorter and less revealing version of the story to most people, she could never alter its tragic tenor. It was important for her to have a clear understanding of what good and bad families are; the stability of her story about growing up in a bad family helped her to regulate her own behavior, which had to be built up on the basis of what she imagined "good" people and "good" families are, and not on the basis of personal experiences within her family. Considering other possibilities seemed to unsettle her. Her efforts to move away from her troubled history and find her dream house with a "white picket fence" seemed to depend on the stability of her narrative.

Another participant had a story of childhood difficulty, with physical handicaps and medical treatments that delayed his development and undermined his school achievement. The integral links of each facet of the story with others made it very sturdy. Efforts in the interview to encourage him to shift his story in any significant manner were relatively unsuccessful. He acknowledged the possibility, but he did not change his account.

For each of these participants, the importance of maintaining a stable story was paramount. Although they had not questioned the rationale for retaining the same narrative prior to this research experience, they were unmoved by the possibility of change. The story as it stood was central to their identity formations and seemed to be strongly supported by others in their social worlds. For certain people, a highly structured and stable story, without a great deal of flexibility in the important structural details, is orienting in terms of their life goals and comforting in terms of emotional satisfactions. Whether or not it is disciplinary or oppressive discourse is not a pertinent question for these people.

A somewhat different outcome after the interview occurred with a participant who had a very solid story related to his job history. In this story of job loss, Fred was convinced that he had made a dreadful mistake that had an adverse affect on his employment history that could not be rectified. As a result, he seemed saddled with a troubled identity marked by an act of stupidity and subsequent job loss. During the interview, he remained stolid in his resistance to changing his story. However, following the interview, he approached me on several occasions with brief comments that indicated revisions in his seemingly impervious story. Each of the revisions contained a message of hope that deconstructed the worst elements of his previous story. It appeared that my suggesting the possibility that there were other stories to be told about this event set in motion options for retelling that helped him reevaluate his seemingly foolish act of many years before. The upshot of the interview process seemed to have been an increase in feelings of well-being and self-esteem for Fred. This experience led me to consider the notion that there might be a "boomerang" effect in the interview process, in which aftereffects of an interaction with a narrative analyst could produce lingering effects that would alter the teller's story in meaningful ways.[19]

The Postmodern Exception: Jiggling Jill

Only one of our ten participants caught the drift of the possibilities inherent in telling stories anew with a very different theme. Perhaps this was not surprising, as she had had the most exposure to the social constructionist literature. Having told an adolescent tale of mischief and merriment, she pondered how she might change the story if required to do so. She responded by saying,

> I could tell a story of tragedy, of how so many of my friends died in car crashes or from being hit by a drunk driver. A "Live for today, for tomorrow we may die story." Or I could tell a story about how dark and depressing it all was, and how miserable I felt. Or I could tell a story about how lucky I was, never in a car crash, never arrested, never suffered any bad consequences.

She sensed the potential for elaborating her story in many different ways, ways that led to many different trajectories in her adult life. She was able to recognize the potential for telling a multiplicity of stories, without necessarily settling on any of them. To her, it was an intellectual game. At the same time, it did not appear that she was involved equally in each telling. It seemed as though she was satisfying my demands, the demands of the interviewer.

The Impact of the Interview Situation: Relational Havoc

Narratives as Co-Constructions

Despite the rage for consistency that many storytellers seem to have, at least within the encounter in which the story is told, the moral of the Jiggling Jill story seems to be that, under the right conditions, a wide range of stories might be told, with some awareness that such stories are new constructions. A second aspect of her interview that is important is related to the notion that she was sensitive to my presence in her narration. To enlarge on this viewpoint, I would suggest that looking at narratives as the construction of a single individual, without regard for outside factors, is too narrow a perspective. Rather, narratives might better be defined as co-constructions within a context, involving at least two people. If the time, place, or actor is shifted, the nature of the narrative is also vulnerable to change. Among the pertinent shaping factors are the identity of the inquirer, the questions asked, the temporal-spatial characteristics of the interview, and the relationships among these various elements. A police interrogation, therapy session, cocktail party, and funeral are very different venues for storytelling. While the differences are too numerous to name here, they are not hard to imagine.[20] Once we recognize these relational complexities, an interesting conclusion can be reached—if we take the notion of narratives as joint constructions seriously.

Narratives as Joint Constructions

It might be said that the narratives revealed in a research study are themselves by-products of the relationships of researchers to respondents. The mutual gaze, subtle signs of agreement or disagreement, silences, smiles, frowns, and comments related to shared or diverse experiences all lend shape to the story being told. If the storyteller is the same age, race, and/or gender as the listener, certain assumptions of similarity may lead to embellishments on themes that might be avoided were the listener someone completely different, and vice versa. As the story is co-created, it loses its unique authorship and becomes something mutual. It is not clear who should be given the final authority under circumstances of a story heard or even read. Thus the researcher is within the stories researched. In this context, we must ask how a researcher can distinguish herself or himself from the narratives collected in order to claim authority to conduct narrative analysis of an independent object? Or perhaps the question must be changed: If the "it" of the narrative, as an independent entity, has disappeared and instead it is defined as temporary, saturated with situated and contextual essences, and belonging to no one in particular, what new challenges have indeed arisen?

Sailing for the Horizon

"I write because I want to find something out, " said Laurel Richardson (1994) in a passage on writing as a search for meaning (p. 517). For me, this has been a similar adventure. What do I discover with my narrative of my narrative research? (Or is it *our* narrative of *our* narrative research?) What are the implications of these explorations for the field of narrative analysis? To end the story of my travels, I shall focus on some possibilities.

Counting Our Blessings

To begin, I appreciate that engaging in narrative research involves an exciting commitment to interdependent, contextualized, value-laden work; that narratives are potent ways of understanding relationships in motion and relationships from the past as they appear in the present; that narratives can help their tellers to feel happy and healthy or sad and sick; that narratives are not necessarily stable, nor are they altogether flexible; that the stability of a narrative depends in part on how important it is to one's sense of self, how it structures one's life, and also on context—the place, time, and conversational partners; that narratives belong as much to a culture as to a person; that living reflexively may subvert narrative stability; that narratives are geared to certain social roles, such as gender and age, and that when narratives are missing, so are potentials for living. Doing narrative research entails accepting that the subject matter of the field is a temporally and spatially sensitive cultural creation, produced in the liminal space between the teller and the told. As such, a narrative comes into existence as a facet of relationship, not as a product of an individual.

Recasting Our Treasures

My chapter with Sara Davis in our feminist-social constructionist reader (M. Gergen & Davis, 1997) ends with this question: "What are the benefits of accepting that there are no final answers to the questions posed?" (p. 255). To wit, can we live with the ambiguity presented by the meltdown of the individual life story within narrative analysis? It seems to me that if we take seriously the ambiguity of narratives in all aspects, then we must also accept that any accounts we give, as narrative researchers, are equally tenuous. We also act within a relational context, of journal editors, readers, book publishers, and colleagues.

If we do acknowledge that narratives are not simply about others, can we still value them? If we accept this perspective, should we still do narrative analysis? Is the beauty of narrative forms and their promise of generative potential for living enough? Perhaps. After all, we seem to live within the kingdom of our stories and the promises they behold. For those of us who engage in narrative work, I think there may be more to it as well. By re-creating the object of our study as temporally evanescent and co-constructed, we introduce new potentials for our studies. We can invent new ways of analyzing and describing our interpretations. We are encouraged to collaborate with our participants in the collection of narratives; we are inspired to write in ways that honor our multiplicities, as speakers, writers, and analysts.[21] We cannot extricate ourselves from our material any more than other psychologists and social scientists ever could (M. Gergen & K. Gergen, 2000).[22] Being a part of the game, can we still play the game? How might the game be changed?[23] These are the questions that narratologists need to address. Many new doors to a relational narrative science are opening. I am optimistic about our potentials to create.

Notes

1. See Jerome Bruner (1990) and Jack Martin & Jeff Sugarman (1999), who argue that psychology overvalues the methods of the natural sciences, particularly its efforts to create causal statements about events.

2. See Kenneth J. Gergen and Mary M. Gergen (1983, 1988) and Mary M. Gergen and Kenneth J. Gergen (1986) for more detail.

3. For a more detailed summary of this research and the development of the story line, see Mary M. Gergen (1988a).

4. The great controversy in the psychology of women between those who supported the notion of repressed memory of true stories of abuse and those who

were skeptical of the viewpoint is indicative of the serious differences that occurred on this point. (e.g., see Herman, 1992; Loftus, 1993)

5. See Josselson (1996; Josselson, Lieblich, & McAdams, 2003) for examples of narrative studies that emphasize these points.

6. Research on narratives indicates that the nature of a current relationship greatly influences the way the past is storied (Holmberg & Holmes, 1994).

7. This and other research was published as "The Discourse of Control and the Maintenance of Well-Being" (M. Gergen & K. Gergen, 1986).

8. See "Finished at Forty" (M. Gergen, 1990). Emily Martin, a noted anthropologist, has looked at medical texts and discovered the ways in which women have been described quite differently from men (Martin, 1987).

9. I remember receiving a book for Confirmation about the lives of girl saints, an inspirational guide intended for my spiritual growth. There was a central plot in these stories, too. While remaining faithful to her religion, each girl faced a terrible fate. The girls were, in some dreadful combination, raped, stoned, starved, imprisoned, burned, stabbed, beaten, driven mad, and/or killed by various heathen men. There was not a happy ending in the lot.

10. All who write about the missing stories of girls, as well as the perversions of girls' stories, are indebted to the work of Lynn Brown and Carol Gilligan, especially their 1992 book, *Meeting at the Crossroads: Women's Psychology and Girls' Development*.

11. It is important to realize that, in the 1980s, there were almost no active heroic stories about girl characters. The Powder Puff Girls were still unborn; Charlie's Angels may have been a lonely exception. And there were almost no women holding important positions. Great strides were made in the 1990s in terms of women in the public eye, such as in cabinet positions in the Clinton administration, Secretary of State Madeline Albright, and Supreme Court Judges O'Connor and Ginsberg. By the end of the 1990s, almost half of the medical and law student populations were women, an enormous change from early decades. It seems likely that the stories for girls have also become much more active, although I am unaware of research that affirms this contention.

12. I avoided analyzing autobiographies that were primarily written to appeal to literary critics and, instead, chose popular books in order to maximize my connection to the reading public (see a summary of this research in M. Gergen, 2001).

13. For this reason, I am not a convert to computer software programs.

14. I am reminded here of the title of the song that characterized the civil rights movement and the leadership of Martin Luther King in the 1950s and 1960s, "We Shall Overcome."

15. As Michel Foucault might suggest, the cultural forms of organizing how to behave are subtle and embedded in commonsense forms of intelligence. The language available and the stories that can be told enforce proper conduct. Foucault (1979) also suggested that one can resist the totalizing effects of these disciplining discourses.

16. One might speculate that in most of world for most of the time, the uniform narrative, comprehensive and coordinated with others, has been a good description of the power of narratives to organize life.

17. It is to oppose just such forms of narrative that Kenneth J. Gergen and I have become editors of the Positive Aging Newsletter. In it, we amass materials that cast aging in a very generative light, and we proclaim it in our editorial policy as an unprecedented time of growth and development. It is found at http://www.positiveaging.net

18. The metaphor of narratives as existing as a repertoire of cultural assets may be somehow misleading in that it stresses the singularity and solidity of the narrative form. I no longer think this is the ideal construction. The paradox as I see it now is that we must gain the experience of learning the stories of the culture we are a part of in order to tell the stories of our lives, and yet, each time we tell a story, we reconstruct (and alter) the stories of the past. In this sense, narratives only come into being in their tellings.

19. The consequences of a boomerang effect can be salutary, as in this case, or negative.

20. W. W. Charters & Theodore Newcomb (1958) similarly showed that if college students were reminded of their religious ideals, they would describe themselves as more ethical than if they were not reminded of their ideals.

21. Karen Fox (1996) writes about her interviews with a convicted sex abuser grandfather and his granddaughter, who is also his victim. She juxtaposes the interview materials, creating a text of three columns, one column for each of the participants—the man, the woman, and the researcher—to speak, seemingly to one another, about the experience of child sexual abuse.

22. See James Anderson's efforts to struggle with this issue and others in his 2003 article, "A Psychological Perspective on the Relationship of Brothers William and Henry James."

23. The book *Conversation as Method: Analyzing the Relational World of People Who Were Raised Communally* illustrates how researchers engage in a dialogic form of studying narratives collected through different research experiences and analyzed with different methods (Josselson, Lieblich, Sharabany, & Wiseman, 1997).

References

Anderson, J. W. (2003). A psychological perspective on the relationship of William and Henry James. In R. Josselson, A. Lieblich, & D. McAdams (Eds.), *Up close and personal: The teaching and learning of narrative research* (pp. 177–198). Washington, DC: American Psychological Association.

Barrows, S. B., & Novak, W. (1986). *Mayflower madam*. London: Futura.

Brown, L. M., & Gilligan, C. (1992). *Meeting at the crossroads: Women's psychology and girls' development*. Cambridge, MA: Harvard University Press.

Bruner, J. (1990). *Acts of meaning*. Cambridge, MA: Harvard University Press.

Campbell, J. (1956). *The hero with a thousand faces*. New York: Bollingen.

Charters, W. W., & Newcomb, T. M. (1958). Some attitudinal effects of experimentally increased salience of a membership group. In E. Maccoby,

T. Newcomb, & E. Hartley (Eds.), *Readings in social psychology* (3rd ed.). New York: Holt, Rinehart & Winston.

Denzin, N. K., & Lincoln, Y. (Eds.). (2000). *Handbook of qualitative research* (2nd ed.). Thousand Oaks, CA: Sage.

Foucault, M. (1979). *Discipline and punish: The birth of the prison* (A. Sheridan, Trans.). New York: Random House.

Fox, K. V. (1996). Silent voices: A subversive reading of child sexual abuse. In C. Ellis & A. Bochner (Eds.), *Composing ethnography: Alternative forms of qualitative writing* (pp. 330–356). Thousand Oaks, CA: Sage.

Gergen, K. J. (1973). Social psychology as history. *Journal of Personality and Social Psychology, 26,* 309–320.

Gergen, K. J. (1985). The social constructionist movement in modern psychology. *American Psychologist, 40,* 266–275.

Gergen, K. J. (1999). *An invitation to social construction.* Thousand Oaks, CA: Sage.

Gergen, K. J., & Gergen, M. M. (1983). Narratives of the self. In T. R. Sarbin & K. E. Scheibe (Eds.), *Studies is social identity.* (pp. 254–273). New York: Praeger.

Gergen, K. J., & Gergen, M. M. (Eds.). (1984). *Historical social psychology.* Hillsdale, NJ: Lawrence Erlbaum.

Gergen, K. J., & Gergen, M. M. (1988). Narrative and the self as relationship. In L. Berkowitz (Ed.), *Advances in experimental social psychology* (pp. 17–56). San Diego: Academic Press.

Gergen, M. M. (1980). *Antecedents and consequences of self-attributional preferences in later life.* Unpublished doctoral dissertation in psychology, Temple University, Philadelphia.

Gergen, M. M. (1988a). Narrative structure in social explanation. In C. Antaki (Ed.), *Analysing lay explanations: A casebook of methods.* London: Sage.

Gergen, M. M. (1988b). Toward a feminist metatheory and methodology in the social sciences. In M. M. Gergen (Ed.), *Feminist thought and the structure of knowledge.* (pp. 87–104). New York: New York University Press.

Gergen, M. M. (1990). Finished at 40: Women's development within the patriarchy. *Psychology of Women Quarterly, 14,* 471–493.

Gergen, M. M. (1992). Life stories: Pieces of a dream. In G. Rosenwald & R. Ochberg (Eds.), *Storied lives* (pp. 127–144). New Haven, CT: Yale University Press.

Gergen, M. M. (2001). *Feminist reconstructions in psychology: Narrative, gender, & performance.* Thousand Oaks, CA: Sage.

Gergen, M. M., & Davis, S. N. (Eds.). (1997). *Toward a new psychology of gender: A reader.* New York: Routledge.

Gergen, M. M., & Davis, S. N. (2003). Dialogic pedagogy: Developing narrative research perspectives through conversation. In R. Josselson, A. Lieblich, & D. P. McAdams (Eds.), *Up close and personal: The teaching and learning of narrative research* (pp. 239–258). Washington, DC: American Psychological Association.

Gergen, M. M., & Gergen, K. J. (1986). The discourse of control and the maintenance of well-being. In M. Baltes & P. Baltes (Eds.), *Aging and control* (pp. 119–137). Hillsdale, NJ: Lawrence Erlbaum.

Gergen, M. M., & Gergen, K. J. (1993). Narratives of the gendered body in popular autobiography. In R. Josselson & A. Lieblich (Eds.), *The narrative study of lives* (pp. 191–218). Thousand Oaks, CA: Sage.

Gergen, M. M., & Gergen, K. J. (2000). Qualitative inquiry: Tensions and transformations. In N. Denzin & Y. Lincoln (Eds.), *A handbook of qualitative research* (2nd ed., pp. 1025–1046). Thousand Oaks, CA: Sage.

Herman, J. L. (1992). *Trauma and recovery.* New York: Basic Books.

Holmberg, D., & Holmes, J. (1994). Reconstruction of relationship memories: A mental models approach. In N. Schwarz & S. Sudman (Eds.), *Autobiographical memory and the validity of retrospective reports.* New York: Springer-Verlag.

Iacocca, L., & Novak, W. (1984). *Iacocca: An autobiography.* New York: Bantam.

Josselson, R. (1996). *Revising herself: The story of women's identity from college to midlife.* New York: Oxford University Press.

Josselson, R., Lieblich, A., & McAdams, D. P. (2003). *Up close and personal: The teaching and learning of narrative research.* Washington, DC: American Psychological Association.

Josselson, R., Lieblich, A., Sharabany, R., & Wiseman, H. (1997). *Conversation as method: Analyzing the relational world of people who were raised communally.* Thousand Oaks, CA: Sage.

Loftus, E. F. (1993). The reality of repressed memories. *American Psychologist, 48,* 518–537.

Martin, E. (1987). *The woman in the body.* Boston: Beacon.

Martin, J., & Sugarman, J. (1999). *The psychology of human possibility and constraint.* Albany: State University of New York Press.

O'Rourke, N. (2002). A social cognitive model of well-being among older adults. *Constructivism in the Human Sciences, 7,* 65–80.

Richardson, L. (1994). Writing: A method of inquiry. In N. K. Denzin & Y. S. Lincoln (Eds.), *Handbook of qualitative research* (pp. 516–529). Thousand Oaks, CA: Sage.

Sarbin, T. R. (Ed.). (1986). *Narrative psychology. The storied nature of human conduct.* New York: Praeger.

Sarbin, T. R., & Kitsuse, J. I. (Eds.). (1993). *Constructing the social.* London: Sage.

Sarbin, T. R., & Schiebe, K. (Eds.). (1983). *Studies in social identity.* New York: Praeger.

Index

About the Editors

Colette Daiute is Professor of Psychology at The Graduate Center, City University of New York. Her publications include *The Development of Literacy Through Social Interaction* (1993, Jossey-Bass) and *Writing and Computers* (1985, Addison-Wesley). Daiute's recent research publications on the role of narrative in development include (with E. Buteau and C. Rawlins) "Social Relational Wisdom: Developmental Diversity in Children's Written Narratives About Social Conflict" in the journal *Narrative Inquiry* and "Writing for Their Lives: Children's Narrative Supports for Physical and Psychological Well-Being" in Lepore and Smythe's *The Writing Cure: How Expressive Writing Promotes Health and Emotional Well-Being* (2002, American Psychological Association). Daiute is currently completing a large research project on children's understanding and action around social conflict, which involved extensive narrative interpretation by children and their teachers. She is also currently editing and writing chapters for *Global Perspectives on Youth Conflict and Resilience*, an analysis of theory and research to explain young people's social problems in different places across the world.

Cynthia Lightfoot is Professor and Program Head of Human Development and Family Studies at the Pennsylvania State University Commonwealth College. Her research and publications focus on adolescent identity development, peer culture, and risk-taking, particularly as they may be understood from a sociocultural and interpretive point of view. Her recent publications include *The Culture of Adolescent Risk-Taking* (1997, Guilford), *Sociogenic Perspectives on Internalization* (edited with B. Cox; 1997, LEA), the special issue of *Culture and Psychology* "Changing Times: Reflections on the Development of Self and Culture," edited with M. Lyra (2000), and *Changing Conceptions of Psychological Life*, edited with C. Lalonde and Michael Chandler (in press, LEA).

About the Contributors

Michael Bamberg is Professor of Psychology at Clark University. He is author of *The Acquisition of Narratives* (1987, Mouton de Gruyter), coauthor (with R. Berman and D. Slobin) of *Relating Events in Narrative* (1994, Lawrence Erlbaum) and (with D. Schiffrin & A. DeFina) of *From Talk to Identity*, in preparation), and author of numerous journal articles. Bamberg is editor of the book series *Studies in Narrative* (John Benjamins, Amsterdam) and coeditor of the journal *Narrative Inquiry* and of several books, including *Narrative Development* (1997, Lawrence Erlbaum) and *Oral Versions of Personal Experience* (1997, Lawrence Erlbaum).

Michael Billig is Professor of Social Sciences at Loughborough University. Among his numerous books is *Banal Nationalism* (1995), which was awarded the Myers Centre Award for "outstanding work on intolerance." Another recent book, *Freudian Repression: Conversation Creating the Unconscious* (1999, Cambridge University Press), provides the theoretical basis for the work presented in this volume.

Sarah K. Carney is completing her Ph.D. at The Graduate Center, City University of New York. Her doctoral research is on women and legal discourse. Her other research interests include the social production of psychological knowledge and cultural constructions of trauma survival and mental health.

Michael J. Chandler is currently Distinguished Professor and Coordinator of Graduate Training in Developmental Psychology at the University of British Columbia in Vancouver. His ongoing research centers on the study of young people's social-cognitive development, especially as such age-related changes bear on matters of interest to developmental psychopathologists and health professionals. Most recently his work has come to focus on cross-cultural comparisons of epistemic and identity development as these unfold differently in Canada's Aboriginal and culturally mainstream

296

youth. His findings, which help to explain the radically different rates of youth suicide in these two populations, are partially summarized in his recent contribution to *Advances in Child Development and Behavior* (Vol. 28; 2001, Academic Press).

Mark Freeman is Professor of Psychology at the College of the Holy Cross in Worcester, Massachusetts. He is the author of *Rewriting the Self: History, Memory, Narrative; Finding the Muse: A Sociopsychological Inquiry Into the Conditions of Artistic Creativity;* and numerous articles on the self, autobiographical narrative, and the psychology of art. Most recently, he has sought to complement his longstanding interest in the self with an in-depth exploration of the category and place of the Other in psychological life.

Mary Gergen, Professor of Psychology and Women's Studies, Penn State University Delaware County, is a founding member of the Taos Institute, a nonprofit organization dedicated to the application of social constructionist ideas to diverse practices. Her most recent books are *Toward a New Psychology of Gender,* edited with Sara N. Davis (1997, Routledge) and *Feminist Reconstructions in Psychology: Narrative, Gender & Performance* (2001, Sage). Her most recent work on narratives, also with Sara Davis, is "Dialogic Pedagogy: Developing Narrative Research Through Conversation" in *The Narrative Study of Lives* (2002, APA Press). *Social Constructionism: A Reader* (edited with K.J. Gergen) was recently published (2003, Sage).

Christopher E. Lalonde is Assistant Professor of Psychology, University of Victoria. His research interests center on social-cognitive development and identity formation in childhood and adolescence. One focus of his research concerns young children's epistemic development and their understanding of the interpretive nature of knowing, which he explores in the article "Children's Understanding of Interpretation" in *New Ideas in Psychology* (Vol. 20, 2-3; 2002). A second research program focuses on the differing ways that culture shapes young persons' thoughts about matters of identity and selfhood. This work examines relations between narrative notions of personal and cultural identity and the incidence of suicide among the Aboriginal people of Canada.

Carol D. Lee is Associate Professor of Learning Sciences and African-American Studies at Northwestern University. She is author of *Signifying as a Scaffold for Literary Interpretation: The Pedagogical Implications of an African American Discourse Genre* (1993, National Council of Teachers of English). She is coeditor (with P. Smagorinsky) of

Vygotskian Perspectives on Literacy Research (1999, Cambridge University Press). She has also published in numerous journals, including *Reading Research Quarterly, Research in the Teaching of English, The Journal of Black Psychology,* and the *Journal of Negro Education,* among others. Lee has recently completed a research project in a Chicago inner-city high school that involves restructuring the English Language Arts curriculum, including assessment, in ways that build on social and cultural strengths that students bring from their home and community experiences.

Janet E. Malley is currently Deputy Director at the Institute for Research on Women and Gender at the University of Michigan. She received her Ph.D. in personality psychology from Boston University. Her research interests are in the area of adult development with a special focus on women's lives, looking especially at how the process of development may be mediated by individual life experiences as well as more broadly based work and family roles.

Ruby Mendenhall is a Ph.D. candidate in Human Development and Social Policy at the School of Education and Social Policy at Northwestern University. She uses a life course and role strain theoretical framework in her work, focusing on the development of various forms of capital (cultural, human, and social) in adolescence and adulthood. She is also interested in the various ways that African Americans, particularly women, have influenced American public policy. Mendenhall is currently writing her dissertation, "Black Women in Gautreaux's Housing Desegregation Program: Their Hopes and Struggles for Better Opportunities."

Katherine Nelson is Distinguished Professor of Psychology Emerita, The Graduate Center, City University of New York. She is the author of *Narratives From the Crib* (1989, Harvard University Press) and *Language in Cognitive Development: The Emergence of the Mediated Mind* (1996, Cambridge University Press). Nelson's current work examines development of self, consciousness, and autobiographical memory in a social-cultural collaborative construction theoretical framework.

Ama Rivers received her Ph.D. in Communications Disorders from Northwestern University. Her research focuses on the role of context in the elicitation of narratives among African American students, and the role that context plays in the quality of narratives they produced. She has extensive experience in working with children with reading disabilities. Rivers is currently the Curriculum Coordinator for the Betty Shabazz International Charter School in Chicago.

Erica Rosenfeld is a Ph.D. candidate in the Learning Sciences Program in the School of Education and Social Policy at Northwestern University. She is the Executive Director of Barrel of Monkeys, a creative arts organization that presents dramatic programming for Chicago area schools. Her research focuses on narrative composing in community-based arts organizations and its function in supporting the healthy development of at-risk youth. Rosenfeld's research interests span cultural supports for learning and the role of the arts in promoting both the development and academic competencies of young people.

Theodore R. Sarbin is Emeritus Professor of Psychology and Criminology at the University of California, Santa Cruz and, since 1987, Senior Research Psychologist at the Defense Personnel Security Research Center. He has been the recipient of a number of awards and fellowships, among them, the Fulbright award at Oxford University, the Guggenheim fellowship, the Center for the Humanities fellowship at Wesleyan University, and more recently, the Henry A. Murray Award from the Society for Personality and Social Psychology. His publication list includes 250 papers, reviews, and books dealing with clinical inference, emotional life, role theory, metaphor, social identity, schizophrenia, and imagination. His current work addresses some of the problems in narrative psychology raised in his book *Narrative Psychology: The Storied Nature of Human Conduct* (1986, Praeger).

Jocelyn Solis is currently a postdoctoral fellow in developmental psychology at UC–Santa Cruz and an assistant professor in the School of Education at Brooklyn College of the City University of New York. She has recently completed a dissertation on the formation of illegality as an identity based on research funded by the Ford Foundation and conducted in a community of undocumented Mexican immigrants in New York City. She has published essays based on this work in the *Journal of Social Issues* and in Laó-Montes and Dávila's *Mambo Montage: The Latinization of New York* (2001, Columbia University Press).

Steven Stanley is a postgraduate research student in the Department of Social Sciences at Loughborough University. His doctoral thesis, which has been supervised by Michael Billig, is a critical discursive study of the dilemmas of being a Ph.D. student in the social sciences. He has published articles about cyberpsychology and is a member of the Loughborough Discourse and Rhetoric Group.

Abigail J. Stewart is Agnes Inglis Collegiate Professor of Psychology and Women's Studies at the University of Michigan and former director of the

Women's Studies Program. From 1995-2002, Stewart was Director of the Institute for Research on Women and Gender. She has published over 100 scholarly articles and several books focusing on the psychology of women's lives, personality, and adaptation to personal and social changes. Her recent coauthored books include (with A. Copeland, N. Chester, J. Malley, and N. Barenbaum) *Separating Together: How Divorce Transforms Families* (1997, Guilford) and (with M. Romero) *Women's Untold Stories: Breaking Silence, Talking Back, Voicing Complexity* (1999, Routledge). Most recently, she coedited (with her Women's Studies colleague A. Herrmann) an extensively revised second edition of the anthology *Theorizing Feminism: Parallel Trends in the Humanities and Social Sciences* (2000, Westview). Her ongoing research focuses on the intersection of life-span personality development, social history, and social structure, via several longitudinal research studies, most recently on a collaborative project exploring generation, gender, race and class as they shaped work and family values in the Midwest in the 1950s and 1960s.

Ulrich Teucher trained and worked as a children's nurse in a pediatric oncology ward in Hamburg, Germany, before embarking on a program of interdisciplinary studies in the fields of psychology and literature. He wrote his dissertation, *Writing the Unspeakable: Metaphor in Cancer Narratives*, on the use of language in cancer discourse. Currently, Teucher holds concurrent postdoctoral fellowships in developmental psychology at the University of British Columbia, sponsored by CIHR (Canadian Institutes for Health Research) and MSFHR (Michael Smith Foundation for Health Research), examining cross-cultural constructions of identity in the narratives of North American Aboriginal and non-Aboriginal adolescents.

Brendesha Tynes is a graduate student in Psychological Studies in Education at UCLA's Graduate School of Education & Information Studies. She received a bachelor's degree in History from Columbia University and a master's degree in Learning Sciences from Northwestern University. Her current research focuses on ethnic identity and socialization on the Internet. Tynes's other research interests include narratives in online contexts, Internet ethnography, and the ways the Internet can be used as a tool for K–12 education.